On the Advantages and Disadvantages
of Ethics and Politics

Studies in Continental Thought

John Sallis, *general editor*

Consulting Editors

On the Advantages and Disadvantages of Ethics and Politics

Charles E. Scott

Indiana University Press

Bloomington and Indianapolis

The paper used in this publication meets the minimum require-
ments of American National Standard for Information Sciences—
Permanence of Paper for Printed Library Materials, ANSI
Z39.48-1984.

Manufactured in the United States of America

Library of Congress Cataloging-in-Publication Data

Scott, Charles E.
    On the advantages and disadvantages of ethics and politics /
Charles E. Scott.
        p.   cm. — (Studies in Continental thought)
    Includes bibliographical references and index.
        ISBN 0-253-33073-4 (alk. paper). — ISBN 0-253-21076-3 (pbk. :
alk. paper)
        1. Ethics.   2. Political science—Philosophy.   3. Philosophy,
Modern—19th century.   4. Philosophy, Modern—20th century.
I. Title.   II. Series.
BJ1031.S368   1996
170—dc20   95-53713

1 2 3 4 5   01 00 99 98 97 96

For Susan

Contents

Acknowledgments

FOR HELP ALONG the way in writing this book, I am grateful to Linnea Wilkins, Michael Jarrett, Michael Hodges, Ben Pryor, Beth Ondo, and Kim Johnson. Several chapters, some in altered versions, have appeared in journals and anthologies, and I wish to thank the editors and publishers of those publications for permission to use them in the present volume. "A (Non-) Passing Sense of Tragedy" appeared in part in *Heidegger Studies*, edited by Parvis Emad and Kenneth Maly, under the title "*Adikia* and Catastrophe: Heidegger's Anaximander Fragment"; "Responsibility and Danger," in *Ethics and Responsibility in the Phenomenological Tradition*, the Simon Silverman Phenomenology Center, Duquesne University, under the direction of David L. Smith; "Self-Fragmentation: The Danger to Ethics," in *Research in Phenomenology*, vol. 22, edited by John Sallis, under the title "Foucault, Ethics, and the Fragmented Subject"; "Democratic Space," in *Politics and the Human Body*, Vanderbilt University Press, edited by Jean Bethke Elshtain and J. Timothy Cloyd; "Thinking Noninterpretively," in *Epoché*, vol. 1, edited by James E. Faulconer; "Nonbelonging/Authenticity," in *Reading Heidegger*, Indiana University Press, edited by John Sallis; "A People's Witness beyond Politics," in *Ethics as First Philosophy*, Routledge, edited by Adriaan Peperzak.

Selected Works Cited

Martin Heidegger

BT   *Being and Time*, trans. John Macquarrie and Edward Robinson (London: SCM Press, 1962).

GA   *Gesamtausgabe*. (Frankfurt am Main: Vittorio Klostermann, 1975–).

BW   *Basic Writings*, rev. ed., ed. David Farrell Krell (New York: Harper-Collins, 1993).

EGT *Early Greek Thinking*, trans. David Farrell Krell and Frank A. Capuzzi (New York: Harper and Row, 1984).

VA   *Vorträge und Autsätze*, Fünfte Auflage (Pfulligen: Günther Neske, 1985).

Emmanuel Levinas

OTB *Otherwise than Being or Beyond Essence*, trans. Alphonso Lingis (Boston: Martinus Nijhoff, 1981).

Friedrich Nietzsche

T   *Twilight of the Idols*, trans. R. J. Hollingdale (New York: Viking Penguin, 1968).

GM   *On the Genealogy of Morals*, trans. Walter Kaufmann and R. J. Hollingdale (New York: Random House, 1969).

Michel Foucault

A   *Archaeology of Knowledge*, trans. A. M. Sheridan Smith (New York: Pantheon, 1972).

PPC *Politics, Philosophy, Culture*, ed. Lawrence Kritzman, trans. Alan Sheridan (New York: Routledge, 1988).

FR   *Foucault Reader*, ed. Paul Rabinow (New York: Pantheon, 1984).

PK   *Power/Knowledge*, ed. Colin Gordon (New York: Pantheon, 1980).

HS I *History of Sexuality*, vol. I, *An Introduction*, trans. Robert Hurley (New York: Pantheon, 1978).

HS II   *History of Sexuality*, vol. II, *The Use of Pleasure*, trans. Robert Hurley (New York: Pantheon, 1985).

HS III *History of Sexuality*, vol. III, *The Care of the Self*, trans. Robert Hurley (New York: Pantheon, 1986).

FB   *Foucault/Blanchot*, trans. Jeffrey Mehlman and Brian Massumi (New York: Zone, 1987).

On the Advantages and Disadvantages of Ethics and Politics

Introduction: Crossing the Ethical by "the" Nonethical

I myself but write one or two indicative words for this future.
I but advance a movement only to wheel and hurry back in the darkness.
—Walt Whitman, *Leaves of Grass*

THE TITLE OF this book is drawn from Nietzsche's *On the Advantage and Disadvantage of History for Life*, an early and, from the perspective of *On the Genealogy of Morals*, anticipatory essay whose value is found in part in its forecast of the thought to which it gives rise. Perhaps all of Nietzsche's thought is anticipatory in this sense: he anticipates thought as genealogical, as cultivated and disciplined memory, with responsibility less to what is remembered than to what is created by anticipation, thought that gives rise to other memories and to thought that in turn anticipates still other remembering and anticipatory thinking. His thought anticipates future thought which anticipates and remembers things that are quite new and that now are without clear connection to us.

The chapters in this book are focused by the question of ethics in the sense that they assume and address the difficult experience that our values and ideals—particularly our highest and strongest values and ideals—may carry with them and perpetuate their own worst enemies. They may add destruction and conflict to the very lives that they would cultivate, upbuild, and harmonize. The question of ethics, as experienced, allows us to participate with alertness in the self-overcoming of values and ideals that form our lives and that are structured by often unattended and intense conflicts. It also allows us to develop values and ways of thinking that form in the self-overcoming process. These chapters also go beyond that problematic by finding access to 'what' is not ethical and not political within ethical and political occurrences. The ethical and political dimensions of our lives are themselves in question by virtue of belonging to 'something' excessive to their own identities. Accompanying those descriptive claims is the ethically and politically strategic claim that when this excess is ignored in our values and evaluations, we will be inclined in our standards and regulations and by virtue of our cultural identity—we will be inclined by virtue of being political and ethical—to eliminate or dominate those values and political structures that are significantly different from our own.

A further claim is that the ignorance of nonethical and nonpolitical excess, excess that accompanies our ethics and politics, has combined with a sense of transcendence in our tradition. In this combination, when the sense of transcendence is threatened, we fear (unjustifiably) the loss or erosion of our ethical and political sensibility. My intention in this book is to write and think in a sense of loss regarding the value and meaning of transcendence and to provide a sense of excess to accompany the ethical and political forces in our lives, a sense of excess that departs from the sense of transcendence. My expectation is that neither ethics nor politics will be lost in this transformation as a sense of excess, which is at least somewhat free of the lineage of the sense of transcendence, permeates ethical and political passion and perception. It is to our advantage to intensify our ethical and political knowledge in the absence of definitive ontological origin and in the loss of our traditional sense of transcendence. This advantage takes place in recognition of multiple, ambiguous beginnings for both the ethical and the political on the one hand and our specific ethics and politics on the other. The ethical does not disclose a transcendent, ethical grounding, and our ethics and politics have their authority only in the communities and traditions in which they develop.

I wish to emphasize the advantage of the nonethical and nonpolitical for ethics and politics, as well as for ethical and political sensibility. The advantage occurs in a consequent reevaluation of difference, authority, and communal identity. The disadvantages of ethics and politics are found in their drift toward universalization and a consequent tribalism that mythologizes their origins and range of authority, their tendency to preserve in submission what they oppose (although this can also be an advantage for their self-overcoming), in their concentration of subjective passions and a consequent identification with static repetition instead of facilitating processes of self-overcoming, and in their elevation of themselves as '*the* ethical' and '*the* political' over the excess that limits their hegemony. To their disadvantage, politics and ethics can function without reserve in passions to be just, good, and true.

The two axes that give critical edge for these claims are the lineages of abuse which accompany our communal standards and habits and our values and language that give us to expect that our communal standards and habits have a right to normative claims beyond the communities that they define. There are also two constructive axes. First, a philosophical purpose of the book is to develop movements of thought and language which carry out and perform the question of ethics, the marginalization of the transcendentally founded value of unity and universality, and the desirability of self-overcoming for thought and language. In this endeavor I shall give attention to the lapses that occur within ethical orders and structures of expectation. I wish to develop a mindfulness in the losses of order and value that occur within orders and systems of value, losses that show nothing determinant or valuable or avoidable.

This is mindfulness in the crossing of the ethical and political by nonethical and nonpolitical lapse. The performative dimension of Nietzsche's and Foucault's thought are particularly significant for this effort.

Second, in close association with attentiveness to such lapse and loss, I also wish to emphasize the question of how we might think in the crossing, in that peculiar openness of indeterminacy that accompanies our determined orders and recognition. This is a question of how we might think and value by appropriating—by giving way to—a dimension of unorder, nonpolitics, and unresponsibility that occurs with our orders, politics, and responsibility. It is a question of thought that has been opened up especially by Nietzsche and Heidegger and in a more limited way by Levinas. They have experimented with thought that is at once nonpolitical and nonethical in our usual sense of the words and, by virtue of being neither political nor ethical, has exceptional significance for reevaluation of our values and orders of life.

I have used the word 'crossing' to juxtapose and connect the ethical and nonethical. The awkwardness of the term lies in the word's suggestion of lack of connection in connection. The ethical and nonethical both belong and do not belong to each other. Each defines the other, but the definition is determined by each not being the other. Neither is able to be the other, and in their crossing each gives the other to pass away in the crossing that connects them and occasions their difference. This difference and ambivalence is variously addressed in the discussions that follow. In our language and lives, the powers that move us—the valences, values—are seamed by difference,[1] by an undoing of the moving power in the occurrence of the moving power, by unvalue's undoing value without power or status or quality. When I speak of the nonethical or the unethical, I speak appropriately only by losing 'its' objectivity in a transforming event of naming or writing or speaking. It is the loss that counts by uncounting, by losing what is grasped in naming, writing, and speaking, by a lapsing that gives departure and indeterminacy in occurrences of recognition and placement.

This is an issue of unvalue or nonvalue in valuing, and not, of course, a question of historical relativity. Or, in the historically formed recognitions and evaluations concerning the nonethical, nonformation occurs that is, at best, only partially addressed within the problematic of historical relativity. That problematic allows one to trace the relative formations of value and to assess their limits, but it does not address the passing away of value in the occurrences of values. For example, the problematic of historical relativism, in both its defense and its rejection, finds neither the crossing of the ethical and nonethical nor the nonresponsibility of responsibility in events of responsibility. Historical relativism and its refusal are tied to a priority of determinate things, whether relative or absolute, that excludes the withdrawing appearance of no determinate being at all.

These chapters thus maintain a tension between a genealogical approach to values and knowledge and the thought of nonethics and nonpolitics. They bring together, for example, Heidegger and Foucault in their considerable differences around the axes of genealogy and thought—not by comparing, say, Heidegger's de-structuring of Western metaphysics and Foucault's account of the formation of the order of representation but by holding together these different accesses to interruption of the ethical and the political which Heidegger and Foucault provide. I do not wish to meld together or to reconcile Heidegger's and Foucault's thought in a way that provides for maximum compatibility. I do wish to provide a discussion in which Heidegger's exploratory work on thinking and language comes before (becomes present with) Foucault's genealogies of our Western knowledge and experience of moral behavior, ethical certainty, and methodological clarity. Heidegger's ambivalence and resistance to positive accounts of the importance of historical and psychological formation in the occurrence of being are in question. A peculiar asceticism in his thought, which accompanies a mixed appropriation of the lineage that combines the thoughts of transcendence, unity, and possibility, is also in question. The genealogy of his own thought, which he taught two generations of philosophers to question, is given a yet stronger impetus and greater dissemination by Foucault's accounts of knowledges and practices, accounts that come close at times to eliminating our traditional experiences of definitive origin and of transcending depth and height.

In the tension bred of this juxtaposition Heidegger's preoccupation with the Western experience of the question of being moves on to a metaphorical plane of spatiality. This transposition relinquishes his preoccupation with heroic and originary figures and reformulates the thought of time in terms of formation of knowledges that are thoroughly invested with traceable mutations of practices and discursive regulations. As one thinks genealogically, things come to presence, as Heidegger shows. Language, as he also shows, lets things come to be. Disclosure occurs, and the way in which a way of thought thinks or does not think the occurrence of disclosure—whether or not things are turned into transcendentally determined realities—makes a culture-forming difference, as Heidegger said it does. But in the genealogical emphasis a particular performance of finitude in the loss of a sense of transcendence takes place, one that Heidegger overlooked in Nietzsche's thought, and one that departs from a preoccupation with transcendental noncontamination by historical and psychological interruptions and irregularities. The resulting thought is more conflicted and less serious than Heidegger's, more predisposed to what I term 'democratic space', more preoccupied with bodies and questions of sorrow and pleasure, less expectant in the lineage of the wise 'men', more impacted by practices of marginalization and privileging, and far more persuaded that highly self-interested power formations infest our tradition's most refined and admirable thoughts and images.

But no one exceeds Heidegger's emphasis on thinking transformatively in and through the ideas and values that have formed our ability to think as we do. Our thought belongs to a destiny, according to him, to a "sending" that calls us out of our patterns of certitude and practices of giving stasis to things by our ways of fixing them in signs and meanings. He repeatedly—early and late in his thought—experienced the overturn of the position and the strategy that gave him his philosophical departure on a given topic. Whether he thematized Aristotle's concept of time or the phenomenological method or the way to language, he found in his thinking the insufficiency of his point of departure and found himself required to rethink the concepts and questions that moved him. He seemed to look for definitive origins, only to show the collapse of the idea of definitive origin. He looked for 'grounds' and found them in the collapse of the language of grounds. *Possibility* for given conditions showed mortal temporality devoid of substantial grounding. He gave priority to presencing and found withdrawal of presence in the occurrence of presencing. He gave priority to being and found, in the sending of being, a *loss* of being.

In such processes Heidegger foresaw a way of thinking that performed its own transformation, a way of thinking that gave way to its own 'disaster' (in the language of "The Anaximander Fragment") and allowed its own passing away *in* its allowance of the self-presentation of beings. One could imagine only with difficulty a thinking that is less concerned for ethical and political values. And yet in such turning and apparent unconcern, Heidegger allows us to see a way of life that threatens its own self-destruction, a way of life no less at odds with itself than Nietzsche's "last man"—the modern European in consequence of a lineage of silent, unconscious resentment and reactionary value formation. Heidegger's nonpolitical and nonethical thinking provides access to descriptions and possibilities that appear to be outside the horizons of ethical and political preoccupation. And in the transformative dimension of his thinking, he suggests a way of turning through this "technological" self-destruction to ways of thinking, knowing, feeling, and esteeming that both see the destructiveness and refigure the life orientation out of which such destruction arises.

In this part of Heidegger's thought, genealogical thinking confronts a relentless encounter with tradition-forming ideas which silently avoid the questions and *aporia* that gave rise to thought in our classical Greek lineage. He describes a way of thinking that falls short of its own question and bewilderment. He shows that lacking an appropriation of its question and bewilderment, Western thought, in determined overconfidence and obscure clarity, determines beings by eliminating their self-disclosive difference from our structures of confidence and clarity. It is a process that exhausts people and things by willful appropriation, a type of strangulation that usually runs unnoticed through our civilization. Heidegger shows that accounts of the formation of our knowledges and practices are not adequate for accounting for the power of reification, the value of largely static identity, and obliviousness to indeterminacy and unpresence in the occurrences of beings. The question of being plagues genealogical thought in its juxtaposition with Heidegger's thought, partially because that question seems so individual to Heidegger's obsession and, perhaps, because it is nonetheless unavoidable. The power of this question for uncovering a troubling distance within Western thought—between a sense of mortal time in the occurrences of all things and a refusal of the pervasiveness of that sense—is clear. And yet Heidegger's accounts of language and thought have not been thoroughly encountered by genealogical thought. By virtue of this lack of encounter, part of genealogical thought's own heritage is not accounted by it.

The voices of this book are not primarily ethical and political, and they are not against ethics and politics. They arise from the experience that oppositions in the area of ethics and politics are too limiting, too attached to eliminations that are disadvantageous to our common occurrences together. Just as it is not a question of support or rejection regarding historical relativism, it is not a question of being either ethical or not ethical. It is rather a question of a different beginning in interpreting our values and practices, of beginning not solely with the imperatives of ethical and political life but with life in which values are necessary and yet made ambivalent by nonvalue, beginning with the hypothesis that this ambivalence does not threaten ethical and political behavior but is advantageous to our common lives, to our lives together with unstable and necessary values to which we both belong and do not belong.

1 | Nonbelonging/Authenticity

THE WORD *nonbelonging* as I wish to use it does not suggest a determinant relation to belonging. We *can* think of the word in such a way that it refers to a state that is necessarily related to but different from another state called belonging. But we shall take *nonbelonging* to cancel this connection and lose its meaning as it appears to fulfill its meaning. *Nonbelonging* refuses a conjunction with *belonging* in the process of seeming to signify such a connection. If nonbelonging were a state to which we belonged, it would be comprehensible. We could define the space that separates it from belonging, and we could place and familiarize ourselves with the distance that separates belonging and nonbelonging. The strangeness of nonbelonging could be located. But *nonbelonging* in the 'sense' that I am taking it would be lost in the familiarizing process. As we lose the 'sense' of nonbelonging and its familiarity, and as we lose our thought of it, perhaps a different thought will emerge, one, no doubt, that we will also lose.

Both *dwelling* and *abyss* are words that arise as Heidegger speaks of dasein's proper appropriation of its mortal temporality. The words unsettle each other: one does not dwell in an abyss, and the continuities of dwelling appear to replace the formless chaos named by *abyss*. Dwelling and abyss do not belong to each other, and their nonbelonging pervades authenticity. Does their nonbelonging unsettle a familiarity of dasein with its own propriety as Heidegger describes it in *Being and Time*? If *Eigentlichkeit* means that dasein comes to dwell in familiarity with its mortal temporality—if dasein's open release in and to its temporality defines the proper space of its existence—abyss and anxiety would be properly located in that space and *nonbelonging* would be an inappropriate word to use when speaking of dasein's proper existence. If, on the other hand, dasein's temporality means that abyss prevails in an erasure of the space of propriety, how are we to think properly of authenticity? And of dasein's dwelling? How might dasein belong to itself? How is *Being and Time* to be read if dasein's propriety possesses no proper space and if *Eigentlichkeit* overturns itself in its own movement and possesses neither *eigen* nor *keit*?

First, is there a case to be made for nonbelonging in Heidegger's account of authenticity? The second part of *Being and Time* shows that dasein is the unifying basis for its own self-disclosure and authenticity. The strong implication is that as dasein comes properly to appropriate its mortal temporality, it may be taken to belong to its being. In section 53, the last section of part 2, chapter I, he sketches out what he will have to establish, namely that dasein's existential structure makes possible an individual's proper (*eigentliche*) being to death. Because this possibility is dasein's own—is constitutive of dasein—it is said to be *eigentlich* or proper, true, and essential. The name of this condition for the possibility of an individual's proper, mortal way of being is the disclosiveness of situated understanding. *Disclosiveness* is to be read in Heidegger's sense of showing forth, opening up, or clearing; and *understanding* is to be read in his sense of dasein's alert, projecting ability to be: dasein's constitutive ability to be is a forecasting process of disclosure that manifests temporality as it projects forward, and in that sense understands, in its historical, social situation.

Heidegger interprets dasein's ability to be in the language of possibility, however, and this language makes problematic the sense in which dasein can be said to belong to its being. In this context it is not a possibility for a future realization of something determinant; nor is it a possibility that takes place at a distance from dasein and can be known objectively by contemplation. Dasein's proper and true ability to be is mortal possibility and is characterized as the possibility of the impossibility of existence: being to death. Dasein's world openness, its clearing for the self-showing of beings, is an ability to be that is sheer, mortal possibility. Possibility (*Möglichkeit*), Heidegger says, is disclosed (*unverhüllt*) as the impossibility (*Unmöglichkeit*) of existence. Being to death, then, is the "meaning" of dasein's ability to be. "Death, as possibility, gives dasein nothing to be 'actualized', nothing which dasein, as actual, could itself be." *Meaning* thus does not suggest any kind of supersensible world or a world made familiar in dwelling. To belong to being to death is to belong to nothing at all as one dwells in the familiarity of one's world.

Vorlaufen, or running ahead, is, with *proper, possibility, understanding*, and *being to death*, the fifth organizing term of this section. It addresses the movement of being to death and possibility. "Being to death as running ahead in possibility first of all *makes possible* this possibility and makes it as such free." Dasein's ability to be discloses itself *in* the running ahead of being to death. It is a movement in which the most extreme possibility of human being, its death, is brought forth and uncovered in its possibility. What is most dasein's own, its ability to be, is not *something* to be realized. Dasein's propriety regarding its being for Heidegger is not a matter of the self's actualizing itself. There is no self there when dasein's ability to be is addressed. Its movement is one of running ahead to its impossibility in its mere ability to be. It is not a movement of self-constitution or of the unfolding of an essence that has a nature to unfold or of a truth that is to find its adequacy in an identity that is constituted on the basis of truth's form or content. The movement of dasein's proper and true possibility is mortal temporality in its difference from the possible identities that we might become, the possible lives that we might lead, and the selfhood that we might achieve.

The movement of mortal temporality is dasein's most essential (*eigenste*) possibility for interpreting its proper existence (*eigentliche Existenz*). Existential understanding, in contrast to interpretation, is found in the projective aspect of dasein's temporal movement. Human being, in its care, continuously projects and designs (*entwirft*) in the midst of its relations. Heidegger has shown in section 31 that its projective character opens up (*erschliesst*) in and to the world as well as reveals the being of dasein as possibility of not being. Projection is being possible. In the section at hand he indicates in a preliminary sketch (*Entwurf*) that the temporality of understanding and its projective character (*Entwurf*) are revealed in its mortal running ahead. Heidegger's intention is to show how dasein "auf eigenstes Seinkönnen sich entwerfen kann"—how dasein can project itself on and by its most proper ability to be. Running ahead shows itself as the possibility for understanding the most proper, uttermost ability to be. If he can show this possibility *and* let it be shown in his account of it, he will have an interpretation that is designed after the temporal and mortal design of dasein's understanding and one that invokes the thought of an abysmal temporality that comes into its own as it passes away. He will then be in a position to show how dasein might live in a way that, like the interpretation of *Being and Time*, opens to its being. Dasein's temporal and mortal movement, its *Vorlauf*, would then be the basis for the way we design our lives, a basis that evacuates itself in its mortality, and a basis that exceeds the possibilities for dwelling and belonging.

This basis has no definitive or determinate nature. Dasein's most proper course of conduct takes place as it lets its disclosure disclose itself in whatever activity one undertakes. Heidegger says that his own work must uncover the structure of running ahead in death as dasein's truest possibility. If his writing succeeds and is proper to dasein, it will be responsive to its own "*vorlaufenden Erschliessen*," to its own understanding *in* running ahead disclosively. That does not mean that the correctness of Heidegger's analysis will be guaranteed if he is true to the being of dasein. It means that an anxious desire for correctness will be experienced in the mortal possibility of dasein's being, which in its occurrence is not subject to correctness or incorrectness; and although Heidegger does not entirely face his own anxiety regarding unity, the impact of his account means that the book's project regarding unity is also in question by virtue of dasein's mortality of design. On the basis of dasein's movement, as Heidegger finds it, even the language of being, running ahead, and design do not escape the unfixing quality of dasein's disclosure. Its truth—the self-disclosure of mortal temporality—comes most clearly to bear as it puts itself in question in consequence of its own claims. Dasein's disclosive running ahead in mortal temporality and the ek-stasis that it constitutes undercut any predisposition to complete certainty, most particularly that predisposition that inclines one to canonize Heidegger's writings or to think on *their* basis rather than on the basis of their possibility for no possibility at all. Heidegger's interpretation of dasein is not the result of "staring at meaning" and coming up with the best reading of the meaning of life. It is designed, rather, to express dasein's ability to be in its disclosive being to death. It clears the way for dasein's world openness as the temporal course of being to death. The account of dasein's authenticity takes its departure from the finite, temporal movement that is the condition of possibility of both meaning and no meaning, that is, from the questionableness of meaning in being to death. Heidegger's own account, in its discipline, suggests that an abysmal aspect suffuses his project of a definitive descriptive account of dasein. *Being and Time* is a book that cannot belong to the circumscription of its own words and thought. It is indefinitely beyond itself in its mortal temporality.

When dasein's *eigenste Möglichkeit* (most proper possibility) is named death (GA 2, 349; BT 307), the meaning of *most proper* or *ownmost* or *most essential* is thus interrupted. Dasein's *eigenste* ability to be, its truest can-be, is not something that properly can be said to be its own in the sense of a property at its disposal. Nor is its truest capacity to be self-relational found in the sense that a subject relates to itself. The continuity of self-relation is ruptured by a course of coming to be that does not reflect or represent the self. It rather discloses human being as nonselflike possibility without identity or subjectivity. Dasein is clear (*offenbar*), not only in its difference from its everyday self-understanding but also in its difference from selfhood. There is a wrenching (*entrissen*) quality in dasein's deathly openness. It lives out its existential understanding as it is torn from the meanings and values by which it makes its way in its society and as it is torn from its inherited interpretation of itself as self-founding. In this wrenching aspect dasein lives its disclosure of its being in the midst of its activities and connections. It stands out of—ek-sists—everything that it lives for. Dasein's deathly openness ek-sists its selfhood as well as its ethos.

Dasein in its most proper possibility is not finally defined by its linkage to people or things. This is not to say that it is not linked to people and things. It is found *only* in social, historical matrices, in its metaphysical history and technological age, and in language that bears the forgetfulness of being. It occurs only in multiple human connections. But dasein is in excess of its definitive way of being. The human world's ability to be, its clearing for all beings, interrupts both dasein's history and the matrix of connections, not in the active sense of doing something to the history and matrix but in the sense of pervading and making possible the matrix without being identical to the matrix or having an existence independent of the matrix. Playing on *Vorlaufen*, we can say that being-in-the-world's ability to be courses through the connections of our individual lives as difference from connections and yields their fragility, their mortality, their disconnection in the midst of their connections. When Heidegger says that dasein's possibility runs forward as dasein's future, is dasein's ability to be, and is being to death, he means that dasein goes forward in this interruption: to go in its most proper being means that in moving into its future dasein never leaves its being to death, its possibility for no possibility. Its futural movement is being to death. "Es geht um sein eigenstes Sein"—it goes about its most proper being. One can see why interpreters have often mistaken this claim to mean that dasein is individually alone in its mortality and that Heidegger is a modern stoic who holds that humans must accept the fate of death with singular courage. But we also see that dasein, as an intrinsically social, historical, and worldly being, is a being marked by difference in its being from the totality of its relations and values. *In* its relations and values dasein is the opening, the *erschliessen*, of its ownmost incapacity to own its being by affirming who it in fact is. It comes into its own by the disownment of the priority of its selfhood in the way it is a self.

How is this interruptive nonrelatedness to be lived? What is proper to it? The paradox in this part of Heidegger's analysis is found in his claim that by disowning the sufficiency of one's connections and identity vis-à-vis dasein, one owns not only one's history and world but also one's being. Just as Nietzsche's self-overcoming in his account of the ascetic ideal echoes the theme of self-sacrifice, Heidegger's interpretation echoes the same thing. The individual individuates itself by discovering the singularity of its being to death and by living its connections with a sensibility informed by that singularity. One loves in the fragility of loving, not in the assumption of its founded meaning. One affirms values with the understanding that one and one's values are able not to be in the possibility of their affirmation. Nothing replaces the individual's life in its living. But rather than thinking in a connection between self-giving and universal principles, Heidegger thinks in the interruption of the meaning of our lives by the mortal *possibility* of living and finds in owning the being's interruption of our lives that we may disown the theoretical and existential sufficiency of our selves for defining our being or our ability to be. Individuation means living responsively in the world with the *eigenstes Möglichkeit* of being to death, which interrupts one's historical and community identity and puts in question the meaning of life. This is saying something quite different from the statement that the individual must die his or her death alone. In owning one's being one owns no one, and that 'no one' is both the truth of one's being and nonbelonging. No one, no history, no community, no subjectivity authorizes the individual's life. The question is how we are to think of being without authority and meaning for life, without self-relational meaning. When Heidegger says that an individual is forced by the forward run (*Vorlaufen*) of existence to take over its most proper and true being in possibility, he is saying that the individual's world and life are decentered and ruptured by the individual's resolve. In this open resolve the thought of selfhood, subjectivity, and self-constitution are set aside. In open resolve one opens out in the world in the "understanding design" of dasein's mortal openness. We are finding that in belonging to its being dasein belongs nowhere in addition to belonging to its everyday world and cultural tradition.

Dasein's situation is thus not one in which it constitutes itself and gives itself familiarity primarily by means of realizing a given potential for selfhood. It intrinsically (*eigentlich*) lacks reality and is able to come into specific kinds of living only by virtue of the historically formed world relations in which it finds itself. The 'wholeness' of its being is found in the stream of possibility—not a determinant possibility for a specific way of being that dasein may realize in more or less appropriate ways. Possibility is never surpassed, even momentarily, by some form of dwelling. Rather, given its history, the very activity of self-constitution proliferates dasein and moves it away from its wholeness and unity, a wholeness that is found in its attunement "to the nothing of the possible impossibility of its existence." Dasein's true (*eigenste*) situation is found in an attunement that has neither subject nor object. It is the mood of sheer, mortal possibility: anxiety. The thought of whole and unity is pushed by Heidegger to a breaking point as he shows that human being finds its unity in nothing present or realizable. In speaking of this opening to dasein's whole ability to be, Heidegger uses a middle voice phrase: "die Angst ängstet sich *um* das Seinkönnen des so bestimmten Seienden und erschliesst so die äussereste Möglichkeit": "Anxiety (is) anxious in the midst of the ability to be of the being that is so disposed and opens up the uttermost possibility." Anxiety discloses dasein's ability to be in a wholeness without substance and in the figuration of possible impossibility. Dasein is most true, that is, it is its own disclosure, in possibility that opens to all values and meanings and stands out from everything that makes an individual's life worth living. The thought of grounding thus falls away in the anxiety that grounds the thought. In anxiety nonbelonging displaces any space that might locate it.

The title of section 53 is "Existenzialer Entwurf eines eigentlichen Seins zum Tode (Existential projection of a proper being to death)." We have emphasized that *Entwurf*—projected design—is closely associated with *Vorlauf*, the running ahead of dasein's possibility as being to death. This section appropriates dasein's proper *Vorlauf* in its *Entwurf* by developing an interpretation based on dasein's existential understanding of its mortal temporality, and in that process prepares to break the traditional thoughts of unity, wholeness, and ground. These thoughts are projected in the forward run of dasein's anxious possibility and can no longer suggest a transcendental grounding for value and meaning. Human being is uncovered in the process whereby the traditional and everyday senses of self and transcendence are ruptured by anxiety, which is the modal aspect of dasein's ungrounded mortality.

In this rupture both dasein and *Being and Time* stand out of the context of belonging. *Stand out* itself is in question. Dasein has no unambiguous stand in its anxiety, and *Being and Time* has no unambiguous place to stand beyond its historical determination. In reference to dasein's determination we can say that it stands out of its familiar world and its self. But there is no determined transcendental field in which to take another stand, no additional and firmer world in which to ek-sist and come to a more proper home. The recoil in the metaphysical history in which *Being and Time* is conceived is radical in the sense that while the book is completed in anticipation of a fuller and more complete account of its own enabling history, and while the authorship of the book is admittedly within the metaphysical lineage that it puts in question, its limits fade out in the possibility that gives it its space of disclosive communication. It does not recoil into a higher truth or into the possibility of greater accuracy and truthfulness. It recoils into no perspective or world view, into no place that would provide a higher standpoint for clarification of belonging. Belonging as it does to an accountable history, *Being and Time* also moves with a timing that gives it no teleological meaning to provide a greater meaning to its history. It finds an ending to its history in the language that gives expression to the *Vorlauf* of its lineage. Neither dasein nor *Being and Time* can belong to the being that discloses them, that is, they cannot belong to their own disclosure, and this nonbelonging appears as mere vacancy as mortality interrupts the determinant connections of their lives.

We can make a case for modifying this radicality. We can point out that dasein's being is metaphysical even as it breaks the hold of metaphysical thinking. We can rightly say that in *Being and Time* dasein's being belongs to the question of being and that that question arises in a quite specific lineage. In this sense nonbelonging might be said to belong to the history of metaphysics; anxiety and the possibility of no possibility are phenomena *within* this history. Anxiety and the possibility of no possibility occur in a quite determinate way: they belong to a tradition that constitutes dasein. We might further point out that in authenticity dasein comes to dwell in a determinant manner by an open vulnerability to its mortal temporality, that nonbelonging is given a home in its appropriated disclosure.

And yet in the process of uncovering this determination, *Being and Time* finds itself uncovered, opened out beyond its history into no history, no determination, no familiarity. This opening out, when made familiar by thematization, impels thought in strange but presumably fulfillable directions. But these directions take their direction from the nondirection of dasein's opening out; and, belonging as dasein does to this transformation, it finds that *in* its belonging it belongs nowhere. Its history is locatable only by reference to its own lo-cations, and its locatability is grounded in nonlocatable indeterminacy. Dasein's belonging belongs to nonbelonging, which provides nothing.

Nonbelonging puts Heidegger's thought at an edge that is dangerous in the perspective of the values and meanings that tells us what is right and wrong at the most fundamental level of our culture. When our essential determinations are undetermined—when our belonging is ungrounded—and when the basis of our creative and ethical passions is experienced as abysmal and unbased, we, in experiencing the importance of universality that is our heritage, are given to believe that the value of life itself is in question. The exhilaration of living on the edge, the passions associated with risk, the freedom of being uprooted: these enlivening spurs to perception and a sense of being that frighten us and awaken our sensibilities to the narcotic of normalcy at its best also forecast the possibil-ity of disruption and catastrophic loss of order. It is not a friendly struggle when we find that at the edge of belonging we can expire with an intensity of living that makes anemic the satisfactions that ordinarily stir in us the deep emotions associated with dedicated affiliation. To live with our ethos and hence with our identities at the limit of recognition threatens exhaustion as well as exhilara-tion. It is one thing to read the *Duino Elegies* or *On the Essence of Truth* in the full assurance of belonging deeply to a way of life that makes clear who we are to be; it is quite another to feel the ungrounding of what grounds us and to be on the line of belonging in the abyss of nonbelonging. How are we to be properly ourselves when we find nonpropriety in the circumference of our being?

The issue is joined in Heidegger's account of *Eigentlichkeit* and *Uneigentlich-keit* in which the propriety of ethics is put in question at the same time that ethics appears to be inevitable. The term *eigentliche* refers to specific ways in which an individual relates to its being. What is the proper way for dasein to live with regard to its being? How is it to constitute itself in its being, which interrupts the very meaning of self-constitution with its possibility of no self at all, a possibility that is dasein's and is most properly so? Our issue is, how does dasein's nonbelonging put ethics in question as Heidegger establishes dasein's proper way to be vis-à-vis its being?

The tension that we have to work with in *Being and Time*, when we consider dasein's propriety regarding itself, its authenticity, is found in Heidegger's em-phasis on dasein's ontological structure as the unifying origin, in the sense of condition for the possibility, of all relative, ontic ways of existing, and in his showing that this ontological structure and its account are in question by virtue of dasein's own disclosure. Dasein's ontological structure provides the basis for raising the question of being, for interpreting its historicity, and for showing how it might exist appropriately with regard to its being. But the basis is more like abyss than like anything that can be properly called normative. Given our in-herited senses of ultimate meaning for reality and the intrinsic value of human existence, this discovery appears at first nihilistic. If we have no solid reference to support the values of individual lives, then anything can be justified. Anything has, of course, been justified in our history, including the most severe repressions, torture, extreme cruelty, wars, and the morbid enslaving and destructive segregation of vast groups of people. The proliferation of norms whereby we justify certain values and contend against other values mirrors our fear of what the world would be like if we lacked an adequate basis for justifying our values and realizing the best possibilities of ourselves. The tension in Heidegger's thought between the search for a normative basis for thought and the discovery of a 'basis' that puts that search in question arises directly out of the fear to which our tradition responds by supporting its ideals and highest hopes with a combination of axioms, authorizing disclosure, and careful judgment.

The tension in Heidegger's thought puts in question the combination of axioms, authorizing disclosure, and judgment, as well as the belief that with a proper normative basis for our values we can hope to overcome the destructive proliferation of violently opposing ways of life. The question we are approaching is whether people can find options to grounded normativity as the basis on which they come to be who they 'should' be. Do options to the traditionally ethical ones arise for our language and thought when the tension between ontological grounding and being that cannot be a ground, but is like an *ab-grund*, defines the space for thought? Does Heidegger's account of the basis for authenticity twist free of its ethical desire for grounding presence?[1]

Heidegger's analysis shows that our 'natural' identities are formed within complex histories and communities that structure our identities as though the inherited values were absolute. It further shows that their conceptual structure is based on the assumptions that being is continuing presence and is simple, that time is linear and quantifiable, that death is the endpoint of life, and that human being has a kind of nature that is available to objective discovery. Our everyday, "fallen" lives are thus the basis of traditional metaphysical thought and the means of evaluation accompanying it in the name of ethics.

The normal is *"uneigentlich"*—improper, not true, not essential—and *"verloren,"* lost. When we hold in mind that the possibility of ethical thought and action is found in traditional 'normalcy' and its history, we see the cutting edge of Heidegger's thought concerning dasein's resolve: as we turn to the possibility of *Eigentlichkeit,* authenticity, we are turning away from ethics as we know it even as we turn to dasein's determining itself in relation to its mortal disclosiveness. Nonbelonging interrupts both our heritage of ethics and the possibility of making authenticity into a new ethics. This turning away from ethics is no less than a twisting free of a body of selfhood that is given in its investment in not knowing its being or its propriety vis-à-vis its disclosure to which it cannot belong. It is a turning that occurs *in* dasein's authenticity. Heidegger's position is far stronger than one that provides only a formal basis for determining what our normative values should be. This metaphysical strategy of formal-positive determination is changed by his thought, which is under the impact of mortal temporality's ekstasis vis-à-vis belonging and dwelling. The question is whether we are able even in our authenticity to recognize the range of our suffering and pleasure or the meaning of the institutions and disciplines by which and in which we become who we are in the expectation of belonging to a way of dwelling that is appropriate to our being.

The "voice" of dasein's possibility "calls" in the midst of our involvements. Heidegger uses the experience of conscience, not its contents, as his phenomenal field. In his account, we undergo a calling away from our identities and selves to the possibility of our being. This call is corrupted by religions and moralities to seem as though it were calling to a specific way of life or ethos and as though it were initiated by specific violations that arouse guilt in a given individual. But the call itself discloses not the power of an ethos but the difference of human being, in its being, from its traditional ways of life. One undergoes, in the disclosiveness of dasein, a continuous "call" to its propriety, its *eigenste Selbstsein-können*, its most appropriate ability to be itself. Dasein's call to itself is like a voice that comes to dasein in the midst of its traditional life, like an appeal or summons to undergo the difference, in its being, from its self. "It gives dasein to understand" that its being is found in the disclosiveness of its ability to be in its possibility of no possibility at all, not in its values or in the objects of its religious and philosophical projections. The voice of conscience, as the disclosure of dasein's being in the midst of its everyday values and standards, functions to make those values and standards uncertain and to "call" dasein to its difference from who it is in its efforts to be someone recognizable in its culture.[2]

The wrenching away from dasein's self and the interruption (Heidegger says breaking into) of our identities by the call of conscience are constitutive movements of dasein that put it in touch with itself. Dasein's self, Heidegger says in section 57, is clearly not in the call of conscience which presents neither a person nor a definitive and definite way of life. Nothing familiar is encountered. In our experience of ourselves we ordinarily say that we are lost when we find no landmarks or customs to which we can relate with familiarity. But in Heidegger's account we begin to find ourselves when we are dislocated and displaced by the disclosure of our being that has no 'stand', no name or heritage in our environment. The wrenching movement and displacement are aspects of the disclosure of being in our everyday world and is hence both our inauthentic and authentic existence. In this "call" we began to hear the "understanding" that constitutes the *Vorlauf* of our finitude. There is no observer, no judge, no clear definitions or standards. But instead of being lost, we are homing in on our being. This wrenching movement means in the context of *Being and Time* that we are being freed from the "lostness" of our familiar world of cultural inheritance and from the surveillance of our identities that make us who we are. To be *eigentlich*—proper to our being—and attuned to our being in our everyday lives, we have to overcome the monopolizing power of valences and exigencies that define who we are.

Heidegger's account of the call of conscience provides for his interpretation the possibility of this overcoming, this twisting free. It further establishes the difference that constitutes our lives and shows that in this difference we, as culturally determined identities, have access to the being whose erasure is part of who we are traditionally to be. To trust our meanings and values by giving them axiomatic status, to stake our lives on them, and to know ourselves in their mediation is to forget our being and the possibility of living appropriately as the being that we are. Only by the severity of the wrenching, twisting movement out of the surveillance and authority of our normalcy and identity can dasein come into its own. But its own is not something defined by belonging. Dasein, in its history, has been on an edge that it has sought to erase; and, coming to its own, dasein finds both the edge and its attempted erasure in the range of identities that it can be. The call of dasein's being, on Heidegger's account, is a call from its history in which the *danger* of its best establishments reveals a mortality that *Being and Time* finds difficult to speak in the radicality and terror that its history has bestowed upon it. And in being proper to its being, dasein finds itself without the ballast that it had come to expect in the technological tradition that makes possible the language of authenticity.

If the being of dasein were determinant and if it provided immediately a nature to be realized by individual action, ethics would not be put in question. We could in principle find out what our nature is and how to meet its standards. But since dasein, in being called to itself, is called to a being whose meaning is mortal temporality and thus has no intrinsic, determinant meaning at all, the structure of ethics as such is in question. To be in question does not mean that we may hope for a time when ethics will be abolished and we will live a higher life, unstressed by the difference between our being and our cultural lives. The "lostness" of everyday life is not to be lost, by Heidegger's account. It does mean that as we follow unquestioningly the patterns of our best ideals and values in a state of mind that knows, at least in principle, what is genuinely and universally good and bad, we are lost to our being and to our mortal indeterminacy. We cannot expect that such a life will unconsciously and inevitably override its mortal temporality by, for example, organizing our environments in systems of value that create totalities of meaning that are invested in ignoring both their own being and the meaning of their being for totalizing meanings. Whereas in the traditional thought of subjectivity one expects some type of self-realization consequent to conformity to the reality of the subject—whatever the subject might be—in the instance of *Being and Time* authenticity means the disclosure of human-being-in-question without the possibility of resolving the question or the problems that follow it. Is it possible that our systems of self-realization and self-sacrifice for higher values make inevitable a maiming of human life that is recognizable only when our best ways of being are profoundly disturbed by the nonpresence of our being? Do our axiomatic values at their best constitute a blindness to who we are and what we do? Does the disclosure of our being and its appropriation, along with the pain and disruption that constitute it and follow it, make possible a profound and thoroughgoing uncertainty that itself reveals the limits of ethics?

The question of ethics in the context of *Being and Time* is a way of being that is concerned in the world and with other people. It happens in language and practice and comes to itself as an individual who is already constituted by relations. The difference of being and everyday existence takes place only in world relations. Hence the emphasis on continuously twisting free of cultural domination *in* cultural life, never outside of it. The terminus is not a life that is withdrawn from culture and history; nor is it found in projected experiences that are ahistorical and purged of corruption. The aim involves an individual's being with others in a specific environment and history and attuned in its relations to the *Vorlauf* of its being without presence. The "perversion" that inevitably occurs in our standards for living is found in their insensitivity to their mortal temporality.

Heidegger articulates his interpretation in the traditional language of being as presence. Existential understanding is "given." Being "presents itself." Dasein "comes to itself." His interpretation is no less involved in the wrenching, twisting recoils than in dasein's authentic movements. In association with this articulation, Heidegger shows that as being presents itself, no subject or substance or nature is disclosed. The possibility for no possibility is disclosed. Mortal disclosure takes place. As dasein comes to itself, no specific course of action is indicated. The given existential understanding has neither a subject nor an object. Dasein's being does not name anything present; rather it names mortal, temporal disclosure that forecasts itself as temporal possibility rather than as a standing nature. The language of presence in this text is thus in a process of twisting free from its own inevitability in the tradition in which it occurs and in which Heidegger thinks. This movement articulates dasein's movement recoiling toward the possibility of authenticity in which nonbelonging is no less invoked than dasein's propriety regarding itself.

The issue of dasein's coming to itself is thus one of dasein's allowing its difference in its being vis-à-vis the status of its life. In this difference Heidegger finds the opening of nonbelonging and the questionableness of the manner in which we establish systems of value. If an individual can allow and affirm its mortal temporality, in contrast to the invested obfuscation of mortal temporality, and can allow also the *question* of the meaning of being in its historical identity, if it can want the 'address' of its being in spite of wanting a sense of continuous and meaningful presence, it can, perhaps, come to appropriate the difference of its own being as it decides its daily issues. This alertness is like a person's affirming or loving another person with a full sense of mortality in the relationship.[3] Or it is like experiencing the validity of a system of values without a sense of certainty or universality. Nothing specific is there to will in dasein's owning its being—hence the anxiety to which Heidegger gives attention. Allowing its being, dasein allows the "calling forth" of its continuous need to take care, given its primordial lack of stasis. This allowing, given the constitution of its identity, is like dasein's unburdening itself of traditional resistances and opening itself to the inevitability of being without foundations. Resoluteness thus cannot be conceived in terms of self-constitution. Rather, self-constitution requires a basis for validation, and authentic experience itself falls into question as dasein comes into its own through its disclosure of its incapacity to belong to its being.

The middle voice gives articulation to dasein's ability to be, its understanding, and its wanting to have conscience, each of which constitutes a manner or *Weise* of disclosiveness (*Erschlossenheit*) that also is not a subject or object with regard to an action. We are in a position to see that in open resolve (*Entschlossenheit*) and authenticity (*Eigentlichkeit*) disclosure discloses and time times, that Heidegger's emphasis is not on self-constituting action or intentional action but is on the (self-)disclosure of dasein's disclosiveness in which nothing belongs to no one. Dasein's disclosiveness is its being. It is being to death, the possibility of no possibility, the *Vorlauf* of no continuing presence. Dasein's being is *its* difference from the finite continuity of its identity and its being in the world. In its most proper being, no 'I' controls and no one belongs to being.

'I' is always situated in a locality of specific determinants. It does not enjoy the benefits of an ontologically founded ideal that can guide it to right decisions. Decisions are made in the power of the values and possibilities for action that are allowed by the situation. This is not a version of historical relativism, however, since the ontological indeterminacy of the specific situation is made inevitable by dasein's being, not by the control of history. The proliferation of values and meanings that characterize our history has its meaning in dasein's being, in its ability to be, as we have seen. The 'I' that resolves properly opens to its being in its situation, twists free from the control of predominant standards of judgment by attending resolutely to its being, and makes its judgments and commitments in the loosening of the bonds of the everyday by virtue of concerned and open regard for its being. As dasein lets itself be called forth in its most proper being, the 'I' is modified by the non-I of its being. It becomes strange to itself in its clarity of purpose and certainty, and it acts forthrightly in understanding the collapse of clarity in its being. No less situated, no less concerned or committed, the individual's attunements and expectations, its perceptiveness, satisfactions, and priorities are conditioned by, as it were, an open door to mortal time that lets in an element different from the presence and totality of value. It acts, but now in the questionableness of the possibility of its actions and in the transgressions of being that mark its living. To be this way is to be resolved, and to be resolved is to attest to the nonbelonging of being in the value-laden situation that one lives in and through.

The tension between Heidegger's language and the language that I have used to speak of nonbelonging mirrors a tension in *Being and Time*: the book's language is facing more than it can articulate; it belongs to a tradition that begins to overturn within it; it speaks with anxious obsession before the mortal temporality that conditions it and that it dreads. This tension, as much as the book's discipline and claims, reveals the nonbelonging that invests *Being and Time*'s tradition as an edge of risk, an edge that puts in question all the effort required to reach the edge. And it forecasts a manner of speaking and thinking that might be alert to kinds of suffering to which we are blind when we belong at a secure distance from something that properly explodes our familiar world into nonbelonging.

2 | Language in a Passing Sense of Transcendence

A Passing Sense of Transcendence

*B*Y THE PHRASE *the sense of transcendence* I have in mind a sense that something that transcends determinations is manifest in determinations. We are predisposed in our lineage to expect transcendence to be characterized by unity and by the positive value of making possible our orders of life, whether that 'something' be God, subjectivity, spirit, or nature in its purposeful unfolding. We are also predisposed to find *in* such unity and value at least indications of sacrality, even if sacrality 'in itself' is not directly manifest. I believe that our strongest options for experiencing differences are characterized by the sense of transcendence; we have difficulty expecting stable orders of life without transcending and grounding unity. This means that the sense of transcendence, even in its most secular contexts, carries in our traditions a virtually inevitable religious or theological implication.

In order to give focus to the passing of this sense, I ask you to allow me for the moment these questionable hypotheses. I will say more about them in the course of this discussion, particularly as I attempt to describe this passing sense in a specific text on language by Heidegger.

As one of its freedoms, philosophy has an ability to engage in processes whereby its own discourses are changed in their words, organizing values, questions, and concepts. This is not an originary, subjective ability but rather one that is given by the conflicts and transformations that are already under way in what is to be changed, i.e., in a lineage's conflicted language, thought, and practice. In this ability, philosophy is in the ken of poetry. Both philosophers and poets can contribute to fundamental changes in the perceptions, knowledges, and valuations that constitute the language in which they write and think. I say *contribute* because language and discourses have lives of their own in the sense that we who speak and know are always within an unencompassable reach and force of language to disclose things. Philosophers can help, for example, to bring toward the center of the discourse words or concepts or experiences that function on the mobile fringe of the discourse or silently in its omissions and thereby help to redistribute other dominant and organizing experiences, words, and concepts. I believe that such redistribution and reorganization happen, for example, *in* the archeological and genealogical knowledge that Foucault develops in *The Order of Things* and in *Discipline/Punish* as well as in Derrida's *Of Grammatology* or "White Mythology." We can also follow the shifting of discourse in Hegel's dialectic or in Nietzsche's transvaluation of values or in Heidegger's thought in the question of being.

Different words and thoughts, different manners of thought, and different experiences may emerge in such changes. The specific process of a change that is under way can play quite a significant role in the development of the differences in knowledges and values. This is the case in Nietzsche's thought in which the performance of self-overcoming and transvaluation exercises considerable power over all ideas and values that had authority by virtue of their seeming permanence or universality. It is also the case in Heidegger's thought as he finds that 'question' and 'way' replace methodological clarity and universal structures in his language about language. In such processes, Gods may lose their positions, what is considered ordinary may change, the very idea of nature might change, and, in our context, the thought and value of transcendence, its sense and the conceptuality that has developed around it, might become questionable. In such processes, a world-shift happens beyond the reach of subjectivities or group responsibilities. Such shifting might be catastrophic or life-enhancing or both, and when one thinks within the shifting far more happens than anyone can intend. How might we think this 'more' and this seeming excess of human determination without invoking the heavily loaded thought and language of transcendence?

In such instances of transformative thinking and speaking, tropes and thoughts arise that are awkward, counterintuitive, and often distressing within the discourse that undergoes the transformation. It is like the experience of changing a language from a classical and officially recognized style to a different and more democratic standard, whereby new words and tropes arise to speak experiences and concepts that are different—at times only subtly different, at other times largely so—from those that could be said in the older usage. Speaking and thinking in the loss of divinity and sacrality mark a considerable change from ontotheological speech and thought and give rise to new experiences, as well as to language that is counterintuitive, for those who sense transcendent presence within the tropes. That change is one that I would like to explore in the context of the language of transcendence. It may well be the case that in some languages of transcendence a metamorphosis of ontotheology occurs that preserves, in spite of the transformation, something like sacrality. And that remainder could well lead us back unawares to something like an ontotheology in the form of quasi-absolute, historical grounds for experience or an elevation of ethnic axioms to universal authority.

We may say in a preliminary way that we can easily expect that art, broadly conceived, provides us with a way to say what cannot be said within the limits of our trained conceptuality. Art seems to allow more space for the performative dimension of knowledge and expression, for something more attentive and mobile in its language before what is other to knowledge and thought. Art can even be conceived as a region of remotion and ek-stasis, one that brings to expression our transcendence not only of the everyday world but also of the limits of disciplined knowledge. What are we to make of such expectation? How are we to think, for example, of Heidegger's expectation that the poet might give birth to words appropriate to their own event and destiny, words that in turn can give the thinker new turns of thought? How are we to think of Derrida's exploratory prose when he ventures into quasi-literary expression?

When I ask how we are to think of such things, I do not mean to suggest that we should think ill of them. I do mean to point out that I see a connection between the conviction that the artist, in the creative act, participates in the universe's transcendent and creative power with extraordinary, performative insight (a conviction that is transformed into a part of Hegel's expectations regarding the movement of dialectical thought) and a conviction, now, about the special opportunity that art affords us to present the loss of transcendent presence and power. While we might not think that lyric poetry or creative narration open, in their performance, to the transcendence of the world-all or the Absolute, we might well find ourselves inclined to find in art an opening to the loss or transformation of the very things that a different age found *in* artistic activity.

I find this reversal attractive, this artistic, performed loss of what was gained by our forebears in artistic performance. The reversal has in it the irony and laughter as well as the mourning that are fitting for the passage of the thought and images of absolute reality. But I also feel caution at this point, a caution that is valued by many when it is claimed that metaphysics is dead and that we can now proceed to a better way of thinking. I believe that I do not need to address the possibility that in art or thinking there is immediate apprehension of something transcendent. Immediate knowledge and insight are not strong possibilities for us. In the broad problematic of mediation and immediacy, Hegel has won the day over Schelling and the later Fichte. But the way in which we conceive of difference in this context might be problematized around what I shall call the sense of transcendence. If we are not alert, we might well conceive an artistic reversal of a sense of participation in absolute reality in terms of difference that transcends us and entices us by its mystery, its dehiscence, its call, or its inexplicable requirements for us. When difference is attached to the sense of transcendence, we may well return to an idea of an indeterminate transcendence which we meet in a determinate way in our creative endeavor.

In broad terms, I suspect that when we conceive of difference we are strongly inclined by our lineage to do so within the power of a sense of transcendence. We might think, for example, of the *loss* of a transcendent absolute as though the loss were in a space of transcendence, as Bataille does. In that case, *loss* defines transcendence, exceeds the space of our ordinary lives and experiences, and incites quasi-religious thought and emotion. Or we might consider our ability to experience and think in terms of transcendence and find in such transcendence the grounds for order, temporality, or value. Our lives would depend on such transcendence as surely as in another age they were found to depend on the continuing presence of God. We will have to see whether such exorbited transcendence or subjective transcendence are linked intrinsically in our language to sacrality and ontotheology in spite of the intention of the particular thinker. In this endeavor we are carrying out one of thought's freedoms that I noted earlier. We are questioning the value of transcendence in the weakening of the traditional power of transcendence to organize our discourses and emotions and, in this process, we shall attempt to find the problematic that relies less on the value of transcendence and sacrality than often has been the case in our traditions. In this process I would like to emphasize the questionability of the sense of transcendence that, in its ambiguity, both pervades our ability to think and speak and that is itself qualified by no sense of transcendence at all.[1]

Language without Transcendence?

We turn to Heidegger's thought, which is heavily marked by the sense of transcendence. I shall not, however, approach his work deconstructively or with a double reading. Such a reading would be appropriate. It could show the play of the sense of transcendence in his thought, its dangers and the compromises that it requires. Rather I shall show the extent to which Heidegger moves through the sense of transcendence to a language that transists out of that sense. His is a way of thinking that puts its own sense of transcendence in question— and at times radically so—as this way of thinking moves through and at the same time releases the hold of that sense.

I suspect that one of the elements that makes rejection of Heidegger's so-called later work attractive is found in the degree to which he succeeds in mitigating in his language the power of the meaning and idea of transcendence as well as mitigating those styles of thought and expression that arise from a sense of transcendence. His later work is made difficult to appreciate especially by those readings of *Sein und Zeit* which are carried out largely uncritical of the sense and concepts of transcendence. Such readings usually treat dasein as a type of transcendental subjectivity, and even treat dasein as though Heidegger conceived it like a monad in the direct lineage of Leibniz. Such readings overlook the extent to which a sense of transcendence, as it comes to expression in *Sein und Zeit*, falls into stress and begins to crumble, and they consequently are unable to follow the movement of that crumbling in his thought after 1927. Part of this complex rejection of his work after 1935 probably has to do with an anxiety over the loss of transcendence and a presumed, consequent loss of a basis for value that transcends regional and tribal difference. While I believe that this anxiety is ill founded, it is nonetheless largely unavoidable today.

I shall address another and more limited aspect in Heidegger's 'later' thought: his ability to think to some degree outside the valence of transcendence accompanied by the consequent strangeness of his language for us when we think within that valence. We shall see in the following section of this chapter how this ability on his part might address the question of thought and its relation to sacrality. Presently I will focus on his 1959 paper, "Der Weg zur Sprache."[2] In this focus I shall take his language and thought as experimental in the sense that it is an *attempt* to speak in the erosion of our language's and thought's representative power and in a quite different group of tropes. Indeed, representation almost becomes an optional trope instead of the form for proper thought and knowledge. Additionally, following the phenomenological direction, he looks for ways whereby to let what 'is' appear other than by argumentation. He looks for the appearing of language in speaking and for a speaking that is appropriate to such appearing. These aspects of his thought that are obvious to a careful reader are offensive, nonetheless, in their performance to the ear of the sense of transcendence. That sense always looks for grounds, mediation, reflective distance, and representational exactness and honesty. In this turn from the sense of transcendence, a return to Husserl (as a necessary condition for understanding Heidegger) probably exacerbates rather than mitigates our difficulty in following Heidegger's thought out of the sense of transcendence.

This experimental effort on Heidegger's part looks for words and tropes that move us away from the role and rule of subjectivity in its manifold occurrences in our ability to know and speak in the presencing of what is. Heidegger looks for a way in which to say things in regard to language that allows 'what' is not representable in language to appear. In our context, we can say that Heidegger looks for a way of speaking and thinking that moves away from its own suggestion of transcendence, which means that he attempts to rethink what we are accustomed to calling 'difference' and 'identity' as well as 'transcendence' and 'immanence'.[3]

When language is conceived within a sense of transcendence it is usually conceived as giving expression to a subject. It is conceived as mediating a subject to other subjects, as giving sound and communicability in a social world. Language is posited as sounding out meaning, embodying it in world relations. In von Humboldt's language, language is a "work of spirit" by which work a "true world" is engendered.[4] As we turn to Heidegger's encounter with von Humboldt's theory of language, I shall address only Heidegger's account of von Humboldt in the context of transcendent subjectivity in order to give focus to

Heidegger's thought. Von Humboldt views language as something that he can know by viewing it. Language is posited by spirit on this account, and *this account* also posits language, sets it forth as something that is to be viewed and known in its view. The knowing subject transcends what is to be known and performs this transcendence as it sets forth what it will know. Von Humboldt carries out the work of spirit, as he conceives it, in the knowledge of language that he develops and, in that process, he develops a view of language that articulates his sense of spirit's transcendence of the world that spirit creates. What he does as he knows and thinks, and what he describes as happening in the coming of language, cohere in the activity of positing, an activity that I shall say is optional with respect to the prominence that it has in the theoretical activity and claims that characterize von Humboldt's knowledge and thought. We find the sense of transcendence *in* this claiming activity. Further, we can say that in this view spirit both transcends the world and is immanent in the world as presented in language.

For von Humboldt, both individuality and totality are presented in the language-world: identity and difference show both the universality of spirit and the singularity of its expression. The found and viewed world is saturated with the subjectivity of "spiritual" activity, an activity whose life is articulated in specific world events as continuing in and through and beyond those events.

This formulation, which moves among the axes of transcendence, immanence, identity, and difference, expresses one of the problematics that must be rethought if the language and sense of transcendence are to lose their formative power for our thinking. Otherwise we will be tempted to retain some version of transcending identity to provide a continuing identity in the midst of change and transition, just as we will want to find for our descriptions a site wherein beings are accessible and conditioned by transcending presence, such as the possibility and experience of obligation and justice. We will be perplexed by the other's appearance and by a relation that allows the other to be other. Mediation will seem to contaminate the other's being, and immediately will seem unintelligible. Such a problematic and the transcendence that it carries, I have said, are found in the manner in which von Humboldt's knowledge and thought proceed. The problematic and transcendence are found in both the performative activity and the conceptual content of his work.

Heidegger, I believe, attempts in the essay before us to avoid a continuation of a modified idealism and a sense of transcendence in his effort to think in a way that gives the experience (*Erfahrung*) of language in the performance of his thought. His way of thinking thus requires of itself that it suspend the authority of what 'we' know about language, turn descriptively to what strikes 'us' as strange about language and outside of our powers of explanation, and carry out an *Erfahrung* of language as thought and speaking that allow language to be its own way to itself, an 'itself' that Heidegger surmises to be nothing other than the way. This thinking would not be a relation of transcendence. It would not be an act of *Geist* or of positing or of any kind of self-enactment of subjectivity. It would be an event of language in which language owns 'itself' on the way to itself, a linguistic event in which language speaks 'itself', clears the way to 'itself', without other basis or grounds.[5]

We can agree with Heidegger when he says of such formulations that they strike us as exceedingly strange. This language constitutes a crisis of communication and understanding—a *juncture where 'we'* can easily feel repelled. Heidegger often sounds unprofessional. We are not before a crisis of disagreement so much as before one of style and sensibility. Heidegger's turn seems wrongheaded. I believe that this kind of crisis arises for 'us', in part because, as we shall see, a traditional structure of transcendence is violated by his efforts toward a performance of thought that abandons the value of the thinker's transcendental position in relation to what is thought, known, and said. As a consequence, the other's transcendence is also abandoned, but not by virtue of claims of immanence, mediation, or identity. And this move is made by Heidegger with a claim to go to the 'thing itself' within a destiny provided by *Seyn*, but without the support of an idea of transcendental subjectivity or a methodology of transcendental reduction or a notion of spirit or the thought of an ideal subject or cause-effect relation or phonocentric interpretation of language or a theoretical turn to thought. I believe that this lack of support achieves—performs—a sense of abandonment and loss of grounds that is part of what Heidegger finds to occur in language's way to 'itself'. "It is a matter of getting closer to what is peculiar to language," Heidegger says.[6]

The way to language—to getting closer to it—is characterized by speakers' *belonging* to speech.[7] We do not belong to speech by causing it or by its having a causal effect on us, Heidegger says. But such assertions only go so far as to interrupt some of our unspoken assumptions about language that are embedded in our operative, subject-oriented knowledge of language. Such assertions function to point us in directions that are largely unapparent to us in both our professional and our day-to-day beliefs. Further, we can address this kind of interruption, debate it, and even assent to it conceptually while living out the transcendent posture of knowers and subjects who know themselves to maintain a mediated or an immediate relation with things: we can continue to live in a sense of transcendence while we address such an interruption. When Heidegger identifies our belonging to speech by virtue of a *Zusammengehören*, however, and says by his phrasing that belonging occurs as hearing, thereby shifting our imagery from the dominance of sight, and when he says that hearing is rifted in its very connection—we could say that belonging to language in its hearing is clefted in its design (*Aufriss*)—when Heidegger says such things in the context of being together in common, he makes awkward, *in that thought*, our own professional knowledge and our day-to-day beliefs. The structure to which we see ourselves belonging in our everyday lives loses its immediate power of persuasion in its occurrence, and we belong to the losing—or to the rift—in belonging to the "design" of Heidegger's language.

This kind of reversal is, of course, a common trope in Heidegger's writing. By it, in this essay, he moves from what sounds strange and bizarre in our disciplined knowledge as well as in our good common sense to a turn of thought in which our commonality is not even hearable in our usual perceptions. At the same time, our deep assumptions about sight and knowledge and the transcendental relation between knowing and what is known are distressed. He reports that he is following by means of thought a dimension in language that is lost to our best, disciplined speech and thought, following something to which we belong largely unawares, and belonging to it in such a manner that in it we are beyond stable grounding—beyond reason, we could say. In effect, whatever unity is found occurs in sounding, rifted, unspeakable bearing-toward-connection in language about which we have no clear knowledge and the very saying of which leaves us puzzled and uncertain in our most honest thought.

My understanding of Heidegger's effort at this point is that he has found in language and in language about language intimations of 'something' quite different from what 'we' think or know language to be. He has found traditional conceptions of language usually to be in the service of things other than language, and he has found that, when he turns to language in its presencing and attempts to think and speak in careful attendance to it, he is required to find different words and movements of thought than those available to him in his philosophical discipline. And even those different words and ways of thinking offer no satisfaction. They constitute attempts, but those attempts in their way-quality, their lack of established, defining rationality, and their appearing to converge out of seemingly disconnected fragments of experience and language—such aspects of the attempts seem to attune him to the 'way' of language. His 'basis' of attunement is considerably different from von Humboldt's. Whereas the activity of positing on von Humboldt's part constituted a spiritual attunement in his thought, Heidegger's lack of guidance and the collapse of the subject's grounding—in a certain sense, the departure of spirit's rule—constitute an attunement to language in Heidegger's exploratory effort. In Heidegger's exploration, the territory takes over from the discoverer and guides the means of exploration by opening or not opening to the activity and language that traverse it. In this case, the exploration is a process that continuously erodes the effective power of the traditional subject, the connections that have traditionally defined language, and the sense of transcendence that has defined the movement and 'place' of language. It is 'the way' that performs the erosion of transcendence, and it is 'the way', I believe, that is most likely to offend us or leave us nonplussed in our professional accomplishment. The very thought of language as the field and medium of objective and representational knowledge now feels misleading in the words and movement of Heidegger's thought. The appearing of language is questionable. Our experience of the 'reality' of language is solicited and shaken. It might be the case that in following language we come to nothing that is essential and rule-governed. When language comes to appear in such unsettling difference, our sense of transcendence also can be shaken. Perhaps language can appear without such a sense, without subjective or objective or positing or sacred grounds, without 'substitution', and without the dominant problematic of identity. Heidegger's direction, of course, is toward the suggestion that language gives presence in a presencing withdrawal of presence. We could blow on the embers of the sense of transcendence by saying that language is like a mystical absolute in its withdrawing presencing. The inclination to save the sacred for Heidegger in that way, however, can be checked by hearing the *es gibt* of language in the exploratory lack of resolution that characterizes his thought. He is not attempting to save any present being, most particularly not a hidden presence beyond presencing and the call of language. In the *es gibt*, the sense of transcendence begins to wither.

If language is not followed in the thought of transcendence, is 'hearing', as Heidegger thinks of it in the context of speakers' belonging to language, a kind of immanence? Hearing and speaking are closely associated: both occur as letting something appear, as the showing of things when speaking occurs. Speaking and hearing "occur simultaneously," Heidegger says.[8] This occurrence of simultaneity occasions the self-showing of what is *and* the self-showing of language. "We speak from language." The self-showing of language is at once a hearing that "lets itself come to saying."[9] As speakers we can hear the self-saying of language: we belong in that hearing to language's self-saying. Perhaps in this language of belonging and hearing we are more than a little implicated in our tradition's thought of immanence, particularly that Platonic kind of immanence by which we find ourselves finitely participating in nonfinite reality because of the kind of disciplined activity in which we engage and which engages us. Just as the soul's immortal part may come to bear in the careful asceticism of dialectical mentation, for example, so perhaps according to Heidegger the speaker comes into an already occurring self-saying in language when the speaker is attuned to it through highly disciplined—i.e., ascetic—*Erfahrung* and *Nachsagen*. If so, we can say that the thought of immanence runs silently through Heidegger's language and that we can expect the complementary sense of transcendence to live there as well—in the immanence of the self-saying of language to which we as speakers belong. Perhaps Heidegger's language lifts us up into the pure and at least quasi-sacred immanence of language's speaking, in which site we might learn anew how to hope for a return of the Gods or at least for a saving sense of sacrality. More than one philosopher has taken such a path of interpretation, and many more have turned up their noses before the "later Heidegger" on the assumption that he leads us toward a restored and romantic experience of the holy.[10] Even if Heidegger is not quasi-platonic in his thought, the issue of immanence remains.

It remains in this way: even though our belonging to language is not specifically conceived as conscious immediacy, our belonging to language—our speaking in the hearing of language's own speaking—nonetheless is without mediation. We *could* say that our determined speaking mediates language. But that is exactly what Heidegger does not say in his thought of *Ereignis*. The way to language is language's own saying, our attunement to which happens as we *lose* our way to language in our best traditional knowledge of it and as we turn to language's self-showing. Language's own saying "holds sway" in all speaking as language lets "what is coming to presence shine forth, lets what is withdrawing into absence vanish. . . . The saying [of language] joins and pervades the open space [*das Freie*] of the clearing [*Lichtung*] which every shining must seek, every evanescence [*Entscheinen*] abandon, and in which every presencing and absenting must show itself and say itself."[11] No mediation takes place: language says itself and shows itself, and our speaking happens *in* the hearing of that saying.

Rather than mediation, Heidegger thus speaks of hearing and belonging. A sense of transcendence could inspire us in this context to use such verbs as *radiates* and *illuminates:* language radiates or illuminates speaking. We might say that in hearing language, one transcends speaking, that the essence of language transcends speech, is at once present in it and continues beyond its determination. This, however, is the kind of language that Heidegger does not use in this essay.

He speaks instead of *eignen* and *Ereignis*, of showing and hearing *in* which things come into *their* own in their coming to be and passing away. The force of Heidegger's language, if I may use such a phrase, is toward the thing's own occurrence in saying and showing itself: toward the things' *enownment*, in Albert Hofstadter's translation of *Ereignis*.[12] Things say themselves. In a more directly middle-voiced grammar we might say that a thing's sound sounds itself. Such self-saying is not caused by something else or caused by means of a subjective act. Beings are en-owning. They are enabled in their en-owning in the very occurrence of self-showing.

Neither this language of 1959 nor Heidegger's language concerning *phenomenon* in his 1927 introduction to *Sein und Zeit* are translatable without severe loss into cause-effect terminology or into a language of transcendence. This language requires a rethinking of what we experience as self or subject. But his language does place an emphasis on what we might call immediacy. There is no mediation between concealing and revealing, for example, or between bestowal and loss. Our belonging (*gehören*) to language is without mediation in our hearing (*hören*) the *Sage* of language, and the *Sage* is without mediation in language's occurrence.

If we take *immanence* to mean immediacy, we will find Heidegger using a language of immanence. But in the deterioration of the language of transcendence, the meaning of immanence as the indwelling presence of transcendent being is inappropriate and misleading. *Ereignis* is not an event of transcendent presence, and I believe that in that light the word *immanence* loses its traditional force and meaning. As we experiment with language and thought in the loss of the sense of transcendence, we can say that the thought of immediacy also changes. It loses a traditional affiliation with immanence and moves outside of a pairing with transcendent mediation.

A Variant Sense

"It is as though a variant sense occupies the old husk, something different is given in unaltered coinage, and a differently scaled sequence of ideas is intimated according to unchanged syntactical laws."[13] With these words Wilhelm von Humboldt, who was terminally ill when he wrote them, described the manner in which time as "a growing development of ideas" can impact a language from inside that language. And these words also speak to Heidegger's own strategy as a thinker. He attempts to write in a different sense from the one that is borne by many of the core words in our lineages, words such as *Wesen, Brauch,* and *Ereignis.* The different sense is usually one that is traced as lost in those words, one that is suggested and obscured in the lineage. Perhaps the coming of time—the timing of time—in our lineage gives far more than the lineage enables us to say. Perhaps there is traced in von Humboldt's words an altering movement—"an enhanced power of thought," in his words—one that is phrased as "the growing development of ideas" but one that opens to a gathering and giving dimension of time in language that is not imagined by historicist views of language. In the image of the dying von Humboldt's writing these lines, Heidegger connects mortality, the coming to pass of our lineage—its temporal *Wesen*—with the coming of time as the enownment of things.

If I am right in saying that the sense of transcendence is passing away in Heidegger's thought, then the excess of language as he finds it vis-à-vis our lineage's knowledge of language should not predominantly suggest transcendence or any present alterity and should not lead to experiences either of sacrality or of sacred images. We find this turn in his attempt to bring language as language to language.[14]

The way language comes to pass is found in the enownment or propriation (*Ereignis*) of whatever happens and appears. Language bears both its own release to saying/hearing and its release of things in *their* saying and sounding. Rather than saying that *Ereignis* is immanent or immediate in language, we must find ways to say that language in its saying and hearing lets things come to presence in its own coming to pass. Heidegger reverts to the middle voice in this thought—"das Ereignis ereignet"—and thereby invokes a voice whose loss may well figure the dominance of cause-effect relations through the dominance of the active and passive voices.[15] If language is to be thought by following its self-enactment and if this self-enactment is thoroughly self-saying, we find neither transcendence nor the immediacy of something that is revealed through language as other than language. We rather encounter things in their saying and hearing without need of the explanatory power of any type of transcendental subjectivity. Such a descriptive claim does not, of course, answer most of our questions, questions which arise from a language saturated with the sense of transcendence. This claim and others like it are calm in a maddening way before the urgencies of our ethos. But the claim is nonetheless offered that if we bring language to language as language we will perhaps hear an attunement to the need and occurrence of things that is outside the range of human and non-human transcendence.

Such displacement of humanity by language and *Ereignis* inevitably sounds quasi-religious in our tradition. It attaches to ages of asceticism in the form of dependence on transcendental meaning and self-denial. Worse still, this kind of displacement suggests a regressive loss of attention to human transcendence and human value, perhaps even a loss of that spirituality that gives priority to human need and suffering. In this context, human transcendence in the form of universal, historical subjectivity seems to promise a development of freedom from just the kind of mystical regression and self-abnegation to which Heidegger's later thought seems to return us. This kind of thinking seems particularly to be saturated with quasi-mystical transcendence when we read it within the operations of the sense of transcendence. And an emphasis on subjectivity or a priori obligation or some other kind of transcendence can appear to be a move away from thought that is captured by the kind of transcendence-immanence dyad that some readers find in Heidegger.

I am saying to the contrary that in a move to recover the priority of a human subjectivity or of impenetrable 'otherness', the sense of transcendence is not only undisturbed but continues to work its way toward a kind of transcendence which, in its momentous singularity and determination, inevitably carries—belongs to—the lineage of holiness and sacrality, that in such momentousness, when combined with universality, the movements of totalization remain in effect quite regardless of our intentions to stop short of the extremity of sacrality.

On the other hand, in Heidegger's thought of *Ereignis* and language's return to language, the sense of transcendence is solicited through the displacement of transcendent presence. Heidegger turns to the *way* to language, and in his descriptive account language is 'waying' without nature, without presence, without transcendence, and without immanence. I noted earlier that Heidegger's thought is a dangerous bearer of the tradition. In this case a tradition of immanent being is thoroughly de-structured and rethought in the valence of

Ereignis-without-transcendence. When we think the connections of things and the spaces that make connection enigmatic, when we think them in a displacement of a sense of continuing presence, the sense of transcendence and its remarkable power may undergo deterioration that allows Heidegger's thought to appear without those mystical trappings that the sense of transcendence can add to it. It is the overturning of mystical transcendence that takes place in his thought of bringing language as language to language—a phenomenology, if you will, without transcendent presence.

"Der Weg zur Sprache" is a part of Heidegger's rethinking of time, a process that von Humboldt phrases in a preliminary way as "time often introduces into [language] an enhanced power of thought and a more penetrating sensibility than it possessed hitherto, and it does so through the burgeoning development of ideas. It is as though a *variant sense* occupies the old husk, something different is given. . . . "[16] The "variant sense" is found in Heidegger's account of language in an alteration of the sense of transcendence, an alteration that requires us to confront the sense of transcendence that marks both our reading of Heidegger as well as our efforts to be moral and responsible thinkers.

I have said that the sense of transcendence pervades our language and thought and enables us to recognize things in our accustomed ways. Hence there is a traumatic dimension to our experience of displacing that sense. Our emphasis has fallen on the value of the displacement and not on what might be the most proper way to effect a displacement of and in the sense of transcendence. I have also said that within the sense of transcendence we are inclined toward an expectation of momentousness, an expectation that would seem to figure Heidegger's Hölderlinean idea that the Gods might return. If there is a deterioration and transfiguration of the sense of transcendence in Heidegger's thought, this hope could well be an articulation of a crisis in his thought, one in which a metaphysical struggle reaches a place of what Heidegger has called *Entscheidung*, a crisis that marks a division in his thought, and one that allows attunement to both the passage and persistence of the sense of transcendence.

If one needs such a momentous idea, the thought that Gods might return in language's enownment calls for experiencing Gods and their difference without transcendence. The discipline includes our thinking difference in the passing of the sense of transcendence. The divine husk seems to be falling away along with altars, sacred piety, and the holy distance between Gods and people. But such thought is speculative and abstract: 'what *would be* the case if the Gods return?' It might be enough for us to think exploratorily in the passing of the sense of transcendence and to give rise to language in the sense of transcendence's loss as we attempt to rethink what language requires of us.

3 | Ethics in a Passing Sense of Transcendence

The Sense of Transcendence

Transcend IMPLIES SPACE AND PLACE. It is opposed to words which denote placement within the limits of something or which denote present standing. In the context of this discussion, the word indicates a surpassing quality, a movement of crossing over, and continuation beyond 'here'. It has an inevitable suggestion of elevation and ascension on the one hand and excess on the other. Something that is said to transcend an individual, for example, is said not only to be present to the individual in some manner but also to escape the limits of the individual's presence and grasp and to be excessive in a way that is usually positive either in value or power. An individual may be said to transcend an intended object by virtue of the individual's structure or power of presentation—by virtue of an excess and difference that we might call an a priori capacity for the appearing of things. This transcendence of the subject is often said to be grounds for truth and order. *Transcend* usually does not suggest badness, meanness, or lowliness.

This combination of meanings for *transcend* and positive value, for example, is particularly evident in our Platonic lineage. A crossing over is thought to take place in every occurrence. Timeless and deathless reality is present to the order and the determination of mortal things. In Aristotle's tradition, too, we expect to find indication of transcending unity in physical movement as well as in time. This sense of transcendence with determination is a part, I believe, of our historically developed ability to think in this sense: as we think or talk we are in lineages that give us to expect that in all specific events something that transcends the determinations is manifest in the determinations. We expect embodiments of something more than the passing occurrences in limited events. *In this way of thinking* we also often experience some kind of transcending unity as the necessary condition for finite orders and hence for finite values.

The connection between transcendence and unity in our lineage is also troubled. We are able to have a sense of unencompassable emptiness transcending us. We are able to think of being as pure transcendence without determinant unity, and we can think of indeterminate transcending possibility. But the issue of unity combined with transcendence is never far from Western preoccupation.[1] Madness, whether in the form of insanity or of nihilism, has often suggested in our history fragmentation instead of a grounding, unifying presence. Our sense of transcendence combined with unity is closely associated with 'healthy' spirituality, hope, and meaning. The possibility of transcending movement without definitive unity suggests fatal disruption of world order, loss of the possibility of truth, and life in a perverted ascendancy of death. The dominant sense of transcendence in our history tends toward feelings of meaninglessness and despair if it is disassociated from a recognition of unity in transcendence.

When our sense of transcendence is combined with a sense of unity and faces experiences of radical difference, we are thus predisposed to undergo a feeling of nonresolution, a threat of disorder in the space of transcendence. If that space is felt to be traversed by differences absent the unity that is 'required' to give them relation and order, we feel a perversion of order within order. It is the crazy-making sense that a unifying, determinate transcendence is disunified by limits internal to its occurrence, as though, for example, fragmentation transcended temporal unities, chaos yielded order, transcendence were nothing but another determination, or historical configurations of experience and practice produced the sense of transcendence. It is as though transcendence were transferred to nontranscendence in a process of discovering the meaning of our sense of transcendence.

Our sense of unity is troubled when difference grows in value in our sense of transcendence, when, for example, empirical objects, nonorganic singularities of disciplined knowledge and truth, or human individuality without transcending human nature forcefully and oppositionally impact our sense of transcendence. In such circumstances *transcend* and *transcendence* can be used to indicate the presence of difference which differentiates beyond experiential and reflective grasp and which gives no promise of continuing and transcending unity. *Troubled*, I believe, is the right word. *Transcendence* is now appropriately associated with highly limited unities or with the loss of a sense of unity, with the crossings over among determinate unities in a departure from singular and transcendental unity. Differences seems to scan transcendence. This experience arises from a different sensibility when compared to that of both philosophers and theologians who discover a resurgence of unity in the transcendence that accompanies 'nature', 'mind', and 'value'. That resurgence may well be the self-articulation of one sense of transcendence in our lineage, its middle-voiced manifestation in some people's recognitions of limited orders. But however such resurgence of unity is found, the sense of unity in transcendence is troubled when transcendence is qualified in its own occurrence by differences-without-unifying-presence.

This qualification of transcendence by differences is probably as old as our traditional and dominant sense of transcendence. A recognition of absence, death, diversity, and time in the possibility of no pervasive unity seems to inhere in the dominant Western experience of transcendence.[2] It is not a question of origins, of whether the sense of life without transcendence or a sense of mortal fragmentation gave rise to a sense of transcendence. My observation is rather that in the sense of transcendence a defining struggle takes place in which the possibility or threat of no defining transcendence is immediately palpable and imaginable. The possibility of no transcendent presence is palpable in the much discussed experiences in ontological anxiety, in mystical experiences of the soul's dark night, and in that doubt of which Descartes has become emblematic. There are many ways to experience and give image *within* the sense of transcendence to the possibility that the sense of transcendence is illusory, e.g., a deceiver God, our existence is only a dream, transcendence is an unconscious and fragmented projection. And there are many ways to counter such experiences and images. I believe that it is accurate to say that the large and diverse lineage that we call traditional metaphysics is defined in part by efforts to maintain, articulate, and build up the sense of transcendence before a contradictory sense that dwells in the sense of transcendence. It is a troubled sense that struggles with its differences, revisions itself endlessly, reexamines its evidence with calm obsession, and rethinks its own sensibility in logics and concepts that both reassure it and reenact the struggle in different patterns of differences that are ordered in a presence beyond difference.

Transcendence, however, is not limited in its meaning to traditional metaphysical thought. It functions even in thought that is governed more by difference than by unity. The other 'transcends' me whether or not there is transcendental presence to define our difference. The other transcends me, for example, in such regional samenesses as species likeness, communal likeness, addresses to me, or likeness of occurrence. Language transcends the individual who speaks; the knowing, speaking individual transcends the known or addressed other; the other transcends the one who experiences it; lineages transcend their expressions and outcroppings; authorities transcend those within their rule; the ruled transcend by their choices those who rule them: difference is transcendence, we might say. *Transcendence* need not suggest unity or even elevation and positive value. Any excess that differentiates itself in withdrawal from total inclusion in its specific determination might properly be called transcending.

Let us attempt, however, to put thoroughly in question the sense of transcendence, to maximize the struggle that takes place within it, to interrupt the powerful suggestion of unity that the sense of transcendence often carries with it. If we intend to intensify the experience of fragmentation in the sense of transcendence and its languages and images; if we agree with the descriptive claim that a certain obsession accompanies the sense of transcendence in its inclusion of its greatest opponent—a sense of fragmentation and mortality without transcendent presence or unity; and if we intend to intensify this fragmentation in the sense of transcendence, we might well wish to set in motion a way of think-ing that holds in question that sense and turns the obsession with fragmenta-tion and mortality against itself, a strategy employed by Nietzsche in Book III of *The Genealogy of Morals* in his encounter with the ascetic ideal. We might well wish to turn toward a language that diminishes the meaning of transcendence on the assumption that that meaning will include, in spite of our intention, not only patterns of thought that inevitably tend toward the reinstatement of the sense of transcendence but also a quiet anxiety before mortal fragmentation. One of the most effective ways to continue our Western obsession with death, absence, and emptiness would be to continue through languages of transcen-dence to reinstate the site of conflict between transcendental unity of whatever kind and difference without transcendental unity (or difference with separate and mortal unities). To the extent that we use the language of transcendence, I suspect that the patterns that we wish to interrupt and break will reassert them-selves in the breaking process. Hence the strategic advantage of interrupting the sense of transcendence and its many languages without an uninterrupted reversion to the sense and the associated languages.

Levinas's thought in *Otherwise than Being* is one of our most sustained at-tempts to interrupt both our traditional thought of transcendental immanence and the thought of transcendental immanence combined with the thought of unity. But Levinas also retains the language of transcendence. In spite of the subtle turning that he effects in his thought as he thinks through and beyond the Western traditions of transcendence, he nonetheless retains a sense of tran-scendence that one could wish that he had put more radically in question. We shall turn to his thought after we consider an instance of thought that combines the sense of transcendence with the experience of withdrawal of transcendent presence, since the language and experience of such withdrawal are definitive of his effort as well as of the effort of this discussion.

Transcendence and Withdrawal of Transcendence

One experience of transcendence in our tradition gives priority to with-drawal of 'presence' over presence. I use the markers for *presence* to indicate, in the first instance, that in this experience transcendent presence is not experi-enced. We might use subjunctive and metaphorical constructions at first, even if we retract them later: it is as though there were presence that has disappeared and that leaves a strange space, as when you sense that someone might have left the room just before you entered it or that someone might be behind you; you turn around, and although you see no one you feel as if someone had been there. Or—and here we draw closer to the language of Hölderlin and Heidegger (particularly Heidegger in *Die Beitraege*)—withdrawal of 'presence' is like times when you are under some necessity in your language and tradition to speak of

God and in the speaking you must also speak of a catastrophic loss of God. The withdrawal (or departure) signals nothing in particular, not even a determinate emptiness, as though God were *here* and God is not *here* any longer. It is like a trace of something lost when you have no clear idea that something was or could have been lost (and not like the trace of something that you are tracking and can reasonably expect to find). All you have are unconfirmable reports and, more important, a language that expects God, for example, to have been here at the same time that you are able to speak only in the loss of all grounds for continuing that expectation.

There are different opinions about how the 'presence' might have been, and different opinions about the withdrawal. For Heidegger, for example, the sense of withdrawal carries with it sadness as well as a hope for kindling a language that restores something of the life and vigor that has marked our lineage—and in his hope he also knows that this withdrawal 'means' the human destiny of open finitude and death and cannot mean that a divine figure once literally filled a now empty space. The tragic loss and almost hopeless sensibility constitute an awareness of the appearing of things in a withdrawal of transcendence as continuing presence, of deathliness, of the immanent division of coming-to-life-with-dying. It also constitutes an awareness that the God's loss can be replaced by another kind of transcendental unity only at the cost of perpetuating 'what' is lost in its lostness. To avoid such substitute theology as might be found in any conception of transcendental unity, we need a language that arises from the withdrawal of transcendent presence and not from the 'unfilled space' of transcendence.

But that way of viewing the God's loss might also occasion relief and not much sadness if we were in a Nietzschean mood. It might be experienced as heralding an overcoming of a long nihilism of ascetic belief and hope, as giving rise to a cautious joy over the possibility of recuperation from both the sense of loss and the sense of a lost one, a release to new life. This difference between Heidegger and Nietzsche, which could be judged as expressing subtle, incommensurate sensitivities, at least has this agreement: we find the opening for whatever appears—a withdrawn 'foundation', if you will—not in any a priori structure or energy, not in any kind of reality, but in something like a space of withdrawn presence the occurrence of which is without reality and foundation.[3]

This linkage of 'transcendence' and withdrawal is lost if 'withdrawn presence' is given literal or symbolic meaning. Hölderlin's observation with regard to tragedy strikes me as accurate also in this context: in the experience of the God's withdrawal, all signs regarding divine presence come to nothing. And Heidegger's observation also seems accurate: a different language from the language that has traditionally given appearance to things is emerging in the awkwardness and uncertainty of these words of withdrawal. For Heidegger this language began to emerge in poets', especially Hölderlin's, sense of mortal being, a sense which seems to arise from the language they are given to write and in which they find their possibility for writing. This sense brings us to our language's own event—its other beginning, as it were, when compared to traditional meaning and thought—in a withdrawal of being that is immediate to the coming of being in the appearance of things. In this difficult language without common sense, language says or performs its own occurrence, as Heidegger finds it, for example, in Hölderlin's poetry. Language appears in its withdrawal—*evaporation, dehiscence, dissipation,* and *caesura* come to mind in thinking of language's performance of its own origin and event. Language begins to give word and thought to its own strange event of coming to be/passing away as it lets its own withdrawal in the presence of things come to word. Such language comes to replace traditional concepts of transcendental subjectivity and of things' own transcendence of their experience and knowledge. A different problematic arises without the organizing power of the language and sense of transcendence.

In this language and its explorations the sense of transcendence is changing radically enough that *transcendence* becomes increasingly unfitting. I doubt that *transcendence* is fitting at all unless there is an operative sense of presence by virtue of a hypostatizing movement of belief, faith, or speculation, i.e., a movement of mind that requires a sense of presence, even if it is withdrawn presence, in connection to the space and transfer that is suggested by *transcendence.* Transcendent presence gives meaning and linkage for the loss that is incurred in the transfer as what is transcended undergoes a movement beyond itself. In Heidegger's language of withdrawal, on the other hand, nothing even possibly present gives meaning to the withdrawal of God or to being or time. No transcendental meaning happens 'there'. The nouns continually evaporate into dispersed aether until they return ontically and absurdly, always unsatisfactory, from their complete loss of reference and nomination.[4] *Withdrawal* in this context is not a word of 'continuation beyond here'. It is a word without suggested continuation, crossing over, ascension, or unity. In this sense I believe that Heidegger is accurate when he says in effect that the language of the withdrawal of the Gods gives a language of mortality that cannot determine its saying by any transcendental reference or movement of transcending.[5]

Of course, *transcendence* does not have to mean the transcendence of some transcendental thing. By accentuating the connotation of excess, we might say that *withdrawal from determination* means *transcendence* pure and simple. Whereas *transcendence* suggests at once determination and lack of determination, on Heidegger's account *withdrawal* does not suggest either determination or lack of determination in the traditional senses of these words, any more than it suggests atheism, agnosticism, or theism. Withdrawal is not *an* excess. It belongs to the occurrence of things' coming to pass, their appearing, their manifestness, in a simultaneous presencing and loss of presence. Things happen as a foundationless loss of presence in presencing. That is not transcendence in a sense of crossing over. It is more like being crossed with no unity, no continuity, and nowhere to go, while one is also a singular and dynamic individual. Even the thought of a law of finitude became more and more doubtful for Heidegger as he thought in the caesura of the withdrawal of being.

Withdrawal marks a way of thinking that leaves the traditional experience of transcendence in the outer turning of the transcending orbit—in transcendence's own withdrawal as it moves, oscillating, from presence-to-consciousness through openings that it gives beyond presence: Heidegger's thought of withdrawal follows a movement of traditional experiences of transcendence, experiences of excess, in which withdrawal marks the movement of transcendent presence. In his thought, transcendence seems to move through itself toward thinking that was lost when presence conjuncted with transcendence.

In the previous discussion I showed that transcendence and withdrawal of transcendence constitute an experience that Heidegger has brought to experimental language and thought. His account of language requires that the persistence in our tradition of the sense of transcendence be continuously interrupted in the formation of a different sensibility and thought. Now, in order to connect transcendence, withdrawal of transcendence, and the question of ethics, we turn to aspects of Levinas's work in which an ethics accompanies a return of transcendence out of what appears at first to be a withdrawal of transcendence in his account of 'the other'.

The Withdrawal and Return of Transcendence

I said at the beginning of this chapter that in our lineage we are determined by both a sense of transcendence and a sense of radical difference. The sense of radical difference defines many experiences of transcendence and troubles the traditional linkage of transcendence and unity. In the preceding section I said that the withdrawal of God, Gods, or being can be thought—and is thought by Heidegger—in a movement of turning out of the sense of transcendence: while one can certainly find the language and images of transcendence in his thought, the language and images of withdrawal turn out of the language and imagery of transcendence toward 'an occurrence' that is not one of transcendence. At this point, that *turning*, with its interruptive effect, rather than an 'occurrence' without transcendence, holds our attention.

I would like to consider the interruption of the sense of transcendence by considering aspects of Levinas's thought in which transcendence submits to its own withdrawal. We can see in his thought a clash between Hebraic and Greek emphases that is thoroughly a part of our lineage, and we can follow this clash in Levinas's way of thinking that both allows transcendence to withdraw and reinstates transcendence-in-withdrawal in a prephilosophical experience of the other that is manifest in the Hebrew lineage and in departure from domination by the Greek lineage. In order fully to allow the question of ethics, we shall want a more intense interruption and release of transcendence than Levinas allows, but that issue at least becomes apparent in Levinas's thought. We shall see that the question of ethics arises out of the withdrawal of transcendence in a sense of transcendent presence and that the positive value of the question of ethics bestows a positive value on that withdrawal.

Transcendent presence is almost eliminated in Levinas's thought.[6] And so is inference from experienced presence to a transcendent and necessary condition for that experience. I say 'almost' because he speaks of a radical transcendence that is known by trust, not because of transcending presence but because of a religious and faithful Hebraic tradition. That means that in the context of Levinas's thought, we cannot *know* philosophically or reflectively any other individual in its transcending movement, i.e., in *its* 'presence'. Such 'knowledge', rather, comes from something prephilosophical—not from immediate experiences so much as from traditional Talmudic and midrashic processes of commentary in their combination with faith.[7] These faithful processes give one to know of a transcendence that is beyond human comprehension and appropriation. Such transcendence is not found to happen originarily in thought, poetry, creativity, or worship. It happens for Levinas in God's lack of immanence in a context of a people's sense of being called by God. God is not present to traditional knowledge of him. One responds in a traditional faith that finds itself under sacred mandate without divine presence. Such a sense of transcendence pervades Levinas's thought; it is a sense that lacks an experience of immediate presence. I want to look more closely at the sense of difference, as distinct to the experience of immanent presence, that so heavily qualifies this sense of transcendence. Does this sense of difference provide a withdrawal of transcendence *in* the sense of transcendence?

When I said that for Levinas the sense of transcendence happens originarily in a people's sense of being called by God and not in God's immediate presence to these people, I could also have said that the sense of transcendence happens for Levinas before the face of the other. The phrasing arises from my conviction that what Levinas addresses when he speaks of 'face-to-face' or of 'before the face of the other' is a thoroughly historical experience in the sense that the experience arises from a quite specific (and highly complex) lineage. Levinas's belief that what is ethically definitive of this tradition is universal in its truth also arises from a quite specific lineage. I do not, however, want to develop this observation. The genealogy of Levinas's belief is less important presently than the extreme emphasis on difference in his experience and interpretation of transcendence. But I want to note and later return to the possibility that 'the other' is constructed by a historically developed body of experiences and values that do not manifest anything outside of a lineage but rather show the core values and beliefs that constitute in part the perception of an ethos. That possibility does not deny the import of the other. It defines that import and interrupts the sense of transcendence more sharply than Levinas is prepared for—because he is still within the force and pattern of the sense of transcendence.[8]

The other, as Levinas writes of the other, takes place prephilosophically 'beyond essence' in the sense that the other is not constituted by 'being' or consciousness or experience. The other is not an event of consciousness, not subject to any ideality, never an aesthetic occurrence, not a projection, not a perceived immanence, and thus is not a presence-to-consciousness. The other makes requirements of consciousness before consciousness is.[9] Transcendence, if we are to use this word—and its use is still in question—takes place in this 'before', and this 'before' is proximity prior to any signification, appropriation, or assignation. Proximity is incommensurable with consciousness; it would not become conscious. Proximity is before appearance. It is contact without visibility, without appropriation in a system of signs and symbols. This proximity is "absolute exteriority." "It is the very transcending characteristic of this beyond that is signification."[10] Or, to use a type of phrasing characteristic of Levinas's writing, this proximity, this 'transcending', is different before there is difference, so different that 'other' must require its signification to pass away into the noncategorical and presignified concrete responsibility of the 'I' for the neighbor before 'other' can, as it were, be 'understood'. The other is 'understood' prereflectively in the 'one-for-the-other', in the self's responsibility for the other that comes totally without benefit of the self's initiation or a priori structure.

In the one-for-the-other, the self is given to be responsible for the other by the other's assigning the self, making the self to be already responsible before the self can enact itself or 'be' itself. The self is already responsible for the other when the self acts spontaneously because the other is always already in calling proximity as other to the self, as unbound and undefined by the self. The self is always in the accusative before the other. In our context, this means that the other's 'transcendence' does not belong to consciousness, selfhood, or any a priori structure of truth or condition for possible existence. This is what I have in mind by 'extreme difference': difference that as difference is totally ungraspable by a knowing identity. And this difference, in Levinas's thought, may be taken as transcendence, not the transcendence of something immanent to the consciousness but of something that withdraws its immanence in its accusative relation with the self. Levinas's term, *proximity*, does not mean presence to consciousness. *Proximity* means, rather, not present to consciousness. The other's proximity surpasses presence in its difference before the self. The self, Levinas says, is for-the-other before it can enact itself.

The self by Levinas's accounting of it thus finds itself already responsible for the other, already "substituted" for the other, already one-for-the-other. The self's (or consciousness') presence to itself is interrupted in its immediacy in the other's proximity. The missing other is missed (is traced) in the self's most intimate event of self-presence, and that missing is testimony to the other's utterly different life outside of the self and testimony to the call of that life in the self's own event: not testimony in presence but in its life before presence could occur, in its call that defines the self's own life and in its interruption of the self's ownness and self-presence. Levinas's sense of transcendence is defined by a withdrawal of presence and something like a remainder of missing and call, by traces of difference without presence. In this context we can say that Levinas's sense of transcendence is one in which transcendence is lost in transcending, that transcendence submits to its own withdrawal in a loss of presence and in extremity of difference.

How are we to describe Levinas's perceptions and descriptions? On the one hand, he clearly intends them to be accurate about human life. He intends to counter what he perceives to be a domination in Western culture on the part of Greek *logos* of a body of experiences in the Hebraic tradition. He thinks that these experiences show 'truths'—not Greek truths but non-Greek ones that are not subject to 'normal' laws of thought and communication.[11] These different rightnesses are right about us in our lives, and if they are learned and lived we would not have such an aestheticized culture that gives rise to and tolerates multiple kinds of murder and human destruction. In his intention to communicate his 'knowledge' to Western thought and to occasion its overturning, Levinas intends for his perceptions and descriptions to submit to the processes that establish their universal validity, although the criteria for universal validity might well change in the process. He does not see himself to be giving a Hebraic homily that is intended only for a believing, Jewish audience, or a poetic articulation of a local piety.

On the other hand, Levinas thinks that his thought arises from something more originary than either thought or consciousness. It arises, as we have seen, from the 'facts' of responsibility, the face-to-face, the one-for-the-other. That is, it arises from something prior even to phenomena, from the already given testimony to the extreme difference of the other and to the self's indebtedness to the other. Levinas's thought arises, I have said, from a withdrawal of transcendence that occurs in his sense of transcendence, a withdrawal richly prefigured in the Hebraic experience of the simultaneity of being a chosen people and of lacking immediate divine presence. As being chosen is a nonvoluntary and definitive aspect of a Jew's life, so is responsibility for the other in the other's call a nonvoluntary and definitive aspect of the self's life. As God is not present in His continuing covenant with the people of Israel, so the other is not present in the other's call before the self.[12] 'Traced as missing', we said following Levinas, but not present-to-consciousness. There is no reason to doubt that Levinas's philosophical thought is prefigured in Hebraic experience (or to doubt that He-braic experience undergoes a considerable change of expression and appearance in his thought). Yet his claim that the prephilosophical origins of his thought are not only articulations of a lineage but also origins for all of us means that on its own terms Levinas's thought is trying to persuade us in the very court of Western thought that he is in the process of overturning. On his terms, the goal is to persuade, not to proselytize. That is part of the meaning of God's call—to bring all people to God's truth. This bringing people to God's truth is not by physical conquest or force but by descriptive accounts of human life in contesting conversations and argument with contrary accounts and by the cul-tivation of a different (not yet dominant) ethic of responsibility for Western cul-ture. War by other means?

The relation of universality and locality is a hard one to bring about in the context of Levinas's work. I want to raise the problem of this relation only this far: the play of originary and prephilosophical grounds for thought in which transcendence submits to its own withdrawal has the effect of returning us again and again—some of Levinas's most fetching prose has to do with obses-sion[13]—to the originary, withdrawn transcendence of the other as though the other were continuously present to the self. That is like the movement and ob-session of a faith that finds its trust as it returns again and again to its originary experience and claims, no matter how severe the doubt and opposition concern-ing them.[14] The returning movement manifests a troubled identity-in-faith, one based on trust of something that is not subject to confirmation except in the language and experience of faith. But in Levinas's thought this locality of faith is attached to a claim for universality. One-for-the-other is not a situation for a few selves or only of Jewish selves. All human beings suffer the passivity of given responsibility. Responsibility implicates all of us. This language of uni-versality suggests a strange continuing presence of transcendence-in-with-drawal as traced in the interrupted self. And it requires in Levinas's account an ethics of responsibility as though such an ethics were commanded. It is not nec-essarily an authoritarian ethics that is to be enforced by an external authority (although Levinas often seems to me to be inclined toward an authoritarian ethics). Levinas's is an ethics that requires each individual to suffer its own re-sponsibility, its own unovercomeable indebtedness to the other. But each of us is under that requirement. The requirement is universal because we are all in a situation of life that is known within the Hebraic tradition. Levinas's is an original version of an ethics that universalizes moral aspects of his own lineage.

The movement of faithful if obsessive return to originary, local experiences defines the almost, when I said that Levinas almost eliminates transcendence. I had in mind this movement of return that has the effect of organizing his dis-course as though the other were present in a transcendent sense, as though the other were present to the self all of the time, by means of its trace, in spite of the loss of the other's immediacy in our experience of the other. The loss of presence in Levinas's thought, we have seen, gives transcendence to submit to its own withdrawal and suggests an overturning of *transcendence* in its power to organize our thought and practice. The returning movement of what we can call 'quasi-faith' in his philosophical thought, however, holds the other in place. Not letting the other go—that obsession—grants a sense of transcendence when otherwise the submission to withdrawal might continue its work toward thought and practice without a sense of transcendence. I believe that this loss of the submission of transcendence to its own withdrawal is due in part to Levinas's commitment to the universal 'truth' of a Hebraic sense of call and responsibility.

Levinas's ethics is thus one that trembles in the sense that nothing literal about the other can be established, and the command of responsibility cannot properly be turned into a prescriptive moral system or a definitive political order. The extreme fragility and tact that characterizes his thought—its unceasing hesitancy before absolutes, its lack of normalizing categories, its refusal of laws that measure abuse and satisfaction while standing outside of responsibility to the other—such characteristics of his thought would appear to put ethics into question. But ethics as such is not only *not* in question for Levinas. Ethics is also inscribed by religious meaning, grave seriousness, unyielding sense of mission, and, as we have seen, a removed and returned sense of transcendence. Such inscriptions remove the *question* of ethics as they accompany thought that places traditional ethics in question. Levinas's thought is ethically saturated.

The *Question* of Ethics

It is often counterintuitive to think that our commitment, our trusting and faithful, if often critical, obedience to a body of values may be generative of some of our most unfortunate suffering. Such a thought means that the manner in which we hold values might be as significant as the content of the values in giving rise to what we experience as worthwhile or as pain and sorrow. The thought becomes less counterintuitive if I hold in mind that what is experienced as worthwhile or as pain and sorrow also shifts, that what can devastate one person can elevate or not affect another. And the thought becomes almost obvious if I also hold in mind that many systems of valuation manifest the tribal characteristic of wanting dominance over other, different systems and of believing that 'this' core group of values will give better times if people will only turn to it and follow it. Usually there is a transcendental presence to the values that guarantees their importance. When strong commitment to a system of valuation combines with a universal intent, we have a movement that makes difficult, if not impossible, what I would call the question of ethics.

If Levinas had thoroughly interrupted the obsessive force of the other in his discourse, I believe that he could have allowed a fading of the tendency to universalize that is at the core of his own ethos, i.e., he could have allowed ethics as he understands it to fall into question and he could have allowed a movement in his own thought toward values that arise from the withdrawal and loss of transcendence. In his discourse, however, and in spite of the nonfoundationalist direction of his thought, the movement of transcendence-in-withdrawal toward a return of the sense of transcendence provides an imperative to ethics as though it were a command from God. Not literally law, but like law in the sense that one finds him- or herself unavoidably under the requirement for responsibility to the other and under the necessity of suffering the passivity of the self as it is occasioned by the other's proximity.

Levinas is speaking of an ethics that at its core opposes murder and other destruction of human life. He says that we are never free of our responsibility for the other's life, that we are under a mandate to respond to the other's need even when the other-in-need strikes out against us. He says that we are living in lineages that lead us away from the other's life, lineages that forget the primal value of human life, forget life sometimes even in the name of God, lineages in which language itself functions in a silently murderous way. Why would a Westerner want to oppose Levinas's values when they arise from the Hebraic heart in the body of our ethos?

The *question* of ethics arises not out of questionable values but out of ethics as such, regardless of the values that compose it. The phrase *question of ethics* does not refer primarily to questions about values but to conflicts and oppositions within the systems of values by which an ethos establishes a hierarchy of goods and bads. Our emphasis now is on the relation of such a hierarchy to universalization. *Ethics* names a way of valuing in which the definitive forces (definitive valences or values) of a tradition—of an ethos—come to expression in more or less normative ways. On the one hand, such normativity appears to be necessary for the practice of the ethos. On the other, the movement of normativity, as it normalizes differences and establishes identity within its domain, appears to spill over to application to different ethea: it seems to tend toward universalization in its sense of right and in the experiences of familiarity and well-being that it provides. The frequent and recent criticisms of universalization are right in their claims that this movement itself, regardless of the specific values, incites something like tribal wars, now conducted as struggles for cultural domination and refusal of amalgamation (i.e., of transformation of identity), and that this movement encourages a sense of universal authority for the ethnic, transcendental beings which ground and justify a people's experience of the rights and wrongs—whether such beings are Gods or transcendental subjectivities or human natures. The *question* of ethics arises from such movements. The question arises from a limited ethos combined with its universalization, which transgresses its own limits, and its claim to authority over other ethea.

Out of this question we may reserve these universalizing, normalizing movements for critical attention. I do not know if an ethics without universalization is possible, but I assume that in our Western lineage universalization is inevitable if our values are founded on universal movements or entities that are taken to be universal. Hence the importance in the context of the question of ethics that I am placing on interruption of the sense of transcendence. Such interruptions are ways whereby we can respond appropriately to the incommensurability of ethnic limits and universalizing.

I do not have an alternative to ethics to suggest. I am convinced that presenting a reconstruction of ethics would be premature until we learn how to think *in* the question. A strategy of interrupting the sense of transcendence and our axiomatic sense of fundamental values appears to be more appropriate. The question of ethics might be maintained not only by giving focus to the dangers of ethics, such as that of universalizing, but also by intensifying the conflicts that disturb the sense of transcendence and by cultivating language and thought that direct themselves away from that sense.

We have considered thought in which the withdrawal of the language of transcendence appears to be required by virtue of the withdrawal of the Gods or the loss of vitality in traditional thought. We have noted the submission of transcendence to its own withdrawal in the thought of Levinas. And we are aware that all of these accounts retain the sense of transcendence in their ways of putting that sense in question. To the extent that the sense of transcendence is in question, the grounding for our universalizing thought appears to be in question. I have said that to the extent that the sense of transcendence falls in question, our seemingly inevitable inclination to universalize our values also falls in question. I suspect that the present renewed interest in transcendence among some philosophers arises out of the feeling that our axiomatic and universalized values are threatened by a growing threat to transcendental grounding. The sense of transcendence weakens the question of ethics to the extent that the sense of transcendence posits a movement that surpasses the locale and gives expanded, universalizing, transcending voice to the local constructions of right, true, and good. That is why the question of ethics in Levinas's thought reverts to an ethics with universal import even when the question is strongest: the question of ethics in his thought maintains a (faithful) sense of transcendence while it radically questions the traditional Western experiences of immanent transcendence.

This discussion raises a difficulty for itself. On the one hand, we find in a universalized locale a perhaps optional source of destructive conflict that is spawned by an ethical sense that some differences in other locales must be changed under the guidance of the universalized ethos. We have said that the sense of transcendence enhances this movement of universalization. On the other hand, we have suggested that intensifying the fragmentation that can be found within the sense of transcendence is worthwhile in order to allow for a more open, less anxious, less protective sense of difference, mortality, and ungroundedness. Such allowance may lead us away from the disasters associated with the traditional ways in which we attempt to avoid experiences of fragmentation, mortality, and difference in the absence of transcendental 'reality'. But the weakening of the sense of transcendence does indeed occasion a weakened sense of unity and commonality. Perhaps it would occasion a weakened sense of human responsibility and human community—a weakened sense of universal humanity. Would that not allow for acts of violence that are free of any ethical sense regarding those 'others' whom we oppose? Would a heightened sense of difference generate values that respect differences? Does not such respect assume a certain transcending and universal human reality? In a word, does not this suspicion of universalized locales with their transcendental grounding lead to a fragmentation of locales with no sense of respect and responsibility for the others, a situation that places no blockage to all-out war for conquest and control?

These questions certainly articulate a well-founded fear in our tradition. Universal values and transcendent 'natures', with the consequences of Western humanism or an obligation to a caring, universal God, have given us hope and hedge against unending wars of conquest. But the patterns of these wars of conquest appear to have persisted at the level of universalization and normalization. Can the persisting patterns that require such conflict be changed? Can the sites of those patterns—such sites as ethics and the sense of transcendence—be changed? Those are questions that motivate our attention to the question of ethics and restrain us in our ethical responses to the question. Hearing the question, changing our languages of evaluation and recognition, changing the patterns of thinking, submitting and resubmitting our ways of judging and perceiving to questions: turning our obsessions on themselves. Not waiting for the Light, but encouraging more transformation without transcendence. Participating in the transformation of the sense of transcendence and the question of ethics without expecting or desiring a new transcendence or a new ethics. Being ethical in the process: such activity is part of thought that is moved by the fragmentation and mortality in our traditional experiences of transcendence and value.

4 | A (Non-) Passing Sense of Tragedy

Heidegger's translation of the first half of the Anaximander fragment[1] reads: "But that from which things arise also gives rise to their passing away, according to what is necessary." Diel's translation says, "but where things have their origin, there too their passing away occurs according to necessity." Charles Kahn translates the words as "out of these things whence is the generation for existing things, into these again does their destruction take place, according to what must needs be." I shall make only one claim about the translations. That claim has to do with the middle-voiced *ginesthai*. Heidegger translates the word *gives rise*. Diel, *occurs*. And Kahn, *does take place*. Each is accurate, but one emphasis is missing. I read the fragment to say that 'whence things come to be, out of this—in and from and with the originary whence—catastrophe (*phthoran*) also necessarily comes to be in the becoming'. Although we could read *ginesthai* in the active voice—as all these translations do (gives rise, occurs, does take place)—when its middle-voiced sense speaks, the verb says catastrophe (or passing away, withdrawing from appearance, ruin) comes to be in the coming to be, in the origin, of things. The middle-voiced *ginesthai* says that with the arising of things, nonarising also arises. Heidegger underscores the aporetic intimacy of arising and passing away when he says that that from which things arise also gives rise to their passing away. That intimacy is preserved still more strongly if we emphasize the, for us, counterintuitive middle-voice construction so that we say that *phthoran* (ceasing to come to be, ruin, catastrophe, withdrawal from appearance) comes *in its own coming to be*: genesis bears in its own becoming the coming of nongenesis along with the coming and passing of beings in their arising to life. In this manner we find that the coming to be of catastrophe—the coming to be of passing away—happens in the *coming to be*— the *arising* to life—of beings. Something of life will be lost if we are intentive—if we do not esteem—the coming to be of passing away. The whence that gives coming to be gives, in the giving, passing away. Arising and withdrawing are of the self-enactment of origin. As coming to be comes to be, passing away, strangely, also comes to be. This joining of coming-to-be-passing-away strikes at the heart of our capacity to think, as we shall see, and it will play a major role in Heidegger's account of the tragic. There is no separation of arising and ruin in the occurrence of *genesisphthoran*. In other words, a continuing presence does not give or create or originate beings. The whence of beings happens in the necessity of both arising and departing from arising. This does not say only that all things are going to die or that dying is the end of finite being. It says something about catastrophe in the origin, the coming to be, of whatever is.[2]

By returning to the Anaximander fragment, do we arrive at a beginning? This question in Heidegger's thought arises with the possibility that our traditional approach to Anaximander has figured an experience of time that is founded in the thought of being as an originary presence. This thought and its accompanying sensibility has lived out the limits of its potential, Heidegger says in the early part of the essay. The sense of an originary being has within it the projection of a full encompassment, a completed beginning and end, a present that is essentially a completion, an eternal now. But that completion, the forms and moments of which we may argue about, has taken place in a strange way. Whether the completion of being—its fullness—is found in absolute subjectivity, the incarnation, absolute spirit, mystical occurrences, or in an *eschaton* yet to come, the beginning and end of being in a perfection of presence are taken to be obtainable, and the cultural consequence, as Heidegger sees it, is an implacable growth of uniformity. The unfolding of our metaphysical heritage out of the thought of being as presence is a drift toward fundamental, common identity with an unavoidable sense that the fullness of being gives the promise of fulfilling our destiny by means of establishing a human community on the basis of common identity. This sense has the consequence that now we need to produce the formation of similarity, to carry out the completion of our commonality in the microstructures of culture. It feels right, for example, to bring other cultures into conformity with practices and values that are taken to represent the best way of living and doing things. We may dispute what the right ways are. But such disputes occur within the context of a larger sense of completion or completability. Our problems are technological in the sense that we need now to find the right kinds of knowledge that will lead to a maximally productive and thoroughly justifiable common life. The petroleum engineer in Saudi Arabia and the metaphysician at State University have this in common: they work within a silent drive to common rightness and are guided by a drive for uniform standards of truth and propriety. Far from catastrophe, we expect the future to allow productive growth and increasing harmony that results from refined uniformity in our values and productive strategies. Our normative, value-oriented approaches to problem solving thus are found to be consequences of a singular and originary quality of a creative and self-unfolding highest being.

The initial emphasis in Heidegger's discussion of Anaximander thus falls on the destiny of being when it appears as a highest being that moves toward completing its own self-disclosure. The consequence of the completion of this destiny in the thought of total self-presence—a thought already projected by

Aristotle in his thought of the completed presence of being in the soul's self-unity, and one that finds self-completion in Hegel's accomplishment of absolute knowledge—the consequence of the completion of this destiny is a sterility that includes an overpowering interest in uniformity and standard connectedness. It is a surprising side of Heidegger's thought, this derivation of secular uniformity from the theological heritage of a highest, self-revealing being. The destiny of being, when being is thought in ontotheological language, is found in a future closed to the withdrawal of being, a future that is closed in the form of progress toward worldwide uniformity. The destiny of the unfolding of a highest being is thus found in part in a progressive unfolding of a greater and greater cultural uniformity. Uniformity, in other words, carries in it a catastrophic closure to being's radical otherness and, in our culture, a closure to differential openness, to counterintuitive eventfulness, to whatever might appear without the authority of logic, grammar, and common meaning. Degenerative deathliness, clarity, predictability, uniformity of standards, commonality of subjectivity, normalcy, the uninterrupted dominance of our accountable past, and a sense of practical mastery, are all correlated with the loss of something to be said in the Anaximander fragment according to Heidegger's introductory remarks.

We can state this in another way. When the Anaximander fragment is read *within* the Platonic and Aristotelian traditions, it is found to be an early anticipation of a more sophisticated and developed metaphysical intelligence. Anaximander's saying is a beginning only in the sense that it is the earliest extant saying of someone who influenced the coming of those whose writing and thought have given us our age. Anaximander is a past thinker whose history remains encased in a metaphysical narrative about the discovery of the thought of nature and the highest being. The fragment, Heidegger says, "belongs to the dawn of early times in the land of the evening" (GA 5, 327; EGT). By belonging to this lineage, it is taken to begin a time marked by a series of great thinkers in the completion of whose thought we live and move and have our being.

But there is another possibility. What if in this fragment there is preserved something that was lost in the formation of our heritage? What if Anaximander thought in a way that is lost, and *that lostness* is definitive of what is necessary in our heritage? And what if the completion of our heritage in the drive to uniformity *makes possible* a departure from our heritage, a departure that articulates our destiny in a way radically different from our heritage up to now? Rather than a narrative of being's progressive disclosure, we might have a sting of radical difference—not a novel idea that comes from a new combination of given thoughts, but rather a thinking in which the completion of being in presence cannot take place. In that case, the fragment holds a withdrawal from our thinking, a lost event the retrieval of which not only gives a destiny other than a technological one but discloses as well the destiny of what occurs by virtue of the loss. What if the fragment shows an origin that never began, or began only by being lost? And what if something occurs in this thinking that cannot occur within the good sense of our best traditional thought? In this case, Anaximander's fragment bears something originary that is other to the positive ideas that gave birth to our dominant tradition, another beginning the loss of which sets the course for what we can normally say, think, and be.

Heidegger says that the fragment gathers the being of beings in the sense that thinking in the fragment's words at this time shows where we have been and the extent to which we have been lost to something silently carried by the heritage to which we belong. The suggestion is that in some way we belong to a lostness, a withdrawal in our tradition, and that our belonging to what is familiar and necessary to us at the same time disinherits us from something that is both withdrawn and originary for us. As we depart from our tradition in thinking with the Anaximander fragment, for example, a simultaneous disclosure of and withdrawal from the highest being takes place. In this withdrawing-disclosure something fateful takes place, and we are gathered in a destiny that we are not able to fully think or speak.

You can see the suggestion that in this encounter with Anaximander's fragment we are approaching a double catastrophe when by *catastrophe* we mean disappearance or withdrawal of both appearing and what appears. On the one hand, there is in the catastrophe a sense of completion in which the *phthoran* of being disappears in a sense of presence. In this sense our normalcy and the passions of our age mislead us terribly. As we sense fulfillment and rightness, for example, in our best efforts to bring to fruition the values of universally present and shared nature—both the nature of our humanity and the nature of the world around us—just then we find ourselves possibly engaged in the disappearance and destruction of the essence of life. Even our most disciplined and refined understanding of essence covers over and loses the life of 'something' that is essential for us. On the other hand, we may well be approaching 'something' that appears so catastrophic that in the dawn of our heritage its elimination seemed essential for life. Heidegger is approaching the probability that this second but originary catastrophe—the catastrophe that the coming of life includes the withdrawal of life—is essential for the vitality that was sought and that is now disappearing. In now thinking through the Anaximander fragment a double catastrophe thus appears to be waiting for us. We might find that our lives bring with them a most feared catastrophe *and* that the *arising* of catastrophe was lost to thought at the dawn of our heritage, a loss that no one produced and a loss which gives passionate satisfaction in the silent disappearing of what we never learned to call being. In this double catastrophe our heroes either flourish or lose their lives in an ideality in which vitality seeps out of their successes and failures through values that encourage uniformity and universality.

We can say this much: in Heidegger's terms, there is no dawn without catastrophe. One catastrophe—that of the drift toward uniformity—we must recognize as we undergo it. Another catastrophe—for which we do not have a name—we must learn to live in and think if there is to be any hope for something other than massive self-destruction in pursuit of good living. The recovery of the thought of catastrophe, and with it the possibility of another dawn, means for him a nonhistoriographical experience of time: Anaximander's fragment must be found in the dawn and loss of a thinking that is radically different from the thinking that has formed us and not in a series of progressive historical events that are uncovered by our best scholarship.

We take a step into our present catastrophe of loving our own destruction when we ask how to translate Anaximander's saying. The usual attempt to reconstruct what Anaximander really meant or what his Greek words meant back then is, according to Heidegger, usually in the manner of calculation. Translating Anaximander is not, for Heidegger, primarily an effort to figure out what he, at another time and in an ancient culture, intended to say and said in that far-off context. Such calculations, in their attempt to avoid arbitrariness, strive to re-present his world and thought. Such an attempt embodies the loss of thinking in which something discloses itself in attunement with its disclosiveness. If we can turn to the disclosiveness of language in our essential bondage with it we may make a noncalculative turn—a turn in this case not to the intentions of an ancient philosopher, but to the coming to pass (*Wesen*) of saying. And in that turn we might find ourselves in the midst of Anaximander's saying. We turn with and out of our catastrophe in this sense: the very historiographic standards of truth and intelligent responsibility which guide the ethics of contemporary scholarship mislead us into a dominance of calculative and representative thinking which *prioritizes* the subject that that thinking includes. The more ethical we are in this context the more we advance the calamity of "man's" domination of being and the fateful suction of the world into the power of technology and intentional construction. We *make* things work: we make things *to* work. And this aggression provides the region of transfer from ancient Anaximander to our time. Translation—the bearing of Anaximander's words to us—is then an operation designed to provide a transfer of his meaning to our intelligence. Something present to him is *made* present to us by its translation. A change of presence takes place with no thought of the catastrophe of no presence at all. The origin that Anaximander then represents is without the fate of loss: Anaximander as an origin does not in this case give rise to thinking and speaking in *to phthoran*, thinking and speaking in withdrawal, disappearance, ruin, separation, and destruction that come with the arising of things in thought and speech. Instead, a disciplined transfer of present meaning takes place. As we turn out of this ethics of accurate representation of present meaning, with the uncertainty and danger that we must feel in this turning, we might turn out of both our experience of time and our ethos of presence to something other than our experience of time and ethos of presence. We might experience both the catastrophe of the dominance of presence and its consequences in technology and the catastrophe of losing our bearings in the world of presence. A double violence occurs. Perhaps Anaximander's saying demands this turning and in this demand a different origin begins to appear in the future of technological catastrophe.

The alternative to calculative–re-presentative thought that Heidegger suggests is called poeticizing. He does not have in mind a more sensitive and less discursive construction than is ordinarily given by philosophers. "Thoughtful dialogue with Anaximander's saying" is the translation of his phrase for an alternative to re-presentative construction. This is not a matter of finding agreement with Anaximander and arriving at a more accurate formulation than that provided by standard translations. This thoughtful dialogue is rather thinking that is attuned to the coming to pass of language that takes place in thinking. In this case, language's origin which gives it to arise and to withdraw is being said and occurs in an exchange with Anaximander. We find not what Anaximander meant but an attunement with his saying in the exchange. In the exchange an origin occurs that lets something lie before us and gathers together at once giving to arise and to withdraw. Anaximander's saying lies before us and in our exchange with it in the catastrophe of our time, its passing away—its withdrawing in its being—also takes place. Language in this case *arises out of catastrophe* in the saying. We cannot say *what* withdraws, but through dialogue with Anaximander's saying we can undergo the unencompassable touch of withdrawal in the coming to be of his saying. Thinking takes place as this exchange gathers together in a dehiscence, i.e., one which lets us read in an opening asunder. This exchange gives not unity but—strangely—gives *genesis* (origin). It is an origin that is utterly different from the one we are given to expect.

I have been using *exchange* to play off of *dialogue*. The initial thought is that in our speaking with Anaximander we can speak within the interchange of arising and passing away. This exchange occurs in the play of catastrophe in our time in which Anaximander's saying both comes to us (arises) and withdraws (passes away). It comes to us in the loss of something essential in our age of production, accuracy, and presence. We have seen that what is lost has to do with how the destiny of our heritage unfolds and with thought of being without the priority of presence. *Dialogue* carries the sense of people's being together *in* an exchange of language. We are gathered together dialogically in speaking with each other. Our language is, in dialogue, thoroughly pervaded by each other's speaking. In a sense dialogue is *Übersetzen*, 'translation', in which those who speak are taken up in an exchange that is not reducible to separate positions. *Zwiesprache* is Heidegger's word that is translated by 'dialogue'. He says, "the *Spruch* (saying) of thinking allows its translation only in the *Zwiesprache* of thinking with what it says (*seinem Gesprochenen*)" (GA5, 328; EGT 19).

I now turn away from the conversational image of dialogue, because we cannot think this saying of Heidegger's if we think of a dialogue with another person. By these words Heidegger says that the issue of Anaximander's fragment is not one that arises primarily in an exchange of words among individuals. While our reading Anaximander in awareness of the catastrophe of our time provides attunement to something that Heidegger hears in the fragment, what he hears suggests something other than an open and alert address that takes place in our reading the fragment. It is rather a matter of thinking's coming to words in the gathering together of things in their origin. This dialogue, Heidegger indicates, occurs *with* language in thinking. In thoughtful speaking, things arise passing away in their being. The origin of speaking-thinking occurs in such dialogue, and Heidegger finds the possibility of thinking in the *genesisphthoran* of beings.

Anaximander's fragment uses the middle-voiced *ginestai*, which, as we have seen, can say in the fragment that beginning (*genesis*) and catastrophe (*phthoran*), in the sense of withdrawal of arising, come together in their coming to be. In our present context we can say that as we think, things come to be, and in their coming to be as we think both origin and withdrawal of origin occur. Our opportunity is to think in the withdrawing origin of being's coming to be—of which thinking's coming to word is the event. That, rather than interpersonal relation, is the site of *Zwiesprache*. So we have moved from an attuning, catastrophe situation of arising–passing away to the occurrence of catastrophe in arising as thinking comes to word. We are not involved primarily in translation or exchange, as we want to think of them, as we read the fragment. Nor are we trying to exchange Anaximander's meaning in Greek for his meaning in English. We are attempting, rather, to think in the withdrawing coming to be that takes place in thinking and saying. We can now say that the double movement that occurs in Heidegger's thought is, in the first place, that of finding Anaximander's fragment to come to us passing away in a time of fateful forgetfulness. The fragment *belongs*, Heidegger says, to the dawn of early times in the land of evening. It can be heard in a mixture of loss and opening. It cannot be heard in—it does not belong to—a laterality full of present meaning. It belongs to the *passage* of the destiny of being's thought as presence.

The necessity of coming to be passing away is found in the catastrophe of our time coupled with a difference of thought that is coming toward us in a forgotten saying of Anaximander. In the second movement, we find the fragment's own saying in the withdrawing coming to be of the fragment's saying. In attending thoughtfully to the coming/passing of Anaximander's fragment in our moment, we are attuned to its thinking the coming to be passing away in the origin of things. By giving full allowance to the catastrophe of our time as we attempt to follow Anaximander's thought, we find the possibility of a *Zwiesprache* with the origin of things taking place in his thinking's coming to word. We are involved in origin that will not translate into our traditional thought. We are involved in a strange recoil of arising and passing away in the coming of things. We are in the midst of catastrophe and the coming to be of beings that will not translate into our good sense.

In this turn on Heidegger's part we have lost our best experiences of conversation and dialogue as models for interpreting our relation to this text, a text that is no longer ancient as defined by a time line but is now, in yet another turn, a saying with which we have not caught up. Neither careful and attentive conversation nor a reliable sense of time can orient us. Exposition is no longer adequate. Understanding is now even more in question than it is in Hegel's thought of *Geist*. When we *understand* Anaximander's fragment, i.e., when we cognize without dialogue and outside of the movement of the question of being, the entire process comes to bear with the thought of origin as full presence rather than with the thought of origin as coming to be passing away. This disastrous divergence from the *question* of being—origin in coming to be passing away without full presence—gathers thought without the catastrophe of *phthoran*: the destiny of being's coming to pass bears upon us in the triumph of unification, technology, and presence. We are before the strange otherness of being's coming to pass in the culmination of being in its thought as full presence. Being's coming to pass in our time presents us with something unthinkable and beyond understanding in the history of being as presence, and we undergo this unthinkable in Anaximander's saying of origin. The *catastrophe* of this time—the ending of being as full presence—gathers the forgotten essence of the origin of things. By this gathering an opening is given to something other than being as presence. Withdrawal and advent come together in a dimension of technology's drive to uniformity. We belong to—are in the hearing of—this dimension. We belong to both the coming to pass of being and the dawn of Anaximander's saying. We are bound, in other words, to both the language of Anaximander's saying and to our own language. Within this bonding a *Zwiesprache* can occur, a dialogue that takes place within the languages. We may note here for later emphasis that the *Zwiesprache* arises out of our language's and Anaximander's language's "belonging to the same" and that the *Zwie*—the two, or the plurality of dialogue—in this context arises from being's being spoken in language. Being comes to speech and thought in the catastrophe of arising-disappearing in unthinkable simultaneity.

Our *access* to Anaximander's language and thought is thus the arising withdrawing of beings *in* their appearing and is not a properly conducted conversation with the fragment, a well-calculated translation based on post-Aristotelian scholarship, or an interpretation of Anaximander that is based on a post-Aristotelian preoccupation with nature. Such conversation and calculation inevitably form part of our reading. But they do not transport us to Anaximander or the fragment to us. That transportation—that translation—occurs in that in which and from which arising and ruin come to be. Our translation takes place in the coming of thought.

Heidegger speaks of confusion, of a ditch (*Grube*) that we have to jump with inadequate footing, and of a shoreless sea of talk about being, when he describes our relation to what is to be translated. In the midst of our thinking is deep confusion, indeed an abyss (*Abgrund*), he says. It is found in our very ability to speak and think of the coming of beings and being. In these passages the catastrophe of loss in the arising of being in our heritage comes to the fore. What we are talking about when we speak of catastrophe comes to be in both its modern form and in its primordial dimension in language and thought.

I pause to note that as we approach the question of the tragic in Heidegger's thought regarding the Anaximander fragment, we find that its site addresses the arising-withdrawing of being, that language and thought are the home of the question of the tragic. The domain of the question of the tragic is not in a conflict of destiny and ideals or in a realm of heroic action and defeat. To raise the question of the tragic is to turn to the coming of beings in the coming (the destiny) of speaking and thinking. We cannot overemphasize the importance of this nonanthropocentric region of the question, since the tragic, tragedy, or their loss, may very well arise *for us* in a turn to ideals and values and away from arising catastrophe that occurs in the very coming of our lives.

We can see that the confusion of which Heidegger speaks arises in an errancy that indwells our clarity and good sense. It is errancy, first of all, that constitutes the way in which the Greeks came to us in our heritage. "It [confusion that accompanies our Greek heritage] arises" Heidegger says, "from the abyss of that relation by which being has brought forth [*hat ereignet*] the coming to pass [*Wesen*] of mankind in the land of evening" (GA5, 335; EGT 25; I have revised the translation). Our coming to pass, i.e., our *Wesen*, arises from the fateful way in which being has come to thought and in coming to thought has given us to arise in the way that we are. The emphasis falls heavily on transporting, sending, and destiny. This destiny does not arise from the nature of things, such that if we understand the nature of things we will understand why we live as we do. We are involved, rather, in Heidegger's rethinking of history by attending to the way in which beings come to be the beings that they are. He sidesteps two major contemporary options: historical relativism and transhistorical normativity. The question of *history* resides in that out of which genesis-disappearing gives rising decline in the coming of beings. *Our* talk of being deceives, he says. But there is something coming forth in the *Zwiesprache* of language that is also in the coming of beings in Anaximander's language and thought. The commonality of the way beings come forth in language and thought, for us and for the Greeks—not nature or values or a singular being—gives a common destiny of which and in which Anaximander speaks. So his language says more than intentional, cultural, or linguistic analysis can account for. In the *Zwiesprache* a saying occurs in which beings come forth in an unovercomeable question. They belong in the question of rising withdrawal. And now there is a gap between the originary question, one which is borne in our language, and the loss of the question. It is a gap that gives shape in a presently inconceivable way to what we have to say and think in the rising ruin of technology.

So when we attend to the deep and unavoidable confusion that accompanies the transmission of the Greek tradition, confusion that is joined to the loss and forgetting of that out of which the arising withdrawing of beings occurs, we attend in a *Zwiesprache* of *genesisphthoran*. This turning occurs in our language that transmits us to Anaximander's saying and occurs as well in Anaximander's language that transmits his saying to us. A dialogue of thinking and speaking begins to occur. Something arises. A genesis takes place in the withdrawal of the coming of being as presence. By attending to the confusion and catastrophe of our heritage we may not be home free, but in being here we belong to an *aporia* that is fateful and dangerous and is far from a technological breakthrough to a thorough grasp of antiquity or to a new age.

Heidegger uses the word *das Selbe* (the same) in speaking of the common occurrence in the transmission of the Greek heritage in our language and thought and in the genesis-disappearance of beings in Anaximander's thought. *Transmission* in this context speaks of sending, of destiny, in which our thinking and that of the Greeks takes place. In the common occurrence, Heidegger says the dawn of thinking comes into the destiny of Western life (GA5, 336; EGT 25). Beings come to be in arising disappearing—in the question of being—and that arising disappearing is compounded by the confusion and forgetfulness that transmit arising disappearing unawares. History, as we know, is to be thought in this fateful transmission. It is composed by the manner in which the question of being unfolds in the experiences, thought, sayings, and lives of beings. The question of being may well be peculiar to our heritage, but it nonetheless gives us to be as we are and to think as we do, and in that sense it *is* our destiny. It composes the transmission of our coming to pass and gives the dispensation, the distribution of things coming to appear disappearing.

We belong, then, to a withdrawal and concealment of being in the transmission of beings, and in this belonging we are attuned to our Greek heritage. That from which genesis-catastrophe arises is lost to thought in the arising of thought. "As it reveals itself in beings, being withdraws" (EGT 26). In this withdrawal beings "are set adrift" (EGT 26) and are at once in the catastrophe of lacking, in their clarity and purpose, distinct bearings to determine the meaning of their being and of the world. Our efforts to establish clearly such meaning bear testimony to our lack of such clarity and compound the *phthoran* of our coming to thoughtful and manageable clarity. We live, Heidegger says, in a realm of error (EGT 26). This means that thought that is unalert to its *aporia*, conundrum, question, and catastrophe is misplaced and disconnected to its own site. ("Error is the *space* in which history unfolds"; EGT 26, emphasis added). And when we pay thoughtful attention to our confusion in the destiny of what we cannot fully think, we are where we belong in our thinking and are, in errancy, directed to the question that has mandated us.

Heidegger thus finds a two-edged necessity in reading Anaximander's fragment. There is, first, the necessity of an originary question of life, written in the middle voice, that not arising arises with arising and that arising ceases to arise in arising. This is the necessity that is lost in the dominant Western thought of being as full and plenteous, lost in the thought that being endures in presence as finite things play out, deteriorate, and die. In this loss, which has come to be definitive of our capacity to think with good sense, being as such, in its originary power, excludes or thoroughly dominates nonbeing. Thus there is the second necessity that arises when the first necessity is lost to our experience of the coming of beings. The second necessity is found in the culmination of being as presence in our culture and controlled and uniforming connections. The second necessity is the fate of losing the necessity of catastrophic arising with the coming of being. I note, however, that finding the second necessity does not indicate an ideal of returning to Anaximander's thought in order to avoid catastrophe. Ceasing to be in the arising of things takes place unthought in our time. Rather than suggesting an ideal, Heidegger is suggesting that as we come to Anaximander's thought out of errancy, we might be able to think and speak in the catastrophe of coming to be as well as in the arising that takes place in things coming to be. Where that would lead us is unclear, but one consequence can be said with confidence: if we are able to think with Anaximander's thought and if our culture were pervaded by that thinking, the *rule* of technology and the blind, suicidal destructiveness of that dominance would be transformed into something quite different.

We might read this part of Heidegger's account metaphysically and say that inherent in the nature of things is a simultaneity of coming to be and ceasing to be and that we are misattuned to our own nature when we forget this fact. Our goal, we might say metaphysically, should be to restore ourselves to a proper relation to being, conform ourselves properly to nature, and live in greater harmony with the nature of things. By this rendering, however, we would make arising–not-arising into a unity to which we could conform ourselves, given accurate insight and right discipline. We would then have a revised understanding of a fundamental and continuing substance of which we are finite instances.

Heidegger's thought takes a different direction. In belonging to the time of the dominance of the thought of being as presence—in belonging to a technological age—and in belonging to another, fragmented origin, a now forgotten one that is written in Anaximander's fragment, we find ourselves in a destiny of passing away as we come to be technologically, a destiny of having to come to ruin as we come to be. Arising catastrophe in any case names the destiny to which we belong. What can be said of that?

We turn now to the second clause of the fragment: "for things render justice and pay penalty to one another for their injustice, according to the ordinance of time." We can say at the beginning—with reference to a standard translation that will be transformed—that in speaking and thinking *we* are the payment of the penalty, we *are* a certain injustice, that the paying of penalty and the injustice are in the occurring of our being. Further, the ordinance of time in some way demands the paying of penalty and the rendering of justice. So human occurrence is of time in which there is errancy, recompense, and penalty. The word that says the *genesisphthoran* of human occurrence is *adikia* (injustice). Two cautionary observations: First, Heidegger's interpretation is in a language that resonates in the Christian conception of the Fall, and if we do not take seriously his efforts toward attunement with our belonging to something pre-Aristotelian and pre-Christian, we miss his movement of thought that destructures Christian metaphysics as he attends to something that is distorted and virtually lost by Christian metaphysics. Second, we are not on our way to a new ethics that is based on a rereading of *injustice, penalty,* and *retribution.* We are rather attempting to think errancy that comes with the coming of beings. This sense of errancy is lost in the Western tradition of ethical thought. I suspect that this second caution raises most of our discomfort. Do we find in the appearing of beings that appearing-disappearing is beyond good and bad as well as beyond good and evil? Do we lose the ethical when we come to think in the catastrophe of coming to be? Is there no ethical presence in this dimension? Indeed, does our ethical passion lead us astray vis-à-vis something that is vital for our lives?[3]

Heidegger takes *adikia* to say that whatever appears disappearing is, in its persisting, out of joint (EGT 41; GA 5, 354; "Das Anwesende ist als das Anwesende, das es ist, aus der Fuge"). The issue of *adikia* is one of persisting in time. Lingering (*Weilen, die Weile*) is the appearing-disappearing that takes place within 'the between' of coming forth and going away. *If* we read such sentences within the framework of a timeline, i.e., if we read them metaphysically, we hear that beings come forth, linger awhile, and disappear. But Heidegger is saying that 'the between' takes place in the lingering; and, rather than being a passage from appearing to disappearing, the between is of lingering's occurrence. 'The between' is in the at-onceness of coming to appear disappearing. ("The lingering appears disappearing [*west*] as transitional arrival and departure" [EGT 41; GA5; translation modified]). Coming to appear disappearing occurs as a strange, aporetic jointure. The lingering of beings occurs as the joining of coming to appear disappearing.

Genesis and *phthoran* come in the coming and lingering of beings. There is no simple presence in appearing or in the coming of what gives beings to appear: no universal, in-place structure, no prime mover, no singular being occurs in or shines through from behind beings in their disappearing appearing occurrence. *Genesis* and *phthoran* do not occur in a reparable disjunction but in a hinge of coming to be passing away that is without rightness or wrongness. They occur without judgment. But *adikia* suggests unjoining or unhinging and is a word that elaborates *errancy*. In appearing in their aspect of being present as distinct from not being present at all, beings may "insist" in their appearing, "strike a willful pose of persistence," "stiffen" for the purposes of lingering, and lose touch not with a primordial connection with a normative being but with the hinge of appearing disappearing, seemingly unhinge themselves from their moment by linking themselves in their insistence to a privilege of presence—"and aim solely for continuance and subsistence," Heidegger says, as though this were the way one had to live out one's time. Here is where *adikia* applies. This disjunction seems to be fated, necessary, not because we are fallen from our nature or a higher being and cannot find our way back into a proper relation with it but because beings persist by identifying themselves with present appearing and consequently lose attunement to disappearing in their appearing.

The hinge of appearing disappearing, on the other hand, gives beings their dispensation. It is the ordinance of time, of the lingering of beings. The hinge is *dike*, the, as it were, custom or manner of the lingering of beings. To interpret *dike*, as *recompense* or *penalty* or to suggest that a wrong has been committed is to lose the nonanthropomorphic thought of Anaximander. The issue is the coming to be passing away of beings and is not moral or civil order. *Adikia* is unhinging in the hinge of appearing disappearing. It names a departure from within an aporia to which beings belong. Beings do not belong to unseamed presence; they belong to the hinge of coming to presence passing out of presence. They belong to a perpetual turning of presence without departure; they nonetheless give *dike* to each other: even as they turn out of the hinge of coming to be passing away, they reveal it as they turn in the coming to presence of their departure. Their coming to be, their appearing, lets them belong to what they depart from. In their insistence to continue they never pass from the ordinance of time in their occurrence. In spite of themselves, they give the *dike* of appearing disappearing to each other in the mutuality of their world.

You can see how we in our technological age—this age of *adikia*—give far more to each other than we can intend and reveal far more than we can know. In our being we give each other departure from appearing that we are made to ignore, and we are of a hinge of revealing concealing that is blotted out in our self-understanding. We belong at once to the almost inconceivable hinge of which Anaximander speaks, just as we belong to the unhinging of beings in the hinge of appearing disappearing. In Anaximander's fragment the hinge that we lost in our passion for making present and holding present comes to us as an opening in our disjointed time.

Heidegger identifies unhinging within the hinge of appearing disappearing as tragic (EGT 44). The tragic inheres in unhinging—in stabilizing or insisting on full presences with the turning of coming-to-be-passing-away—in the fate of revealing that hinge to which beings belong by being as though they did not belong to it. We find the tragic in beings which are of—which belong to—the hinge that their way of being denies. This denial, this 'willful pose of persistence' does not appear to be avoidable. Lingering includes a fate of unhinging as people establish themselves and preserve their ways of life. Such insistence seems to be an aspect of their withdrawal of being. But this is a destiny without *a* continuing and present nature; and the coming of things in the domination of presence of appearing may well trace something that the Greeks found both fateful and tragic.

I use the qualifiers—may well, might have—because Heidegger cannot be sure. It is an historical question, after all, though not an historiographical one. It is a question of how we find being and ourselves sent in the determination of thought and speech. The possibility of finding something determinate that determines the determinations fades from the options for thought that are available to Heidegger. Nothing specific can establish the truth of his thought. He does not take the options of claiming that language and thought are essentially illusions or that relative values make all claims relative. He says something different from these options. He says that our coming to be is pervaded by a question of appearing disappearing, a question that also withdraws, and that in this question and its loss is traced something that some Greeks might have called tragic.

Tragic arises in unhinging in the hinge of appearing disappearing by virtue of insistence or presence here now. The tragic seems to be unavoidable, but there is a doubt or uncertainty regarding this unavoidability. First, the tragic arises from the hinge of *genesis* and *phthoran* as beings in their persistence insist on presence. It is unclear whether this insistence is necessary outside of the destiny of being in our metaphysical heritage. Heidegger suggests a breakage of this necessity when he speaks of an opening in the fragment—another beginning—that comes out of a future different from that of being as presence. Second, this possibility—is it a possibility?—is not fully thinkable. We have only a trace of the tragic in the fragment, something that slips our grasp but gives an attunement to its difference when we withhold assertion of definitive clarity in relation to the tragic. The withdrawal of clarity about tragedy intensifies this attunement. Perhaps, in reticence concerning the tragic, an occurrence without tragedy transpires. Perhaps an opening to *dike*, the hinge, happens now without insistence on presence, an opening that is a beginning other to the first beginning that took place as Western thought and speech turned away from the hinge that gave them their birth.

Heidegger's reading of the fragment suggests such an opening. "What momentarily lingers a while passing away, *ta eonta*, appears disappearing insofar as it allows the adjoining hinge to belong" (EGT 44; GA 5, 358; translation modified). Beings belong to the dispensation, to the turning, of the hinge.[4] If beings reveal themselves to each other in the turning and not in insistence on presence now, something different from the destiny of our heritage begins to emerge.

There is at this point in Heidegger's discussion an important use of *Rücksichtslosigkeit* and *Rücksicht*, which are translated 'inconsiderateness' and 'consideration.' Heidegger is picking up his earlier and seemingly intrusive discussion of the seer. The seer is outside himself or herself insofar as he or she finds beings, not merely in their insistent presence but also appearing disappearing in their unconcealment. The seer is unconstrained by the demands of the present and is thus able to see beings in their *genesisphthoran*, in their unconcealing concealing coming to be passing away. The seer does not preserve beings in their craving to persist as, for example, technology does but in their release from presence in their coming to be passing away. In this manner beings are esteemed and measured in the appearing disappearing that gives them to be.

By translating *tisin* as 'esteem' or even stronger as 'heeding care' (*reck*), and attaching *allalois*, 'to one another', to this word, Heidegger finds that beings heed one another with care in appearing disappearing, in unconcealment-concealment. Like the seer, beings preserve one another in the *dike*, the hinge, of their coming to be. Now far more than insistent subsistence, standing reserve, or passionate persistence is at stake. Beings are with each other by their belonging to the hinge, not *primarily* to presence. They join in the aporetic hinge of appearing disappearing and surpass, like the seer, the unhinging that seems to give the tragic. By letting themselves belong to the hinge, something not tragic would appear to transpire. And yet this allowing of the hinge and this return of presence to its affiliation with no presence at all does not mean that we now cease to insist on presence. Or does it? I shall take Heidegger's experience of hope to occur in the midst of unhinging and its moment of full recognition—which means, in the midst of the tragic and its moment of full recognition—and not to be a hope that suggests eradication of the tragic. The disappearance of the tragic is beyond hope. Or, stated another way, hope comes appearing disappearing in the tragic coming of beings in which the withdrawal of the tragic is beyond our sight.

In this part of his discussion Heidegger turns to an earlier sense of *usage* (*der Brauch*) and turns from within his technological age to a nontechnological thought. In this turn comes a sighting both of the tragic and of hope within the tragic. The question is how *to kreon* is to be read. It is ordinarily translated by the word *necessity*. In Anaximander's fragment *to kreon* speaks of how coming to appear and disappearance are joined: "but that from which things arise also gives rise to their passing away, according to necessity." Coming to appear disappearing—the event of beings—must needs occur. We recall that *Anwesen, Anwesende*, and *Anwesenheit* do not refer only to presencing, being present, or what is present. The *Wesen* in those words indicates coming to be passing away or appearing disappearing. There is not first presence and then a catastrophe of no presence. Rather beings take place losing place. They never happen as straight presence. The question before us is how coming to be passing away is given, how beings are handed over, as it were, in their being. So we are not asking primarily about presence to the extent that we are thinking in the *question* of our metaphysical heritage. The matter is one of the coming to appear disappearing of what comes to appear disappearing. It is not a "matter of the presencing of what is present" (EGT 60, GA 5, 364; my previous sentence retranslates the quoted translation). When *what* comes to appear disappearing is confused with coming to appear disappearing, the giving of *genesisphthoran* is confused with the act of *a* being, and that unalert and unintentional confusion, in which the withdrawal of being in the coming of being is obscured, gives rise to experiences of beings in the dominance of presence.

But this fateful oversight is not the consequence of human frailty. There is something like a nonhuman necessity involved. The disappearance of being in the coming of being is the issue. The lines here are finely drawn. Heidegger is not saying that it is being's nature to withdraw. There is nothing in itself to withdraw itself in the question that gives rise to our time; the coming to pass of being (the *Wesen des Seins*) is in the coming to be passing away of beings. Being comes to us passing away. Rather than saying that being withdraws from us to itself as it comes to us and thereby suggesting that being is a mysterious, transcendent being, Heidegger says that our oblivion and forgetfulness of being accompany being's coming to pass. Being comes to pass in the Greek's thought of being, not because finite minds cannot grasp something infinitely present and beyond human grasping but because the essence of being is found in the coming to pass—in the appearance—of Greek thinking and speaking. There is nothing present there that is to be grasped even by an infinite mind. Being in Greek 'experience' is the slipping passage of coming to be, and in our tradition that means that being is its loss in its thought's grasp. This continuous slippage from presence is for us its question, i.e., the oblivion of being is in the *genesis*, the coming of being in the formation of our heritage. Our capacity for thinking did not begin with presence. It began with the loss of presence in the coming of presence.

Since the tragic occurs in the domination of presence that is consequent to the passage of being and to the impossibility of holding this passage in a per-

sistence of presence, you can see that Heidegger can brook no hope for an elimination of being's oblivion and a consequent elimination of the tragic. But—and
this is a noteworthy transition in his thought—this oblivion which belongs to
the *genesis* of our traditional lives comes with the coming of beings and is part
of what we can call picturesquely the gift of beings or the gift of life. Life is, as
it were, handed over; it is like a translation of coming to be passing away into
a lingering being, viz., into beings that stay as they are for a while. Not-a-being,
viz., coming to be passing away, hands being over to become beings and in the
handing over preserves beings in their passing away, gives them to appear in
passing, and preserves them in this strange lingering.

This handing over, which is the thought of *to kreon* (necessity), is usage in
an archaic but highly relevant sense: to use, in the history of the German word
brauchen, meant "to hand something over to its own coming to pass and keep
it in hand, preserving it as something coming to appear disappearing" (EGT
53, GA 5, 367; translation modified). Our word *to brook* has the same antecedents
and carries the sense of 'to have the enjoyment of', as in to brook a piece of land
or to brook an occasion. The coming of *genesisphthoran* gives rise to things and
at once to their passing away according *not* to an ironclad necessity but rather
according to a usage; coming to be passing away replaces the sense of employ-
ing something for gain, i.e., retrieves the lost heritage of the lostness in which
comes technology and the reign of re-presentation. The word indicates allowance and esteem rather than consumption and utility.

In Anaximander's thought Heidegger finds the passage of being the coming of beings in their appearing disappearance. Beings, in coming to themselves, undergo the loss of being as they accent their own presence. And yet they
nonetheless in their lives hand over a nonconsuming bestowal of being even as
they consume, destroy, and live unattentive to the passage of their lives. In usage
being comes going in beings as they linger in disappearing appearance. Disappearing presence stands with destabilization in being's insistent perduring. Beings lose their attunement with their coming to be passing away as they preserve presence, and they preserve presence in the passing away of being in its
coming. *The tragic* thus seems to name the limit of being in its passage from
insistent presence.

I said earlier that our technological age is suicidal in the sense that the way
that we hold ourselves and beings in presence takes away the vitality of coming
to be passing away and that something other to this obsession with presence
seems to reside in Anaximander's thought. We also noted with emphasis that
attunement with the coming to pass of being might be found in noninsistent
attentiveness to the passage of our technological age, a passage that dangerously trembles between self-destruction and self-overcoming by virtue of what
technology bears in forgetfulness. The hinge of coming to be passing away
turns out to be the insubstantial measure of our turning away from our own

being, and our unhinging turns out to be a turning away from and yet back to this hinge: *in* our tragic loss of coming to be passing away—in our obsession with presence in lingering for a while—Heidegger finds the hope of *to kreon*: our insistent presence is nonetheless let be; by turning this handing over of presence, we find not only the tragic but the *giving* of the tragic in the disappearing of being. We belong both to the hinge of presence and to the unhinging of presence. Without a sense of stability of the securing bounds of a determinate origin, we have found an inseparability of the tragic and hope, a strange joining of catastrophe and vitality whose measure is traced but not fully thought in the heritage that gives us to think and speak.

Connecting the tragic and hope is not a new thought to the extent that tragedy in its presentation has long been considered an act of human courage and affirmation in the midst of powers far beyond our control and beyond the scope of human care and compassion as well. Heidegger's hope, on the other hand, seems at first to diminish the depth of tragic insight. In poeticizing language to allow it to speak in the thinking of *genesisphthoran*, Heidegger speaks of rescue that comes when being advances in its oblivion to its furthest extreme. Ours is the time of this rescue as the hinge seems to be ready to swing back, most probably in Heidegger's thought, the opening whose closure has been the occasion of a fateful swing to a mad cultural departure from our lineage's most giving, vital, if last thought. We are clear, however, that for Heidegger hope is not found in a human affirmation of endurance in the flow of crushing destiny. The tragic, rather, is found *in* the very insisting affirmation of human endurance. It is clear that an ethics of human dignity and worth is not the site of a possible resurgence of life-sustaining value. Rather, ethical affirmation of human worth is the region in which willful persistence most likely will take place. The hinge turns toward hope in a transformation of thought whereby *necessity* is recovered in a language of usage in which bestowal of being, as distinct from insistence on presence, transpires. In the hinge of their occurrence, beings pass through their own tragic unhinging. They give esteem to one another not in valuative affirmation but in belonging, in their being, to the hinge and in letting each other, by virtue of their being, belong to the hinge of *genesisphthoran*. Hope resides not in human affirmation but in beings' belonging to the hinge. To speak within this hearing is properly to poeticize and to speak in the hope of the hinge's occurrence in our time of dominant presence. The extreme danger—we are speaking of a terrible deadening of the world that is no less threatening than the night of the rule of the last man in Nietzsche's poetic thought—this danger does not subside in Heidegger's hope. The tragic arises and persists. But the tragic—*adikia*—does not control its own dispensation. *Adikia* does not send itself. It is the hinge—it belongs to the hinge—that it refuses in a passion for persistence. Hope can thus arise in a passage of this passion and in the passage of persistence. Hope arises in the arising of loss of the tragic. If our language can let itself hear that in which it belongs—if it can take place in *that Zwiesprache*—something barely thinkable that I am calling 'esteem among beings' may take place beyond good and evil, other than a response to a highest being, and quite other to the insistence that we project in our best efforts to survive by yet one more, better structure of values. That kind of belonging indicates the extreme danger in which Heidegger's hope arises, a danger that belongs to the arising of his hope and one that indicates as well the futility of efforts to elaborate the tragic in enthusiasm for a new age. No new age: the coming passage of the tragic. A passing opening out of our age: the catastrophic coming of Anaximander's thought.

5 | Thinking Noninterpretively

THE PROBLEMATIC THAT will guide this discussion is that language, patterns of interpretation, and communities all can bear within themselves, as aspects of their identities, powers which we ordinarily call destructive. This destructiveness, which might well constitute our ability to interpret and to communicate and bond with one another, can take a variety of forms that are subject to description. Examples of this destructiveness are found in interpretations that present themselves as noninterpretive and set in motion countermovements to their own manner of occurrence, or communities whose bonding movements produce a destiny of totalization which obscures the freedom of bonding, or a language which destroys the lives of what it presents. We will narrow this problematic by considering the likelihood that interpreting—as a process of ordering, presenting, and disclosing—includes in our heritage an inevitability of technological representation and that such representation inevitably destroys the essence or life occurrence of what is represented, that for us orders of interpretation and technology cannot be separated. This will be our emphasis as we read parts of "The Question concerning Technology."[1] In this essay Heidegger shows that things as they now come to appearance renounce, *in* their appearing, the life or essence of their appearing. Since interpretive language gives appearance in its ordering of things, his descriptive claim means that interpretive language is in question in its occurrence. And that means that interpretation in a time of technology is in question. We will then consider parts of his reading of Heraclitus in order to raise an option for speaking and thinking that is not circumscribed by interpreting.

The claim that interpretive language is in question is not new. Our tradition of thought was born in efforts to achieve noninterpretive insight into realities that transcend interpretation. Entities so nonordinary that we cannot entertain them in our ordinary lives, although our very lives depend upon them, have been the frequent objects for thought that presented itself as noninterpretive. Such thought could arise only when an individual through severe discipline and often special access achieved a release from ordinary interpretations and ways of life that arrested one's attention in mortal and passing things. To see and hear and speak ordinarily—that is, according to the given standards of clarity and good sense—meant to misperceive what is really present. The power of misperception was considered to be so forceful, so intrinsic to the usual manner of thinking and perceiving, that an agency of perceiving significantly different from that of ordinary agency had to develop in thought and language. This agency is seldom conceived as one's personal self but as something other to the particular thinking and speaking individual, other by virtue of transcendence, deathlessness, extraordinary gift, or purity of essence. I suspect that the destiny of this manner of thought is lived out now in beliefs that teach us to look for true realities to revere, true political values to profess, and true heroes to follow. Such realities, values, or heroes give us a desired transcendence of what is ordinary.

But if the ordering of language and evaluation is itself in question, even the objects of our most special language and evaluations cannot release us from the dangers of self-destruction. Such orders of objects and evaluations in their representation of things and in their claimed origination as extraordinary might be primary bearers of destructive force as they function interpretively to tell us who we are in common, together, as individuals who form a people. The most definitive orders of our culture, as they hold us together, would then be ones that function centrally in our criticism and creative work. As definitive, they will usually be inaccessible to critique and description because they will define the topography and hierarchy within which critique and description take place. Belonging to such a definitive, ordering center might well give rise to an obsession to hold things in place according to silent demands for a certain manner of presentation, such as the demands of technology as Heidegger discusses it. By the force of such obsession, which I will describe as a concentric force of markers and signs, our sense of identity is protected, but the disclosure of identity, its flowing and withdrawing quality, its coming to be passing away in its appearance, might well be obscured. We might well be in a destiny of obsession that produces identities and definitions without a sense for the nonidentity that ungrounds the grounding of identity. One point of departure is thus to find out how to hold in question the valuing and interpretive manner of thinking by which things, people, and their common ties have identity and meaning.

Heidegger begins "The Question concerning Technology" by linking questioning to entering a way of thinking that is not technological and to building a way of thinking that is not fixed on—i.e., not obsessed with—specific claims and topics. Thinking in the *question* of technology might open us in our relations with things to the *Wesen* of technology, i.e., to something nontechnological in technology. As we question technology we need not be controlled by technology. Rather, we can be on a way of thinking that is appropriate to the essence of technology, to its coming to be passing away.[2]

When Heidegger says that technology is not the same as its essence, he is saying in part that there is a difference between *what* technology does and the disclosiveness of technology. This disclosive dimension is the being of technology, its coming to presence in the appearing of things. Heidegger means that we must think nontechnologically if we are to think of technology in *its* coming to presence. The thoughts that we are approaching are that *technology* names the way things inevitably appear at the present time: the word names a manner of ordering which I shall elaborate by Heidegger's terms *Bestand* (standing reserve) and *Gestell* (enframing). In this order of appearance things are at cross-purposes with their lives. When we think in the question of technology we can interrupt the inevitability of technological ordering and find openings to another way of thinking that moves away from the destructive cross-purposes of technology. In the course of the discussion I will show that interpretive thought, when it is viewed in the context of "The Question concerning Technology," is inevitably technological and that Heidegger's suggested alternative to interpretive thought, based on an interpretation of technological ordering by means of early texts in our lineage, is a way of thinking that is structured by conceptual orders. The interruption of technology occurs as we turn to the *Wesen* of technology, to technology's disclosiveness—its letting things come to presence. This turn gives us an opening to a dimension of technology that is not technological. After we follow Heidegger's account of technology we will elaborate an alternative to interpretive thought that Heidegger finds in the work of Heraclitus. By this process we will put in question our ordinary manner of interpreting the events and texts of our tradition and consider the possibility of thought that is neither interpretive nor opposed to interpretation.

The word that Heidegger uses to describe the manner in which technology lets things come to presence, i.e., to appear, is *Herausforderung*, a word that is given in the translation as 'challenging' and 'challenging forth'. This word has the overtone of defiance, as when someone is challenged to a duel or is called out in a challenging way. In a time of technology things are given to appear and to have significance by their usefulness. They are fitted to purposes based on needs, plans, and interests. Things are given value and place in orders of need and use. By drawing on words that I shall emphasize later, we can say that technology exposes things and lets them lie before us with meaning and significance by expediting and dispatching them in a kind of challenge that gives value in defiance of their nonuseful disclosiveness. They have presence insofar as they further something else. They play a role in larger plans, such as the plans of social order, agricultural production, or institutional structure. "Such challenging happens in that the energy concealed in nature is unlocked, what is unlocked is transformed, what is transformed is stored up, what is stored up is, in turn, distributed, and what is distributed is switched about ever anew" (BW 322; VA 20). *Technology* thus names a manner of appearing in which things *are* for the sake of something else. Such orders are dynamic and cybernetic. They are orders of transition and transformation. But the disclosiveness of things, their dimension of nonorder, their lives in their appearing, are not relevant to their places in our lives. And the possibility of technology itself as an occurrence of nontechnological disclosiveness is, within a technological framework, without interest or value.

Heidegger's descriptive claim is that technology in its defiance of disclosiveness, as it provides a space that challenges things forth into orders of useful availability, is disclosive. It is a manner of giving presence. But in its manner of giving presence the *question* of giving presence is defiantly pushed aside. Technology is a manner of disclosure that defies its own disclosiveness. Insofar as coming to presence means the very life of things, technology is a way of being that is defiant regarding its life.

A double emphasis is found in this part of Heidegger's account. Technology is itself a revealing that orders. It is a manner of disclosing. It lets beings appear as the things they are in structures of practical significance. It engenders a specific kind of world. And the things that appear have their lives within orders of useful availability. Heidegger places technology within a history of disclosure. His broad claim, which I discussed in detail in chapter 4, is that Western thought and speech took their origins in experiences of beings in their mortal appearing. Their arising is already characterized by their passing away. Their disclosedness, that is, is characterized simultaneously by the coming and the withdrawing of being. The deep perplexity of mortal disclosiveness is constitutive of Western thought and speech. We will see later that astonishment over and in mortal disclosiveness—as distinct from instrumental mentation and orders of conceptual grasp—is definitive of the appearance of beings in Western thought and speech, even when such astonishment is thoroughly overlooked in particular ways of ordering things. For now I note that technology, which has no interest in astonishment over disclosiveness, is within a history of disclosure, that it is a manner of bringing things to appearance, and that it constitutes an inchoate refusal of its astonishing mortal disclosiveness.

Heidegger's emphasis on a history of formation in the way things appear is part of his releasing his own thought from the power and priority of subjectivity in modern conceptualization. "Modern technology, as a revealing which orders, is . . . no mere human doing" (BW 324; VA 22). We have our existence within orders of unconcealing, orders within which things and humans occur significantly in reference to each other. We are not only born into a society of possibility defined in part by financial resources. We are also born into cultural orders that allow us to communicate within orders of use. We must refer to things and people in their hierarchies of instrumentality and availability and participate in economies of technological exchange. We come to be in such orders. They condition our ability to recognize ourselves and think of ourselves. In Heidegger's account, we are able to conceive of subjectivity, historical relativism, and humanism because of the priority of use within a history of human formation that occurs in defiance of disclosiveness. In this history, people and things are in relation by virtue of their availability for projects based on communal and individual needs. They constitute a standing reserve (*Bestand*). The name for this framework that has already brought things together in such a manner is *Gestell* (enframing). Technology's inevitability, not subjectivity, provides the unity of appearance in our common lives.

Thus within technology things are disclosed—that is, they occur with meaning and names, and they belong in a community of human beings—as they are enframed, as they are set and arranged and regulated according to the needs and interests of communities of people, communities that are themselves under the demands of a defying manner of disclosing. On the one hand, *enframing* names the disclosiveness of things within technology. On the other, communities render things real by structures of purpose, use, and availability within the sway of disclosure as enframing. I note now and will return later to the thought that words, concepts, and thinking generally are 'things' in this context. Our thoughts occur with purposes and within histories that give them purposes. Words are for use. Words and thoughts, for example, that lack relevance or political values or institutional goals for human survival are naturally considered merely aesthetic or abstract and impractical within the dimension of *Gestell*. Whether there is political importance in an *absence* of relevance for politics is a question we will pursue later.

Presently our emphasis falls on Heidegger's claim that *Gestell* names the *unconcealment* of technology. It lets be, gives presence, and withdraws from grasp in its own disclosure. *Gestell* is not only a being but is the disclosiveness of beings in a time of technology. In our ordering of things—i.e., in our governance, in our processes of arranging them with meaning and significance—we thus belong to *Gestell*. As interpreters we belong to enframing.

A second emphasis falls on Heidegger's claim that the revealing/concealing of technology, its *Wesen* or coming to pass or waying or essence, is not technological. What is technological about technology is closed to its own nontechnological coming to pass, to its own essence. Technology's disclosiveness and its self-disclosure in enframing are outside the *grasp* of enframing thought, language, and practice. It is, for example, counterintuitive to question the *Wesen* of technology within an enframing state of mind. Such questioning has no cash value and is, in that sense, senseless. This means that as an enframing community or state of mind lives out its essence it closes itself to its own coming to pass. Technological life is thus at odds with its own occurrence. We are "called" to reveal things—to give them presence—as ready for use, and yet this call to let things come to presence falls outside of a readiness for use. It is 'useless' in its address.

Heidegger's descriptive claims are that when we turn our attention to the essence of technology, we turn in and out of the power of enframing and we find ourselves, as technological beings, in a course of revealing that provides us with a surprising history. The second point first. Heidegger's word for what I called "a course of revealing" is *Geschick* and is translated 'destining': "When we consider the essence (*Wesen*) of technology we experience enframing as a *destining* of revealing" (BW 330; VA 20, my emphasis). We can say in an introductory way that revealing rather than technological ordering has given shape to the course of our tradition and our world. He is not saying that 'disclosure' or 'revelation' name something present that has molded our history. He is not saying that there is a primordial, self-enacting being from which the world unfolds. His thought behind the claim that we experience enframing as a destining of revealing when we consider the essence of technology is that the question of the *Wesen*, the coming to be passing away, of beings gave rise to thinking in our lineage. And this question was experienced, thought, and spoken in the earliest reaches of our history as the coming to be passing away of disclosedness. Not of a pervasive sub-*stance*—not of something already there when we turn to think—but *Wesen* as arising and passing away occurring at once together in the appearing of things. This questionableness of arising and passing at once in things' appearing is not separate from thought and speech. Thought and speech give things to appear and thus belong to the *wesentliche*, the essential, question of being.

So revealing has given shape to our lineage and world as the element in which Western thought has arisen and as the element by which things have come to be thought. As things *appear* in whatever order they appear in, and as they come to be in chains of significations, they bear in them a *history* of disclosedness that *sends* them to be in their tradition. We are attempting to avoid the idea of something preformed and present as we speak of destining. And we are attempting to keep a distance from the language of historical relativism that thinks a continuing presence negatively. Heidegger's thought of destining suggests a way of thinking that is not based on something present but on the *question* of coming to passing away in the appearing of things.

As we turn to the *Wesen* of technology we find ourselves turning into a history of disclosedness that takes us to the origins of Western thought and away from the power of technological enframing: "When we once open ourselves expressly to the *essence* (*Wesen*) of technology we find ourselves unexpectedly taken into a freeing claim" (BW 330–331; VA 29). Our thinking comes more into the inheritance of disclosure and comes to belong to it rather than to orders of significance and meaning within a time of technology.

There is danger not only in technology but also in the turning of which we have been speaking. On the one hand, *disclosedness* and *Wesen* name ways through technology to freedom from the encompassing power of technology. On the other hand, *enframing* names the disclosedness of technology. In technology disclosedness has turned against itself in orders and arrangements that are designed *not* to open to the question of being, the coming to be passing away in the appearing of things, or whatever else in technology is not technological. It is rather a revealing that defies revealing by calling out beings—giving them to appear—with no attunement to their own course of disclosure. This counterplay, I have said, has a suicidal aspect. It constitutes a life against its own being. "The destining of revealing is in itself not just any danger, but *the* danger. . . . when destining reigns in the mode of enframing, it is the supreme danger" (BW 331–332; VA 30).

There are many dimensions to this unusually rich thought. The one I want to emphasize now is that as interpreters we are necessarily involved, by Heidegger's account, in technological disclosure and its dangers. This involvement not only means that some beings appear as the source of truth. It also means that access to texts and thoughts that developed outside of technology is possible only by turning within technology out of it. We are thus considering the likelihood that in a time of enframing even the art of interpretation with an emphasis on community might embody a danger of destructiveness to which our language and thought are blind. We began with the suggestion that when thinking takes place in questioning it follows a course that interrupts technology. Questioning thought may turn in technology out of technology. The questioning that we have followed concerns the essence of technology. By this questioning Heidegger has *interpreted* both the time of our lives and technology itself. His interpretation has taken the forms of description, clarification of both words and active, structural components of a use-oriented culture, elaboration of some texts, and claims about the formation of time in our culture. Above all he set the question of technology within the context of the history and forecast of the question of being—its coming to be passing away in the appearing of things—and that is a major interpretive move.

But in what we might initially call the 'performative' dimension, Heidegger opens his thought to an excess of interpretation. Nothing in his thought is based *solely* on the accuracy or interpretive meaning of his claims. The interpretive dimension in "The Question concerning Technology" occurs *within* the occurrence of questioning in which the process of appeal to meaning and significance is interrupted by an indictment of significance as a standing reserve. There is something about a highly disciplined way of thinking in question and not in quest of certainty, when it is not thoroughly determined by the beings under consideration, that gives it the possibility for speaking after (*entsprechen*) and addressing an opening in excess to the occurrence of those beings. Such thinking, in its dimension of nondetermination—its being in question—is strangely determined by an excessiveness that Heidegger addresses as the question of being. This question takes place in the performative dimension of Heidegger's thought as he puts in question the adequacy of *his* interpretive claims. Something other to his interpretation is suggested and left unresolved.

The turning of the question—its movement in his thought—is thus not only an interpretation or an action that individuals perform. Such turning does not create an order of thinking or function as a formalizing agency. It is like a springing away within structures from those structures, like a billowing out of an excess within a given identity. The turning of question arises within given contexts but gives rise to something that incompletes the completion of the given context, like the arising of the question of the essence of technology within a context of ordering that is not only ill-suited to address such an issue but positively ill-disposed to the possibility of having an essence. The turning of the question is a danger to the integrity of its host; but in posing a danger to its context it also may turn danger to disclosure, to an *exposure in the turning's excess*.

You can see that we are bordering on a political matter when we put in question the adequacy of any politics—any ordering—as we put in question the values of clear certainty and ordinary sensibility. We are approaching the possibility that the nonusefulness of excess opens a way of thinking that exposes the danger of interpreting by turning out of interpretive thought, by occurring as thought that turns from standing reserve and enframing. The possibility is that the danger of interpretive thinking will be disclosed in a departure in interpretation from interpretation.

Heidegger does not place emphasis on the adaptive ability of a way of interpreting that changes and mutates by changing circumstances. Flexibility is not the issue. Nor is there a positive claim about the presence of a transcending reality that moves thought beyond its momentary fixations. We are clear that any such presence would be, in a time of technology, an instance of enframing thought and would most likely function as a standing reserve that causes formations and produces meaning. The edge in Heidegger's thought that we are approaching is an occurrence of questioning that releases thought from its secret obsessions and fixations and in that release opens to de-veloping (i.e., taking out of darkness) disclosures with alertness to their arising and passing away in excess to all causation. We have no reason to be optimistic that such release in Heidegger's thought will persuade us to change anything essentially or will set in motion a new politics. We have every reason to think that this is another interpretation to be evaluated, treated with fair critique, and placed within a hierarchy of options for human benefit.

But even without optimism Heidegger *will* speak of saving. Although this language would be mistaken if we heard it as another version of *Herausforderung*, it nonetheless provides a challenge and calls us out to another way of hearing and seeing. He begins this part of his discussion, as he usually does, with a series of interpretations as he addresses the thought of saving, and by these interpretations he follows a development of thought that exceeds interpretation. Our question will be whether he thinks saving in the *turning* of the question concerning technology or whether the turning stops in this aspect of his thought. If the turning stops, his thinking would have been encompassed by interpretation, and the question of technology would probably be left in something like a standing reserve to help his interpretations when they need it.

Heidegger does not speak of saving power as the translation suggests, but of *das Rettende*, which means 'the freeing and protecting'. *Das Rettende* gives protection to disclosure and hence to human beings when it is recovered in our lineage by freeing the essence of technology. The word *saving* in this context does not mean retention of something for later purposes, that is, it does not suggest a version of standing reserve. Nor does it suggest a being that causes or does something called saving. The thought of ontological difference is fully in play here, and *das Rettende* does not name a being and certainly does not name a power. Rather a draw of the *Wesen* or essence or coming to pass of technology, a draw in an absence of power, allows an opening that returns things from their retention for use and significance to their unuseful being, to their disclosiveness, their appearing in ceasing to be as they come to be. The American philosopher Richard Rorty has given an archetypically technological response to this language by calling it esoteric. It sounds to him like language for an inner circle of devotees. But the point has nothing to do with devotion to Heidegger. The issue is one of turning in our interpretive circle of relevance, *turning* by means of excessiveness in the disclosure of things *through* the values of usage, availability for usage, encompassing organizational structure, and productivity to the disclosive excess. This turning of language in attentiveness to excessiveness that occurs in the appearance of things in language and thought is in the draw of the disclosive coming to pass or waying of enframing. This disclosiveness is excessive in that it escapes or exceeds enframing. It cannot be enframed, and by this freedom from enframement saving occurs.

Heidegger takes the thought of saving and preserving from Hölderlin's "Patmos" and the lines "But where danger is, grows / The saving power [*das Rettende*] also" (BW 333; VA 32). In Hölderlin's poem Heidegger finds a coupling of danger and saving. Even though the disclosure of things in a time of technology sets things against their disclosiveness, their disclosures also carry the draw to disclosure in excess of technological ordering. And Hölderlin's poetic language performs the draw to disclosure. It attends to *das Rettende* in the midst of the danger on which it relentlessly focuses. By following Hölderlin's language Heidegger finds that his own language is turned out of the reflective orders that now mold philosophical thought. Hölderlin's poetry is excessive to philosophical good sense as it speaks of the danger that occurs in the losses that define what we can and should mean when we speak carefully in a context of technological order. In his attention to danger and in speaking of it, and *in* it his language begins to turn to the disclosure of danger in its excess of danger. And by following Hölderlin's words Heidegger undergoes a turning in his own thought to something that he could not think if he followed the movements that have come to define philosophical mentation. The *danger* of technology comes to appear in Hölderlin's poem to be the bearer of a saving excess vis-à-vis the strangling hold of technological disclosure.

The danger in technology, as we have seen, lies in its yielding, issuing, and bearing things in a way that defies them in their appearing or, as we shall say later, in their shining. It distorts the disclosive bearing of things in its bearing of them. Or we could say that technology in its disclosiveness produces things as though it were not disclosing them and as though they were without disclosure. But the seemingly normative edge to this language is misleading. It is not that things have a particular nature, an inner identity that is distorted. The phenomenological side of Heidegger's interpretation is found in his thought that things lack such a nature in their essence, that their essence occurs in appearing, and this difference from natural identity is a locale of excessiveness that escapes substantive categories and nomination. Sending and granting as *Herausforderung* makes things to be useful and "blocks" the sending and granting that come to pass but do not produce or use or defy. But it also bears the nonuseful disclosedness of things.

In this context Heidegger uses the word *poiesis* to elaborate a manner of disclosure that is not technological. The *Wesen* of technology, as we have found, is in a lineage of appearing: our tradition was born in an unresolvable question of the appearing of things which was experienced as mortal, as coming to be passing away. Things came forth passing away. They appear in deathliness, i.e., in withdrawing from appearance. In deathliness things are alive. When people attend to mortality in the ways they relate with things and when language or art lets things appear meaningfully and relationally in preservation of their deathliness, the appearing of things is also preserved. Their being is allowed. The keeping of things keeps their coming to be passing away and does not merely hold them in presence for use. *Poiesis* names a manner of speaking, presenting, and, if we are careful with the word, 'ordering' that is attuned to their coming to be passing away. Not technological order, but an uncovering of things, a way of bringing things forth in language and practice that remains in affirmative touch with the mortality of the very process of appearing. The poetic language of Hölderlin constitutes such a *poiesis*, and Heidegger's thought is in part a mimesis of Hölderlin's language in which Heidegger's thought responds attentively in the poetic enactment. This enactment, which I addressed earlier as the performative dimension of Heidegger's thought, returns us to a pretechnical aspect of technology which we shall discuss in relation to Heraclitus. For the moment I only note that in poetic speech and thought something both present and lost in technological disclosure is retrieved, and when this retrieval is attuned to the danger of technology a nontechnological *poiesis* of technology becomes possible for thinking.

Wesen does not appear as a category or as any structural element for interpretation. It does not happen either as an order or as a part of an order. This interpretive claim means that we must exceed interpretive arrangement and discursive order if we are appropriate to the essence of technology. We find Heidegger's interpretive thought turning out of interpretation in its attempt to follow a noninterpretive dimension of technology which is noted by the word *Wesen*. The *Wesen* of something occurs as it comes to pass, that is, as mortal appearing which, as we shall see, gathers things together in passing. Our translation uses the word *develop* for this occurrence: in their *Wesen* beings open out from obscurity, they *de*-velop or unfold or come into disclosure. I am noting now that in the coming to pass of technological things—in the midst of the technological world—something other to interpretive arrangements develops. *Excess*, we have said. And this excess is of the disclosures of thought and language and appears to be recovered when language is attuned to nontechnological disclosure, an attunement that I have marked by Heidegger's use of *poiesis*. By this turning to excess and *poiesis* the relation of interpretive thought to truth is coming into question. And as it comes into question the relation of interpretive thought to technology gains emphasis. *Does interpretation arise from a kind of ordering that projects itself and thus closes on itself by means of its primary values and place in reserve a body of meanings by which funding interpretation gives itself meaning as a totality?* Whether interpretive thought inevitably totalizes, even when it allows for transformation and internal process, is a question that I reserve for the moment. But we can say now that by this language that is esoteric in technological hearing Heidegger appears to be following a development of noninterpretive thought, namely a manner of speaking and disclosing that develops in attention to a nonintentional dimension of enframing. His thinking suggests unenframement, freedom from thought that determines things—i.e., places them—by values and that produces things by structures of significance.

As people turn out of the attunements of enframing to attunement to disclosure, their existence changes. This is an unexpected descriptive claim by Heidegger. The nonpolitical excess of disclosure can occasion a shift—and I believe it to be a radical shift—in our way of being with each other and with the things of our world. We no longer belong entirely to the enframing values of a technological time but come to belong to the mortal disclosure of whatever appears—including, of course, our own lives. This transformation suggests that our ways of presenting ourselves and things would change, would not be ordered primarily by use, relevance, and economies of productive exchange, that interpretive thinking would change in the draw of disclosiveness. Letting something appear in its coming to be passing away, a text for example, would demand a way of reading that does not attempt to fix it in a productive order, such as an order of relevance for the production of knowledge or the production of value. Techniques of interpreting and discovering would belong to processes of letting the appearances of things follow their disclosiveness, their coming out of no particular 'where' into the life of existence. "Keeping watch over the un-concealment," Heidegger calls this attentiveness (BW 337; VA 36). The histori-cally developed being—human being—that has come to be as it is in a lineage born of the question of disclosiveness comes to itself in an essential (*wesentliche*) way as it opens to the disclosiveness that has given it its historical course. Hu-man being turns to its own disclosedness as it attends to the nonorder of the disclosedness of things: "It is precisely in enframing, which threatens to sweep man away into ordering as the ostensibly sole way of revealing, and so thrusts man into the danger of the surrender of his free essence—it is precisely in this extreme danger that the innermost indestructible belongingness of man within granting may come to light, provided that we, for our part, begin to pay heed to the essence of technology" (BW 337; VA 36).

Keeping watch over unconcealment thus means that one develops touch with something originary in our capacity to speak and think. The originary, far from being something like a first cause, is that to which we humans belong by virtue of what gives us in our lineage to be human, namely the coming of unconcealment with uncertainty, a nonresolvable question that develops in the development of speaking and thinking. For better or for worse, human being comes to be—unfolds and develops—as question in passing. That is the send-ing, the timing, of our being, and as we attend to the unfolding of this question we give way to our *Wesen*, our being other to *Technik* and to all forms of resolu-tion in the guise of enframements.

These words of mine are, of course, interpretations of Heidegger's interpre-tation of human being and of time, of their emergence, of how they are endan-gered in their contemporary development, and of Hölderlin (among others). As interpretations Heidegger's words and mine define their subject matter. They definitively place the matter before themselves and establish limits whose ac-curacy is necessary for their validity. But Heidegger invokes a noninterpretive option.

There was a time, he says (interpretively), when *techne* was experienced as *poiesis* (BW 339; VA 38). Artistic presentation in this *techne* revealed something in its appearing, its unconcealment. For a time in Greece, *poiesis* was experi-enced as letting something arise out of darkness. It included attention to the thing's unordered shining forth as it comes to pass in its presentation. This in-terpretive claim is not meant to suggest that we should attempt to do things as the classical Greeks did them. It rather says that our lineage of presentation, of which technology is a part, bears an originary dimension of *poiesis*. *Poiesis* and *techne* are not technological and do not give presentation primarily by orders and certainly not by orders of relevance and usefulness. Technology is made possible, is "sent," and, ironically, has its essential meaning in a lineage of non-technological disclosure. The noninterpretive aspect in Heidegger's thought is found in its interruption of technological order, and hence of interpretive order, by the question—the uncertainty—of technology in its limits and danger. The self-interruption of his interpretive work is found in a reading of Greek experience that follows *poiesis*, which is lost as it is interpreted. This questioning opens by its interpretation of something whose occurrence exceeds interpretive movement. It accounts for its own danger in its recognitions of the danger of technology and of the present incomprehensibility—in that sense, the mystery—of presentation and disclosure that occur outside the broad reach of *Gestell*.

In questioning, as Heidegger develops it, something other to interpreting thus gains emphasis. One phrase that he uses in this emphasis is "bear witness to the crisis" (BW 340; VA 39). In questioning without expectation or hope of resolution, even the limited definitiveness of open-minded interpretation is interrupted and exceeded. The crisis or danger of technology opens to its disclosiveness, its coming to pass in which no standing reserve of value or meaning is suggested. Thought seems to come into its own as it undergoes this movement in alertness to the danger of technological order and sees its own danger in the midst of its accomplishment. Astonishment develops before nonresolution and incomprehensibility in the coming to be/passing away—before the *Wesen*—of technology, and one blinks, perhaps, and listens again, listens not for something definitive but listens in astonishment over being astonished in the dangerous limits of technology. Heidegger's report is that in such listening things come to stand out in their excess to all frames of reference, particularly in excess to the frames of reference provided by our conceptual, interpretive structures. He does not say that we should refrain from speech or thought regarding things or that we should stop thinking about them and interpreting them. But he points out that what speech and thought say and mean, as they develop in question and in crisis, loses the authority of valuation and meaning as things become clear in their passing occurrence.

Thus far I have emphasized the value structure of interpreting within the framework of *Gestell* and its inevitability. That is, I have structured these remarks that put interpretation in question in a manner that places emphasis on the order of interpretation. I am clearly thinking within the force *Gestell*. I have suggested that valuing in a time of technological disclosure cannot avoid the *Gestell*, that interpreting is unavoidably dangerous by its reserve of meaning and its silent demand for relevance. And I have reenacted this danger in my critical account. My interpretation of Heidegger revolves around a *concept* of danger, a *grasp* of technology, and an *interpretation* of the limits of technology. You cannot hear in my interpretation the orderless coming to be passing away of disclosedness. Within the structure of these remarks, the danger of technology thus continuously shows itself and confirms, I suspect, the accuracy of what I propose. I have adopted a certain spareness of style in order to accentuate structure and the limits of structure and to avoid the confidence and draw to emersion that occur in poetic discourse. And I have developed in addition to addressing the danger of order in a technological time an aporetic structure that you have probably discerned: the *aporia* of interpreting the uninterpretable. The uninterpretable *Wesen* of technology accompanies the occurrence of interpretation but is not a part of the order of interpretation. By this *aporia* I hope to have accentuated and brought to thought the difference between the order of interpretation and the unorder of the coming to presence of technology.

Another aspect of the danger in interpreting is an inevitable movement from an interpretation back to itself. I would like to accept without elaboration an implication in Heidegger's account of world and interpretation in *Being and Time*, namely that any arrangement of things constitutes a lived interpretation as people live in and through these arrangements by means of significances, structures of reference, etc. A grammar that arranges words and their functions, for example, is as much an interpretation as a room's arrangement or an institutional structure or the formation of a book. We live in interpretations that refer back to themselves by the signifiers, markers, and normal meanings that provide place, use, referability, and community. To live within interpretive frameworks is also to produce the otherness of whatever does not fit within the framework, whatever exceeds the framework by its place or movement within it, or whatever occurs mutely, meaninglessly, outside of it. An interpretive movement turns toward itself in producing alterity—or it produces alterity by moving always toward itself. An interpretive movement is thus like subjectivity in this regard. It arises from itself, projects itself, and functions as though it grounds itself by providing the basis for its own validation. An interpretation that interrupts its self-validation is surely one that is in question.

I can only note the similarity between subjectivity and interpretive structures, their requirement for self-validating perspective, as we elaborate Heidegger's interruption of interpretive thinking by turning to a few paragraphs in his reading of Heraclitus's fragments B 16 and B 50, and I make this notation in order to emphasize that Heidegger's movement away from the dominance of the subject in thought and language is a movement away from interpretation. We shall have to see if his interpretation, which is governed by the question of disclosedness, that is, the question of being, allows a movement in thought and language that is not concentric, as subjectivity and interpretation appear to be. If such concentric movement is broken and exceeded and if we think in the occurrence of breaking and exceeding, we shall have the possibility of an occurrence of thinking and speaking that is not interpretive. We will also have an occurrence that is not structured finally by meaning and significance and one in which presumably the dangers of valuation and *Gestell* are interrupted. I will pursue the possibility that Heidegger's interpretation of Heraclitus's interpretation allows and attends to an excess of interpretation.

Heidegger begins his reading with a meditation on the strangeness of a combination of obscurity and lucidity in Heraclitus's words. Heraclitus attempts to say the lighting—*das Lichtende*—in such a way that the language of thinking calls forth the shining of the lighting (EGT 103; VA 250). (We shall see that this shining is excessive to its interpretive movement in Heidegger's language.) Heraclitus attempts to think *a-létheia*, to think not only the shining forth of beings out of utter darkness, or *léthe*, but to think as well the shining of the lighting out of *léthe*. The fineness of Heidegger's reading here is measured by his attention to the shining in its difference to *what* shines. The shining gives the possibility of interpretation and is not itself an interpretation. And yet Heidegger's reading is an interpretation. This *focus* on lighting and shining, their very names, in the thought of both Heidegger and Heraclitus narrows the field of attention, includes definitive distinctions, arises out of a history of amazement before the occurrence of things, and contrasts to another history of confusion over shining and what shines. Further, Heidegger is not proposing a special faculty of discrimination that characterizes mental agency and that sees shining after proper exercise and discipline. Nor is he proposing an occurrence of special revelation. His interpretive claims are that a specific occurrence named *alétheia belongs* to Heraclitus's thought, that this occurrence has been blurred and forgotten by later thought, and that its recovery will put us in touch with something originary for our Western ability to think and speak. But he also claims that the occurrence of shining out of darkness, *alétheia*, does not happen solely within this circumference of interpretation and conceptualization and that in interpreting *alétheia* we do not think what we are talking about. To give proper place to this obscurity, its shining, and their excess to interpretation in Heraclitus's words, Heidegger gives in his reading priority to *Erstaunen*, or wonder and astonishment. "We need . . . to take up . . . wonder as our abode," our *Wohnsitz* (EGT 104; VA 251).

"Wonder," Heidegger says, "first *begins* with the question, 'what does all this mean and how could it happen?' How can we arrive at such a beginning?" He thus begins by appeal to a state of mind that not only keeps everything unsettled and in question—a state of mind that is not grounded in knowledge or belief. It is a state of mind that attends to obscurity and shining together and that holds our attention to them *in an absence of clarity or resolution*, i.e., in an absence of concentric movement. Wonder is in stark contrast to interpretive thought: interpretations of what Heraclitus says work toward correctness and the elimination of questions, Heidegger says. "Wishing to pursue the 'objectively correct' teaching of Heraclitus means refusing to run the salutary risk of being confounded by the truth of a thinking" (EGT 106; VA 253). And rather than seeking correctness of interpretation, Heidegger wants to point to something noninterpretive which he calls *das Ereignis*, or the event.

So we can say that by holding resolution and correctness in question, by thinking in question, Heidegger wants to touch something outside the authority of interpretive thought, outside the circumference of significance and meaning, and outside the concentric movement of interpretation. In this sense his interpretation is designed to break what he says about Heraclitus and *alétheia*. He wants to think noninterpretively in this excess of interpretation, and his access to this possibility of thinking is questioning and wonder. By questioning and wonder Heidegger hopes to enter into thinking and speaking, which are appropriate to a noninterpretive dimension of Heraclitus's thought and speech in which excess of interpretation occurs.

I emphasize the importance of interpretation in the occurrence of the excess of interpretation. Questioning and wonder do not take place in a vacuum. They are not empty. They are not pure states of mind that one reaches by reduction. Questioning and wonder are *Greek* experiences that are originary in combination with their being obscured and forgotten in the formation of *our* Western capacity to speak and think. But something is lost in this originary experience when orders of interpretation control how and what we think: *alétheia,* or the bestowal of presencing out of nonpresence, is lost. We cannot overemphasize in this context that *alétheia* does not name a reserve of meaning, that it does not validate the *meaning* of the question of being, so much as it gives uncertainty to the entire discourse and leaves the field of signification ungrounded by anything that could possess meaning or even possess the virtue of attacking reverence and the nomination of *holy.*

Insecuring, by a careful reading of Heraclitus, what is present and our everyday representations of things around us is thus a measure for entering the noninterpretive dimension of thinking in which things come to presence unsecured.

As Heidegger turns to the lines we shall follow, he has given an account of truth as the "bestowal of presencing" in the Heraclitus fragment B 16 (EGT 118; VA 268). This phrase, the bestowal of presencing, names the event of lighting, of things coming to light, their coming to be things in the world, and it—the event—never comes to completion in a grasp, meaning, or order. It withdraws from the existence of things as it occurs in giving presence. To follow Heidegger's interpretation with agreement, we need to affirm with him that Heraclitus's words give expression to an experience that is primordial in our heritage. We need to agree that the question of being shades and hovers throughout Heraclitus's thought and the primordial experience to which he gives word. We need to agree that when we return to Heraclitus's fragments without interrupting the provenance of technology in our thinking we cannot hear what he says. And, as Heidegger says early in the essay, we will never know with certainty whether his reading is right and those who disagree with him are wrong. But we approach a region of noninterpretive thinking by means of his interpretation regardless of agreement and disagreement. It is not primarily a question of judgment any more than the experience of a play of light in a Rembrandt or the experience of death in a late Cezanne is circumscribed by judgment.

Rather than judgment, Heidegger undergoes a dialogue with Heraclitus's words as they have been retained and encounters something "unuttered," something elusive and obscure that comes to presence and withdraws and occurs as question (EGT 120; VA 271). Rather than closing an argument, Heidegger opens his reading by giving attention to a current of simultaneous coming to presence and withdrawal from presence that takes place in Heraclitus's language. This strange occurrence manifests an incompletion in Western experiences of the world that both stirs thought and eludes conceptualization. The question arises in careful investigations of Heraclitus, investigations that are based on thorough knowledge of the language, culture, and relevant scholarship. They arise in well-prepared dialogue, not in flights of speculation. If the questions arose without such a careful encounter, they would lack disciplined engagement with the lineage from which they arise. The question of disclosure occurs in a crisis of interpretation, not in avoidance of interpretation and its requirements. The crisis happens as an interpreter finds (perhaps undergoes), through words and thoughts, withdrawal from conceptual order when that order operates with disciplined rigor. One comes to find, Heidegger reports, that the words say more in the dialogue than orders of meaning can express or retain.

Through the question of disclosure that arises in Heraclitus's fragment, Heidegger also finds that Heraclitus found himself before questions that he could not directly articulate but ones that he could 'say' in combinations of obscurity and lucidity. Heraclitus's thought is *in* question, and his art is found as he lets the question arise in a strange mixture of darkness and light. *Alétheia* takes place as the question arises—comes to presence—in the withdrawal of presence and clarity. Thinking in question is not at all like thinking within the circumference of interpretations. It is more like thinking in an *aporia* that accompanies the presence of whatever is there and is recognized interpretively.

Those who think in the question of coming to be passing away, in the *aporia* of the arising withdrawal of being, "hearken to and belong to the lighting"; they are the "der Lichtung Zuhörende und Zugehörige" (EGT 120; VA 271). They are the ones whose thought arises from astonishment in beings' coming to presence passing away. "We have heard [*gehört*]," Heidegger says, "when we *belong to* [*gehören*] the matter addressed" (EGT 66; VA 207). We belong to something when we *let* it lie together with other things before us, when *its* presencing in its environment has sway in its time and place. When we think and speak in the obscurity and clarity of Heraclitus's thought, without resolving one into the other, when we thus speak and think in the question which arises in his thought, we may find in such a dialogue that disclosedness arises in *its* time, i.e., arises in question in our thought. He is not speaking of a question identical to Heraclitus's or one that is posed in identical concepts but the same question of disclosiveness in its excess of specific frameworks, the same arising-withdrawing that hides in even our most technological orders, the same coming to be passing away to which technology blindly belongs.

Far from constructing a handbook on learning how to think in attunement to the question of disclosure, Heidegger's thought, in dialogue with Heraclitus's thought, interrupts his own interpretations. These interpretations are surely within the formation of *Gestell*. But they also break that formation by their attention to a radical difference from technological disclosure in the Greek experience of *poiesis* and *alétheia*. By attending to the question of technology's dangerous disclosure and by following the question of disclosure in Heraclitus's thought, Heidegger thematizes and loses his thematization of disclosure. In that combination he finds a way of thinking that is not interpreting, but something else that he calls meditative and for which he knows that he lacks both an adequate name and an adequate interpretation.

If Heidegger is accurate in his descriptions of technology's danger, the sharpest edge to the danger is found in our deep and largely unconscious conviction that when we think at our best, value with greatest care, and act with political respect and passion, we address danger from outside the danger. In the thought of this account, the danger is *greatest* when we are secure in our communities, assured in the meanings that hold together our best sensibility, and clear about our responsibilities. This danger qualifies not only our politics, ethics, and religion but our scholarship and reflective thought as well. The danger inheres in our lives with each other and with things. Within the problematic of this discussion we might wonder over the possibility that the recognition of the danger of interpretation is interpretive, that the recognition which would motivate us to allow our convictions to break and our passions to falter opens us to far more than we can recognize. The coming life of noninterpretive disclosure appears to depend on interpretation, and interpretation appears to belong to the noninterpretive occurrence of its own event. This mutual dependence constitutes both the danger and the opening to renewed life through the danger that I am addressing.

6 | The Ascetic Ideal
Nietzsche *contra* Heidegger

THE INTERRUPTION OF an ethos—of values, ideals, practical and theoretical axioms, and habits of mind and heart—can be an occasion for the entrance of possibilities for thought and action that are either suppressed in or foreign to what is ordinary in a culture. When the issue concerns the suffering, destruction, and oppression that are constitutive of an ethos, an interruption of the ethos can make perceptible, if only obscurely, some of the pathogenic elements that are otherwise invisibly a part of the ethos.

One pathogenic aspect of our Western ethos is the ascetic ideal. It is characterized by many types of refusal and denial regarding the manner in which human life occurs, and in Nietzsche's account the ascetic ideal reinforces this denial with a habitual insistence on the continuous and uninterrupted presence of meaning in all dimensions of life and being. In our ascetic withdrawal from life we join forces with hopelessness, suffering, death, and helplessness by giving them a meaning, in our appropriation of them, that far exceeds their living occurrence and that subordinates them within a scheme of meaning and hope. The rule governing the ascetic ideal is found in its incorporation and blind expression of the hopelessness and meaninglessness that it is designed to overcome through its hope and meaning. This incorporation and dissemination of what it is designed to overcome constitutes the ideal's nihilism for Nietzsche: the affirmations within the ascetic ideal project their opposites and produce a spiral of unwitting and inevitable violence in the spirituality they create. The denial of life within the affirmations of the ascetic ideal continuously reestablishes the destructive power of the ideal. But when this movement is broken by a self-overcoming like that in Nietzsche's genealogy of the ascetic ideal, the rule of the ascetic ideal is interrupted and a possibility is opened for life-affirmations that do not suppress by hope and belief the most fearful occurrences involved in being alive.

The affirmation of life without the illusion of continuous meaning, the affirmation that Nietzsche found in early Greek culture, was lost, according to his reading, in the course of the increasing cultural dominance of those whose nerve had failed before the disheartening flow of life. The ascetic ideal expresses this failure in its insistence on meaning and in its persistent manufacture of hope out of illusions bred of the failure. Heidegger is perhaps at his most non-Nietzschean point when in his Rector's Address he turns to the Greek division between the everyday and the question of being. This is an ironic moment in Heidegger's thought: he traces the origins of his own move to separate the future of the German university from the German *Volkstum*, that is, from dominant popular culture, to the emergence of the separation of thought from everyday life in Greek culture. But this move is not associated with the affirmation that Nietzsche uses as his reference in delimiting the ascetic ideal. According to Nietzsche's genealogy we have lost an earthly affirmation of life *in the midst of* not finitude or contingency but the specific suffering of everyday life. Nietzsche wants fully to face the brutality, the fateful shattering of hope, the disappointments that break people's lives, the individual and social tragedies. The debilitation of minds and bodies is juxtaposed to people's savoring food and drink, enjoying sexual pleasure—juxtaposed to friendship, the energy of ambition, the struggle between competitors, the mixture of desperation and exhilaration in efforts of accomplishment: Nietzsche's move is toward affirmation in the midst of chaotic living when he speaks of what is lost in the blind and self-deceived chaos of asceticism that is ordered by the illusion of continuous meaning.

In this affirmation one has an awareness, presumably a full awareness, of the otherness to human interest that radically distresses us. People's attention is delimited by it. Rather than escape or turn away from it, people are delimited by it in their relations with things. Rather than appropriate the suffering of life in ascetic self-denial, human beings stand with its otherness, its unthinkableness, its density. They need not attempt to embody it in forms that seem to shape it to human and thinkable dimensions. They live in the inappropriable, meaningless dark vacuity, with it and other to it, out of it and in it—angel and animal, Nietzsche said. Not to be lost, not to be redeemed, not to be overcome, it is connected to a will to live, an affirmation with and not in spite of the chaos. This affirmation does not promise an end to butchery and chaotic insensitivity, but it does provide an awareness of misery, a region for the fullness of its sounds, that is not to be escaped by ideals, goals, and visions that often define our subjection to what we must consider to be the best way of life. The affirmation that Nietzsche uncovers interrupts those satisfactions that are governed by the ascetic ideal and makes a place for the miserable chaos of life that is most feared and covered over, yet held and carried forward, by the ascetic ideal.

Heidegger's move, on the other hand, is toward a break in Western history that makes possible a questioning, an attentive thought that, by the effect of the question of being, is drawn away from everyday life, while nonetheless attached to it, and toward a way of living that appears to be more ethereal than Dionysian. Thus it appears—from the perspective of Nietzsche's human, who never leaves the earth even when transported into ecstasy. The factor of withdrawal from the everyday and earthly is more pronounced in Heidegger's thought than Nietzsche's, although the conflicting emphases are shaded and not always distinct. Zarathustra, for example, withdraws from human society at the beginning, in the middle, and at the end of Nietzsche's poem. We are not to be trapped by the virtues of everyday living, according to *Beyond Good and Evil*. Better to withdraw than to live happily in the herd. But the zigzagging drive of Nietzsche's thought is nonetheless toward the body and earthly life-affirmation in the midst of continuous dissolution of meaning and sense, that unspeakable other of life vis-à-vis human mentation. Nietzsche's withdrawal is away from a traditional escape from life and toward the earthly life that has been all but lost in subjection to ascetic ideals.

Heidegger's thought suggests connectedness in being which, though neither presence nor meaning, gives the basis for hope of retrieval and preservation of something lost and not yet thinkable. In his Rector's Address, for example, the cadences of mobilization and marching are toward a discipline of nontechnical thought that will be far beyond the authoritarian measures initially necessary to galvanize German society to the point of willing the true essence of its culture. Our question now addresses the extent to which Heidegger's thought brings to bear the ascetic ideal, the extent to which it includes a process of subjecting the animal, the chaotic, and the meaningless to something that infinitely transcends them and, by its splendor, humiliates them—in spite of the absence of voluntary participation in such a project on Heidegger's part. Does his language give priority to a seriousness of mind that is inevitably associated with a will to truth? Is there within it a desire for redemption and salvation, in some sense of those words? Is his thought akin to a traditional spiritual quest— in spite of its intentions? Is there a self-overcoming of spirituality like that found in the writings of Nietzsche and Foucault? Is there in Heidegger's thought a silence of remove, a wincing silence, before the chaotic flow of appearances in the midst of senseless cries of both pain and pleasure, a silence that delimits the distance between being and beings, one that finds fulfillment in meditative and preserving attention to the highest things, one that is nurtured by distaste for the corruption that accompanies mortality, taints it, and makes it repellent to a sharply honed Western sensibility? If the ascetic ideal, without a movement of self-overcoming, is an element in Heidegger's thought, we might discover our closeness to his thought, our affiliation with the ascetic ideal, in what we now find to be his limits. It is possible that the quiescence of his meditations and the elements of silence that accompany it are already attractive to us in our desire to find a way of life that eliminates evil and that eventuates in a community that preserves primarily our difference from animality and from the meaningless glare of being who we are.

In *Being and Time* and *On the Essence of Truth* we find that the questionableness of our thought and values takes place in dasein's standing out of its presence. This ek-stasis takes place in the occurrence of temporality, which Heidegger interprets as the disclosiveness of human being and the world-openness of human being in which beings occur in their own disclosures. The draw of the question of being includes a withdrawal from (and in) the dominance of ordinary language, meaning, and value. The withdrawal is a necessary part of the interruption and of the questioning thought. In this withdrawal we find a mysterious kinship with being in its withdrawal from presence. One of its effects is a severe delimitation of "the everyday" and of traditional philosophy, whose values, meanings, and problematic are within the domination of the everyday. To remember that the question of being is forgotten in its own heritage is to begin a process of retrieving the division of thought from the everyday that has given our heritage—or at least the German heritage—its temporality and its destiny. This 'otherness' to the tradition of Western thought, this 'otherness' that Western thought traces by antiphrasis, 'defines' temporality in two senses: it opens human time to its own ek-stasis, to its own radically noneveryday dimension, and its interruption of continuity constitutes the mortality of our inherited 'foundations' for life and truth. *Ek-stasis* thus interrupts mortal temporality, the essence, that is, the *Wesen* or coming to pass, of the Western heritage, as well as the ontological difference between being and beings in dasein's ecstatic occurrence. Dasein's propriety is found in questioning and questionableness, and no account of human being, including Heidegger's, can be taken as definitive and certain and also be proper to dasein's being. Because of the meaning of temporal ek-stasis in Heidegger's thought, his own work is self-overcoming.

The elements of withdrawal from the everyday, beings' difference from being, and dasein's standing out in the disclosiveness of being—the very elements that hold ethics in question and provide the basis for recoil in Heidegger's thought—constitute Heidegger's vulnerability to the ascetic ideal. Does the question of ethics, as it takes place in his thought, reinscribe the ascetic ideal? Dasein's questionableness, its mortal temporality, is not a selfsame identity. It is not subject to categorization. But it is 'uncontaminated', in Derrida's phrase, by everyday life in its difference from everyday life, and it is conceived with a seriousness of mind that complements the most heartfelt endeavors of traditional thought. Is this the spirit of seriousness, in spite of Heidegger's holding 'spirit' in question?

The unbroken seriousness of Heidegger's thought seems to be appropriate to the forgetfulness of being and the disastrous control of calculative thought that accompanies this forgetfulness. In it our heritage is at odds with its own temporality, its *Wesen* or essence or coming to pass. But in this great danger, Heidegger's turn of mind—the turning of his mind—up to 1933 appears to promise a listening that *connects* with and counters the destructive forgetfulness, an ekstasis of thought that is closer to rapture than to a rupture's senseless spasm. There is a continuity between this seriousness of mind regarding being and its forgetfulness, on the one hand, and the cadences of the Rector's Address that are preparatory to essential thinking, on the other: Heidegger's early thought harbors an expectation of single-minded endeavor that is unified by a singularity of occurrence; and in spite of his clear insistence that the question of being and the disclosiveness of the world are steeped in the pathogenic contamination of forgetfulness, in spite of the recoils that occur as he thinks through mortal temporality, *disclosure, error, being, essence,* and *ekstasis* inspire a seriousness that draws him toward not just an avoidance but also a purging of the contamination of forgetfulness, however subject to failure this elimination may be. Such seriousness bestows meaning on his thought far in excess of what we might expect from the abysmal difference of being.

Is this seriousness itself preparatory? An overbearing prelude to a lighter touch? Or does meaning override meaninglessness in Heidegger's seriousness of mind and revert to the ascetic ideal? If he had thought the 'contamination' of the forgetfulness of being in such a way that it could not stand opposed to thought, especially to essential thought, if the interruption of the everyday world were taken as a disruption of mystery as well as of meaning and not only as provisional vis-à-vis a recovery of essential thinking, and if the question of dasein's propriety were lost in multiple experiences of thought, I believe that the interruption of ethics, which characterizes *Being and Time,* would not have seemed compatible with the unifying force for mobilization that Heidegger invoked in his Rector's Address or with his national self-identification.

In what sense could dasein's transformation to *Eigentlichkeit* be ascetic? Although one's relations to others and things change in the transformation, although one opens to one's temporal openness and to that of all others, and although that includes a different relation to bodies, a relation not governed by control, mastery, or usage, there is nonetheless an absence of sensuality, dissemination, and, in Foucault's terms, a play of bodies in Heidegger's language. The unity that he invokes, which cannot be a being of any kind, lacks all connotation of body or of the body's dispersions. Such unity is thinkable on Heidegger's terms at this time of his thought only in movements of mind that are presently not describable except in the effects of destructuring the patterns of clarity that have defined Western thought and in retrieving the question that interrupted the complacency of our early history.

An ascetic self need not be formed in this process, a self that constitutes itself by denying its pleasures and its lack of meaning. And yet, the ekstasis of dasein does not appear to be attuned to bodily pleasure and distress or to find its propriety in the dark, confusing, and often unsatisfying muck of human life. The pleasure and distress of bodies and the senselessness of life are as secondary in this context as they are in most types of elevated spirituality in the West. Does that mean that suffering bodies are also secondary? I am not sure. Does that mean that the other's cry is best heard when it is 'spiritual' anguish and not when it is merely abused or starved? Again, I am unsure. But Heidegger's

thought is often closer to a way of praying than it is to an intermingling of bodies, and this meditative dimension waxes rather than wanes as his work pro-
ceeds. Saving and preserving the world in a dimension of care-filled listening
before the disclosure of beings is one hope in his thought, and Nietzsche's ghost
might well rise up in a passion of suspicion over this stolid presence of serious
good faith. The danger of the ascetic ideal in Heidegger's thought will not be
addressed until preserving, saving, and meditative thought are themselves interrupted and put in question. Surely the world, the language, and the situation
of thought and action are too muddled, too filled with cross-purposes, counter-
valences, and unsolvable dilemmas, to allow any saving power or any intensity
of careful, thoughtful, deeply informed attentiveness to give them a cleaner,
purer, rapturous return to an ungraspable and originary essence. The retrieval
of the question of being is as fraught with danger as the forgetfulness of it is,
and I suspect that if we forget that we shall be easy prey to an unbridled desire
for meaning and truth, however they are interpreted, at the cost of the very shattering that Heidegger has introduced so powerfully into twentieth-century
thought.

   We thus begin this discussion of the ascetic ideal in Heidegger's thought
with the double possibility that the interruption of ethics provides an opening
to hear what is inaudible in our ethos and that Heidegger tends to close that
opening in aspects of the thought that is intended to maintain the opening. The
closing element is the work of the ascetic ideal in Heidegger's effort to twist
free of the forgetfulness of being, particularly, as we noted, in aspects of his
thought of ekstasis. In this thought ethics comes radically into question, and in
it the ascetic ideal also appears to recoil back on itself, instead of away from
itself, and to reintroduce a new ethics of thought.

   We turn to the *Letter on Humanism* to question thought's relation to ethics
and the unfolding of the ascetic ideal in Heidegger's later thought. By following
the unfolding of the ascetic ideal in this letter we will be able to see more clearly
both the ethical dimension of his thought in his breakage of the hold of ethical
thought and the danger of ethics in his thinking.

The Unfolding of the Ascetic Ideal in the Unfolding of the Appeal of Being

Thinking in the Drawing Appeal of Being

   In the first paragraph of his *Letter on Humanism* Heidegger advances a
thought that figured in a preliminary way in his Rector's Address: thinking
finds its *Wesen* (essence) in an intrinsic relation to being.[1] Thinking carries out
the appeal of being to the essence of human being. *Carries out (vollbringen)*
means to unfold something in the fullness of its essence, its *Wesen*, its coming
to pass. So thinking may unfold the appeal of being in the fullness of its coming

to pass in human being's coming to pass. I have interpreted *Bezug* by translating it as 'appeal'. In its *Bezug* to human being—its relation to or draw on human being—being is more like a call in dasein than something standing over against human being, relating to it. "Thinking does not make or bring about the *Bezug*." Rather, the *Bezug* of being is "handed over" to thinking from being; it is like an "offering" that happens as thinking thinks. A double middle voice is audible: as thinking thinks, being (is). Being comes to pass as human being comes to pass thinking. The manifestness (*Offenbarkeit*) of being is in the coming to pass of thought.

The structure of Heidegger's thought in this paragraph is similar to that in his discussion of *Eigentlichkeit* in *Being and Time*. As thinkers (and poets) "watch over" or take care for being (in the sense of 'have a care for'), they come to their essence in the watching or caring. Although thought and being are not identical, a sameness of *Wesen* unfolds, not as the subject or object of an action but as being happens in regard to itself, that is, in a middle voice. The thinking that Heidegger has in mind is being in the middle voice.[2] Heidegger's emphasis is on the *Bezug* of being vis-à-vis thinking because it delimits and interrupts our inherited interpretation of *human* and provides a basis for rethinking *human*. Our emphasis is on this *Bezug* because it indicates that in the interruption of our ethos by the appeal of being we find an accord that goes far beyond any community of agreement that we might construct. The accord of being and human being makes manifest not an essential or defining structure—an essence in that sense—but a quality of belonging that is not at all clear to our usual ways of thinking, one that is close and intimate, like a dwelling that infuses the dwellers and gives them the space of passage that constitutes them. Although such an accord is not a structural continuity and has an abysmal dimension, it nonetheless, as accord, provides unity in the sense of sameness for being and human being. Although it is not a structure of meaning, is not subject to meaning, and in thinking defers the circumscription of meaning, this accord appears to be suited to the metaphors of dwelling, giving, and offering. The proper role of the thinker and poet is approximate to that of a shepherd or to a careful and devoted guardian who by alert attentiveness preserves the manifestness of being. In this attentiveness one comes to pass in the unfolding, not in the vacuity or dispersion, of being. Heidegger speaks of "the simplicity of the manifold dimensions' rule" (GA 9, 315). Being is the "element" of thought that "enables" thought and brings it to its essence. Thought "belongs" to being; and being "bestows essence as a gift," makes thinking possible in being's coming to pass, is thought's "may-be," its finite, ecstatic, temporal coming to be.

A releasing serenity, which Heidegger meditates under the name of *Gelassenheit* in another essay, pervades this thought—a striking contrast to the cadences of Heidegger's preparatory rhetoric in his Rector's Address. It is not the serenity of dogmatic certainty or of theoretical clarity but one of deep, virtually unspeakable propriety of being in which nothing in everyday life is privileged.

The may-be of being means that the full range of finite possibility—death and suffering as well as pleasure and happiness in everyday life—is allowed in the fitting accord of thought and being. Heidegger's play on *Mögen*, or favoring, and *Mögliche*, or possible, in the term *Mög-liche*, or may-be, gives emphasis to the disclosiveness of human finitude in the context of being's giving, bestowing—"enabling" (*Vermögen*)—the essence of human being. Being enables thinking to be thinking and is of thinking's disclosive process as thinking's disclosive process is of the enabling disclosiveness of being. Allowance, even the *gift*, of life in its simplicity accompanies the despair and ruptures of living as well as its moments of peace and congruence. *May-be* suggests the difference of being in its company with existence. In its allowance and affirmation one lives through the difference and is not totally circumscribed by one's travail and success.

Serene joy in the midst of life is clearly projected by this thought. Being's allowance of life, the sameness of this allowance in all divisions of life and in the midst of life's dispersions—the thought (of) being, this middle voice—is not ruptured by the ruptures of life. It gives the possibility of releasing serenity in its difference from everyday life. The thought of *its* ontic rupture would be nihilistic for Heidegger. Being is not to be overcome by the disaster or disruption: it is without the possibility of ontic hernia. Nor do the ruptures of living have any privilege in disclosing being. They show the finitude of existence, and they can provide the shock necessary to give vitality to the question of being. But being is voiced in a primordial accord with thought and language, a quiet power ("*stille Kraft*") of favoring and enabling that is quite other than the wreckage or the satisfactions of life. This accord is beyond—other than—the erotic, consumptive, dispensing, establishing, deposing, nurturing, killing, competitive, impotent, controlling, loving, hating, despondent, suffering, abusing, warring, negotiating, peace-bestowing elements that constrain us to be human. The accord pervades these elements. It saves them in the sense that they *are*. Rather than a reign of chaos, it illuminates them, gives them moment and voice beyond their discourse. Being in its accord means more than the whole of human meaning. It gives unity beyond any formation, thought beyond conceptualization, and being beyond the lives of humans. The accord of being thus has a redemptive aspect that bestows "the gift of essence," interrupts mere nothingness, as it were, and saves the being of all beings that are destroyed, consumed, or neutralized in the world of humans. Or at least so it seems. These are indications whose thought is still beyond us, but they are vaguely audible in our belonging to being as this belonging comes to us in our heritage.

More meaningful for Heidegger's thought than meaning itself. More important than the whole of our values. More hale than our most robust vitality. More affirming than our highest love. Beyond our satisfactions. Saving of essence even in our helplessness and hopelessness. Beyond the limits of identity and causality: this dimension of Heidegger's thought is both ascetic and ideal. It restores a seamless mystery of being in the midst of effecting the sharpest cut into twentieth-century thought. It tells us that human being belongs to being and that being, although abysmal and severe in relation to all that we value, is beyond the travail and limits of our common lives. In Nietzsche's terms, the angel, rather than the animal and the rupture of the angel, provides the stimulus for thought. There appears to be no Dionysus in the coming of thought's essence, although there is an abundance of mystery. The withdrawal of being and the nonessence of its event are interpreted in the language of mystery under the aegis of bestowal in this aspect of Heidegger's thought. He speaks of chaos only in relation to the dispersions of a life that has forgotten its essence. It seems in essence that the bestowal of essence is *the* thought. There appears to be a continuing triumph of being over chaos, and for Nietzsche that *is* the ascetic ideal.

This much is given and forecast in the first three paragraphs of the *Letter*. The stakes are high. Without the accord of thought and being, thinking becomes instrumental (GA 9, 317–319). It teaches, elaborates, explains, and solidifies itself into positions to be defended and expanded. It becomes like an ethos in that it both nourishes identity and closes people to differences that threaten the autonomy that sustains them. Chaotic confusion is the result: people confuse essence with the subject's autonomy, public openness with the enabling openness of being, role-dominated communication with a speaking proper to the human essence, subjective self-possession with essential relation to being. The essence of humanity is thus threatened, and this extreme danger is not apparent to us because our language, rather than homing in on being's bestowal of humanity's essence, covers over the truth of being and "surrenders itself to our mere willing and trafficking as an instrument of domination over being" (GA 9, 318). The dispersion of human life in this confusion of dominations and manipulations and its resulting demeaning of human life and indeed of the entire world has lost the quiet sameness of being. Heidegger does not project a totalizing society, but rather one in which the differences of beings—their disclosiveness, not the uniqueness of their roles but their essential relation to being in their disclosures—are heard, attended with gentle care, and preserved in their address by our ways of being with them.

This is far from the pastoral romanticism that some readers find in Heidegger and either attack as obscure or appropriate by cultivating rusticity or early twentieth-century ways of life that are unburdened by some of our conveniences. Just as mortal temporality, according to *Being and Time*, is the meaning of all events in dasein's world, so the bestowal of essence is concurrent with everything in human life, including its perversions and horrors. But Heidegger's intensity of conviction, his desire to be faithful to the appeal and draw of being, his prophetic sense of both doom and hope, provide a setting for single-minded, even obsessed, concern for the simplicity and sameness of being. One expression of this intensity is found in the Rector's Address. Another is found in this letter in which the corrupt dispersion of human life is held in judgmental contrast to what appears to be the purity of being—purity at least in relation to lives that are unclaimed by being. Heidegger's rejection of democracy or any other communal system is not the issue. It is rather his longing for reunion with the lost "claim of being" that propels him toward language and thought that struggle not for the thought of mere difference or of disjunction without unity but for the thought of being that unfolds in the *fullness* of its essence (GA 9, 319). The demands of this quest drive him to separate from the inessential part of the world in an almost priestly way: in the world, but not of it. Is there an inessential part of the world?

That question raises the further question as to whether the question of the essential is itself inessential, in the sense that it does not bring us to anything that is ultimate or that has ultimate value for people, and in the sense that it is not the primary question of our tradition. Without ultimate value, people and beings are heard in the 'mere' quality of their life struggles. Their hierarchies and roles are at best conveniences in a given way of life. Without sanctity their anguish and happiness can be clearly heard—not necessarily heard, but possibly heard—in the interruption of the inherited claims to ultimacy, claims that suggest a staggered range of importance concerning who is anguished or happy. An absence of ultimate importance levels us all, discloses us all without the sanctions of the many orders of our lives. In such an interruption of ethics the ascetic ideal of Heidegger's approach to being, *this* part of our Western ethos, is momentarily suspended, and the question of ethics affects the beginning steps that one might take toward retrieving something in our tradition that has been lost. The lostness, our common lack of essence, not what has been lost, affects us and provokes us to think in that moment.

Nietzsche and Heidegger are separated by the issue of whether the simple lack of an "ontological" 'home' and the consequent question of being and its loss move through and define our history. On Nietzschean terms, Heidegger misreads our common history by his thought of the claim of being. *That* claim and Heidegger's attraction to it give voice to the ascetic ideal, the ascetic force that shapes both the claim and our history in its hope-giving, meaning-giving obsession before the chaos and homelessness of human being. The claim of being overrides the accidents and randomness that riddle our economies, thought, and practices. *A* being's claim on human being and its difference from human being—such elements are found by Heidegger to be ontic, and the governance of ontological thought by beings and their many differences constitutes nihilism for him. The issue between Nietzsche and Heidegger at this point rests with quasi-historical claims: for Heidegger, our history is constituted by the claim of being, its manner of thought, and its being forgotten; for Nietzsche, our history is constituted by a conflict between those who can live fully in the meaninglessness of life and those who must hide chaos in order to survive it.

"... Man essentially comes to pass (*west*) only in his essence (*Wesen*) where he is claimed by being. *Only* in this claim 'has' he found that wherein his essence dwells. *Only* in this dwelling does he 'have' 'language' as the home that preserves the ecstatic in his essence" (GA 9, 323). There is something consumptive in these onlys. Heidegger intends to set apart human being by virtue of its ecstatic relation to being. "Such standing in the clearing of being I call the *ek-sistence* of man. *Only* to men is this way of being proper" (GA 9, 323–324; emphasis added). This ecstatic relation makes reason—*ratio*—possible, as well as human essence. Human being is completely unique in this "standing." Rather than ratio joined to animality, the human being is singular in its body: the whole body is found in the relation to being. As Heidegger shifts the terrain of thought from a mind-body dualism, he puts the meaning of animality in question just as he has already put thought in question. It is not a question of adding qualities to animality; it is a question of rethinking human being in the singularity of its essence. The biological sciences, medicine, and psychology are also put in question. We cannot know properly the human mind and body by disciplines that are based in the mind-body division. The human body is not an animal-like object. Although the facts of the sciences are not necessarily wrong, their structures of knowledge and interpretation skew whatever they discover by the assumptions about body and mind that are built into their perceptions and verifications. Heidegger's claim is that these disciplines must be rethought in reference to the question of the essence of human nature. *Ek-sistence* is the leading thought for this reconsideration, because human being is found *only* in its *Bezug* (appeal) to being. Human being comes to pass *only* in the clearing of being. The disclosure of being is the truth of human existence.

The 'only' means that humans are separated from each other and from other creatures by an "abyss" (GA 9, 326). However other creatures are known; they do not stand ecstatically in the lighting-concealing advent of being. Human being is the provenance of the truth of being. This means, I believe, that although human being inevitably turns away from being—error delimits it in its ekstasis—nothing in the human is utterly dumb to being, nor is being completely erased for any aspect of human being.[3] The human body is singular in its ekstasis. Ekstasis thus eliminates kinship with creatures—an abyss separates us from them. *Ekstasis* finds part of its meaning in an *only* that suggests a totally unique relation with being, an *only* that erases the thoughts of 'no clearing at all', simple darkness, dumb juxtaposition, or meaningless convergence. The abysmal mystery of being thus appears to consume our kinship with other creatures, to imprint human being with an encompassing destiny of being that makes singular every dimension of human experience and provides a pervasive sameness for human being, however that sameness is thought.

Have we moved beyond the ascetic ideal by shifting the provenance of thought from its traditionally dualistic mind-body character? Probably not, because undwellable chaos has been consumed in an assurance of dwelling that, no matter how mysterious and questionable, elevates our cries and our laughter by an ekstasis that finds its fulfillment in our conceived thinking and saying of being. Is animality rethought, or merely lost? In Heidegger's thought we find our essence in the ecstatic coming of being, in a departure from unspeaking earth which—no matter how mortal—is nonetheless saturated with meaning in meaning's loss. Perhaps the human cry is never like an animal's because it is infused and constituted by meaning. But failure to hear the radical delimini-tion of meaning in the cry is one aspect of the ascetic ideal, and we wonder about what we are unable to hear in our ethos in which meaning reigns even in our spasms, twitchings, and murmurs of satisfaction. Does the 'abyss' that separates 'us' from the animal constitute an opening in which we might hear mere suffering and death, mere happiness that is interrupted continuously by the abyss, a glow of meaning and a depth of essence that find their intensity by an absence of gift that accompanies them? A strangely equalizing body of sounds in which elevation, enlightenment, and superior cultural sensitivity mean nothing? An equalizing body in which the question of the meaning of being has no suasion over folly, in which the cry cries and pleasure pleases, in which there is neither rank nor governance—the equalizing human body that puts in question the claim of being and the thought of being as meaning and essence come to pass, passing away in the body's earth as it shifts under the impact of whatever cataclysm or nurture befalls it?

Recollection of Being—and Nothing Else

The *Letter on Humanism* is like the Rector's Address and *Being and Time* in the sense that it is largely preparatory to a language and thought not about be-ing but of being. The clear change from the Address to the *Letter on Humanism* is that a nationalistic appeal is no longer a part of Heidegger's preparatory strategy. His preoccupation with human destiny and human lostness is impor-tant for both works, and his conviction is consistent in both pieces that people are homeless to the extent that their lives and thought are oriented *primarily* by a specific ethos rather than by the essence of their language and thought, which becomes manifest in an epoch-making interruption of the Greek ethos.[4] If we retrieve a sense of homelessness in the midst of our familiar environments, says Heidegger, we make an initial step back to the forgotten essence that will lead us, as humans, home. The preparatory work includes an interruption of our sat-isfactions with our identities and our ethos—it includes the emergence of the question of ethics—in the context of the question of being. The ethnic interruption of Heidegger's initial steps toward the thought of being is aligned with the primordial interruption in Greek culture. The interruption's importance is governed by the question of being which circumscribes the interruption and gives it a quite specific meaning and destiny: that of returning us to the abysmal essence of our language and thought. Our return to essence-giving being in its ungraspable mystery is like a homecoming.

In our heritage the thought and saying 'there is being', which comes to us in Parmenides's fragments, is the one that continuously moves thought (GA 9, 334). Being is not an object to be contemplated or a prime mover, but takes place in the coming to pass of language and thought and in this coming to pass is world-governing. Being clears for beings in the middle-voiced sense of clearing clears. Clearing is the region for the appearing of beings. Instead of nothing at all, being (is), and beings are. When thought and language think and speak in an open address with beings and also, at once, are fully attuned to their own clearing event, 'there is being' is said, as distinct from forgotten and left unsaid, in the very process of thinking and speaking. As a person thinks and speaks in this alertness and attunement, he or she is predisposed to allow what is focused to be delimited by the clearing, by the 'there is being'. The ungraspable mystery of being then pervades thinking and speaking that address and relate to beings.

In Heidegger's reading of our heritage, thought began in the clearing interruption of the question of being. We felt the impact of the clearing effect that can accompany an interruption of habitual patterns of certainty when we asked if an interruption of the question of being would clear the air for the sounds of human suffering and pleasure that are otherwise drowned out by many valuable things. Heidegger's claim, however, is an explanatory one as well as a descriptive one. Thinking begins in this clearing interruption in Greek thought; this beginning is fateful in the sense that it delimits the future of thought— thought is forever coming to the interruptive clearing of beings; it emits or sends thought in our heritage; thought is always in the hegemony of the sending and clearing of being, that is, being (is) or gives itself in thought so that beings come to stand as something; and our heritage is made up of the ways in which things come to stand in thought. Human being thus ek-sists in the "nearness of being" as the dispensation of being unfolds in human history (GA 9, 342). Human being is a continuous process of nearing and falling away from being in this dispensation: it is its own continuous interruption of being's interruptive closeness in the midst of unthinking endurance.

Our language thus serves, protects, and preserves thought to the extent that it allows a 'saying' of this dispensation as it speaks of things. Heidegger's preparatory work is not necessarily a saying of being. It is an attempt to prepare the way for recognition of the importance of thought and language that is oriented to being. It is responsive to the originary interruption of the question of being and the originary bestowal of thought in our heritage. It maximizes an awareness of its own inability to do what it projects as most desirable. It provides a continuing diagnosis of our consumptive endurance and our forgetfulness of our proper essence. And, as preparatory, it steadily undercuts its *own* prescriptive authority. But we have found that it also does not put in question the originary preeminence of being. The pattern of certainty that accompanies this trusting service to the importance of being, not only in our tradition but in the very movement of thought, is where we have located the power of the ascetic ideal. That being is continuously near is known without doubt in Heidegger's discourse. Hence his language speaks of the thinking that is yet to come, thinking that bears in mind the truth of being as "meditative recollection of being and nothing else" (GA 9, 358).

In this 'nothing else' we have found the body of desire, mere living, the viciousness and crudeness of ordinary life, the division of bruteness from civility, and the meaninglessness that pervades meaning: all such elements of human living are subjected to the provenance of being. This subjection has a muffling effect in the sense that the giving of being, the continuous 'it gives', casts the mere desire of thought, the ordinariness of thought and its meaninglessness, into the role of a falling from thought proper. Proper thought is to be clear, simple, and clean. It is to be filled with care for being, never aversive in its proper realm—critical diagnosis, though necessary, bears witness to thought's fall, and the thought of this fall will protect the falling in *its* being and save it from fallen obtuseness. The longing for home that Heidegger thematizes is a longing for essence that always puts dispersion, ambiguity, and discord in their proper place. Dispersion takes place in the process of twisting free from the hold of forgetfulness, but it too is retrieved in its being in the process of turning to being, a process that allows a clearing rule of thought, and one that allows dispersion to dwell in the language that is the "house of being" and the 'place' most fitting for humans.

And when we suffer in our mere living, or when we experience simple pleasure? When we 'only' exert ourselves to make something, to carry out an ambition? When we undergo the normal senselessness of everyday dispersion and distraction, or when we merely conform, that is, when we live ordinarily?— does the thought of nothing but being attune us to our ordinary misery and happiness? Only to the extent that it tells us that there is something *much* more important than ordinary pain and the enjoyment of everyday things. We can read Heidegger as saying that everyday things will be elevated by the simplicity of proper thought, but the question is whether they are everyday in their elevation. The 'saving' of the everyday from the everyday, the preserving of what is proper in the midst of the ordinary, appear to eliminate the very thing that is to be preserved and saved: the everyday.

The quasi-sacramental quality of Heidegger's thought regarding being betrays the ascetic ideal in Nietzsche's sense, an ideal that obliterates the meaninglessness of the mundane by an ever-giving, elevated, and ontologically different essence that destroys much of what it is designed to save in the saving process. When this loss is not interrupted by the ordinary senselessness of life, we are ensnared in a group of values that easily lose the mere burst of hilarity, the everyday struggle to survive, or the cry of simple desperation: lose them in an effort to elevate them and to give them more than they have—meaning beyond all everyday meanings and truth with a quality of 'ever'.

I doubt that we can hear each other well until we interrupt our senses of privilege and elevation and interrupt as well the meanings by which we perceive salvation from that from which none of us is saved: the ordinary meaninglessness of everything that gives us meaning and the simple disruption of all of our presumed continuities. Nietzsche's account of the ascetic ideal is right in this, that whatever in our tradition saves and preserves seriousness concerning truth and meaning saves and preserves the very elements that are taken to be overcome by truth and meaning in their seriousness, and also that this inaudible preservation makes soundless the senselessness and disruption that it is intended to replace.

In one paragraph in the *Letter on Humanism*, Heidegger says that proper thinking is manifest in a part of his letter. This part goes beyond preparatory thought and enters into a more fitting saying of being. Prior to this observation he says that "historically only one saying belongs to the matter of thinking" (GA 9, 358). Essential thinking "lets being be" (GA 9, 358). It guides humans in their ek-static bearing with being into the region where healing arises and beings become hale (GA 9, 359). This healing does not mask "evil" but makes it all the more apparent. "The essence of evil does not consist in mere baseness of human action, but rather in the malice of rage. Both of these, however—healing and raging—can essentially occur only in being insofar as being itself is what is contested" (GA 9, 359). The nihilation of rage illuminates itself, is cleared, as having an essence, too. Destructive rage is in the history of being, albeit perversely. Its lost essence is the nihilation that belongs to being. Being's nihilation is found in its not being a being; in its essence (it) is not, (is) other than existence. In that sense being's withdrawal is nihilation. It is like a no to everything that is. Everything possibly definitive falls away from being. In its healing favor, however, being grants the fall; and when, in its falling away *from* being, human being closes on itself and is closed to being's favor, a compulsion to degeneration and calamity takes place. Only if this rage that accompanies forgetfulness of being, the rage that is expressed in a society of consumption and manipulation, for example—only if it is thought in the healing gift of being can it undergo a quiet regeneration by returning to its favoring, never-destroying, granting essence. When falling from being is thought in its fall from being, dwelling in the house of being can take place (GA 9, 358–360). Then the rage of separation from being is quieted before the granting that clears even for this rage. Malignant rage is never nothing. It too exists. Without the giving of being, instead of rage there would not have been . . .

Because the granting of being is always other than what is granted, the 'evil' that comes with the granting clearing of existence does not, in Heidegger's thought, occasion a contamination of being. For Heidegger, being is not stained. We are seeing, however, that its freedom from contamination constitutes the pervasive stain of the ascetic ideal in the thought of being. This thought of being appears to be impossible without the ascetic ideal.

Further, from human "ek-sisting in the truth of being" can come the human's true fortune and lot in life (GA 9, 360–361). People can find their directions from the dispensation of being: one "abides" in the truth of being (GA 9, 361). Human economy is 'ruled' by this dispensation, which, although it never tells a person what to do, provides the gift of being by which all things can be truly minded. In such minding of being, the human "deed" exceeds objectification. Thinking then "towers above action and production, not through the grandeur of its achievement and not as a consequence of its effort, but through the humbleness of its inconsequential accomplishment [*Vollbringen*]" (GA 9, 361). Ek-sisting then can come to language: "for thinking in its saying merely brings the unspoken word of being to language. . . . Being comes, clearing itself, to language" (GA 9, 361). Then, "ek-sistence thoughtfully dwells in the house of being. In all this it is as if nothing at all happens through thoughtful saying" (GA 9, 361).

At this point Heidegger says, "but just now an example of the inconspicuous deed [*Tun*] of thinking shows itself. For to the extent that we expressly think the usage 'bring to language', which was granted to language, think only that and nothing further, to that extent we retain this thought in the heedfulness of saying as what in the future continually has to be thought, we have brought something of the essential unfolding of being to language" (GA 9, 362). The moment of thinking to which Heidegger refers is not preparatory to essential thought but breaks through separation from being to the thought of being as the words "bring being to language" and do what they say regarding "being that comes, clearing itself, to language." In this "deed," this event that unfolds the appeal of being in the fullness of its essence, human being comes to its essence and, by coming to it, thinks and 'says' its essence. Its essence is brought to language. We have a moment in which "the *sole* matter of thinking" is thought, a moment that is joined by 'the Same' to essential thinking whenever it occurs in our heritage (GA 9, 363, emphasis added). No evil can dwell in this moment, no technological madness, no misuse of beings. The danger, Heidegger says, is that we confuse 'the Same' with a being, with something self-identical. Then ambiguity and "mere quarreling" constitute the danger, and essential thinking does not occur. But without this confusion we can be in the dispensation of being in a fitting way: "the fittingness [*Schicklichkeit*] of the saying of being, as of the proper sending [*Geschick*] of truth, is the first law of thinking" (GA 9, 363). Not the necessity of self-overcoming, not its own dangerousness, but the fit of the saying and the sending of being is the first law of thinking. Although being means for thought a continuous process of self-overcoming and experimentation in the preparatory aspect of thought—an aspect that is largely definitive of the best thought available to us—in the destiny of being, proper and fitting thought in a "deed" beyond manipulation and objectivation, in this abyss-like mystery, there is neither self-overcoming nor corruption nor destruction. There is rather saving power, whose *Sagen*, saying, is the first law of thinking.

Further, the knowledge that being's dispensation is saving power, that being is the sole matter for thinking, and that language can be fitting to the self-sending and fortune of being—that knowledge appears to be the lot of the essential thinker. This knowledge has the practical effect of providing certainty outside of the self-overcoming processes. A dispersion of the Same would be no less than the raging madness of language and thought ensnared in forgetfulness of being. That would be the effect of thought out of touch with its own being and proper heritage. The proper thought of being is not subject to dispersion or ambiguity or to any interruption other than that of its own advent. Instead of interrupting his own approach to being or interrupting the thought that being can be thought in a fitting way, Heidegger suggests a strategy of preparation that is based on the secure knowledge that being is the sole matter for thinking. He says that attention to the propriety of thoughtful saying means that we consider carefully when and whether we say anything regarding being. We must time our saying carefully—now assuming that our thought and language give being its proper sway—with reference "to what extent, at what moment of the history of being, in what sort of dialogue with this history, and on the basis of what claims, it ought to be said" (GA 9, 363). The rigor with which we call being to mind, the carefulness of saying, and a frugality with words determine the strategic piety of this thought. Such careful gathering of language into "simple saying" restores thought "inconspicuously" to "the poverty of its forecasting essence" (GA 9, 364). At this point in Heidegger's thought the die is cast for the indelible stamp of being. A version of poverty, chastity, and obedient humility deeply marks this die.

Heidegger's claims about beings seem to place essential thought outside the sway of an ethos. On the one hand, he has relegated values to an activity in which the subject takes priority over being; he has seen that valuing is correlated with warring over the highest and most objective values. The effort to prove the objectivity of values is bizarre and foolish, he says—this effort does not know what it is doing (GA 9, 349). Being is beyond value and valuing and puts ethics as such in question. But Heidegger exempts the thought (of) being from evaluation and judgment. It is set apart from the vicissitudes, accidents, and collisions of its heritage. Nothing intrinsically chaotic takes place in its proper middle voice. Contrary to Nietzsche's thought, Heidegger's is never interrupted by the serious consideration that the essential thought of being is an *error*, that our philosophy has its origin in an error whose only 'value' is the negative one of interrupting the experience and life of the senses.[5] Rather, it means that humans exist in an openness that has no disruption in its mystery. Its disruption of ordinary life is at once a calling of human life to its totally nonordinary and nonsensuous essence. Being (is) dispensation that sets the standard for interruptions, but is also openness that grants and never vacates.[6] One part of its destiny in Heidegger's thought in the *Letter on Humanism* is thus to forget its mortal temporality and to cast its mortality in a self-denying valuation that holds at bay its own interruption. In this sense, his thought (of) being, in its presumed and unqualified openness, seems to fall prey to its own thoroughly ethnic quality, which privileges the Greek and German cultures and which sees no alternative to nihilism if its mysterious difference is traversed by nothing at all. In this dimension it exhibits the anxiety typical of the ascetic ideal.

7 | Transition
"What Is Paris Doing to Us?"

Heidegger makes a descriptive claim that both weds his work to the history of Western philosophy and incites a turn within this history. This is a combination that defines one edge of his originality. The claim is that Western thought carries and perpetuates a questionableness that takes place in its own occurrence, a questionableness that takes place in the *happening* of everything that appears in thought. This questionableness, as it emerges early in our lineage, does not invoke something present and permanent that strikes wonder in people and gives rise to reflective activity. His historical claim about the question of thought in the absence of ultimate or eternal presence sets him apart from another claim that is dominant in our tradition about the origin of thinking. That claim states that thought at its best belongs to the enactment of a primordial being or to a nontemporal order. Heidegger's different claim is that our heritage of thought has its inception in the utter strangeness of things whose appearing arises in an occurrence of simultaneous coming to presence and losing presence. Our ability to think is formed by a nascent experience of being's happening as mortal temporality in a double movement of presentation and withdrawal from presentation. There is, however, agreement on this classical idea: *thought* names a kind of mentation that is different from calculation, computation, and practical intelligence. Thought, which is the occurrence that defines a philosopher, arises as some people are stirred by excess to our meanings and clarity, an excess to which human being seems essentially to belong. Such people are stirred to thought by a mood which seems to be connected to this excess. This mood might be articulated by such questions as these: What are things really made of? Who are we in common beyond the differences that divide us? What is the meaning of mortality? How do beings begin? Is everything that happens characterized by sameness? These are questions whose emergence requires mentation that is distinct to solving problems. They require the cultivation of perceptiveness that is strangely related both to something that is not comprehended and to the occurrence of human being.

Heidegger's claim that Western thought takes place in the perpetuation of the questionableness of its own occurrence and of that everything that appears in thought means that all beings, including our own being, appear in the absence of the possibility for graspable resolution or of perfection of being.

Thought has its continuous origination in what he calls the question of being—not in wondering in the overwhelming presence of something that escapes our grasp but rather wondering in a loss of presence that accompanies things' coming to presence. The appearance of things led some of our early predecessors to think in the questionableness of appearing, to think not in a quest for a presence that explains beings' coming to be and passing away, but to think in a manner appropriate to the mortal and presenting occurrence to which thought belongs. He develops and supports this claim primarily in his readings of Greek thinkers, details of which I have discussed in previous chapters. Presently, I wish to note that by his claim that our thought finds 'the condition of its possibility' in perpetual questionableness he eliminates the priority of presence for thought and provides a basis for showing that when thought gives priority to either transcendental or imminent presence it works at cross-purposes with its own occurrence.

These are claims that are as controversial as they are momentous. In thinking them and their consequences Heidegger set in motion an overturning of the phenomenological and ontological transcendentalism in his own specific Aristotelian, Kantian, and Husserlian lineage. I emphasize the importance of this *movement* of overturning in his thought. It is the movement of overturning transcendental thinking from within that constitutes one of his primary works as a philosopher. Without following and participating in this movement one cannot follow what happens as Heidegger thinks. That is the reason why many appropriations of Heidegger fail to uncover what is original in his thinking. There is certainly within his work the strong influence of Plato, Aristotle, Thomas, Kant, Hegel, and Husserl. Those influences, however, occur *in* the overturning movement of the *question* of being that defines his thought. That question ungrounds the traditional grounding of thinking, includes the supplement of withdrawal of presence, and transforms thought in the nonresolution of loss of presence as beings come to presence. Thought belongs to question and does not find its destiny in answers, systems, or certainty. If we use the word *essence* carefully, we can say that for Heidegger the essence for thought happens in the *question* of being. It does not reach completion in any form of conceptualization or assertion. Its essence occurs in the coming to be passing away of both thought and of whatever happens to appear in it.

In the work of such French philosophers as Deleuze, Lacan, Blanchot, Foucault, and Derrida, the questionableness of thought operates as a guiding phenomenon. They do not base their work primarily on Heidegger's. Heidegger, rather, brought to expression a possibility for thinking that emerged in this century, developed it with singular power, and provided a place of departure for these Frenchmen. We could also follow the influence on them of their fellow countrymen Bataille, Sartre, and Levinas, all of whom were less affected by Heidegger. We could trace the rereading of Descartes in recent years as the mark of a radically changing environment for thought in France. We could follow their revolt against Sartre, Marxism, and traditional allegiance to Freud. In such studies we would find the heavy influence of Descartes, Marx, Freud, and Sartre in the manner in which they are overturned. And we would find the movements and formation of language as the field for signal departures from the thought of subjectivity. We would find the impact of Sade, Artaud, and the Theater of Cruelty, of Saussure, Mallarmé, and many others who are foreign to Heidegger's philosophical world.

Foucault has noted the singular influence of Jean Hyppolite on a generation of French philosophers. Whereas new readings of early Greek thought provided Heidegger with a base for his claims about Western thinking, Hyppolite's re-reading of Hegel may well have provided for many contemporary French philosophers a focus for rethinking the occurrence for thought. The young philosophers that Hyppolite taught were to become, like himself and like Heidegger, thinkers whose work focused on figures within their own lineage. As far as I know, none of the French whose names are associated with what we popularly name 'postmodern' did serious scholarly work in Eastern thought. They made the history of Western philosophy and culture their field of research within approaches often beholden to Hegel and, as we shall see, to Nietzsche.

Foucault says of Hyppolite:

> Instead of conceiving philosophy as a totality ultimately capable of dispersing and regrouping itself in the movement of the concept, Jean Hyppolite transformed it into an endless task, against the background of an infinite horizon. Because it was a task without end, it was also a task in process of continuous recommencement, given over to the forms and paradoxes of repetition. For Hyppolite, philosophy, as the thought of the inaccessible totality, was that which could be rejected in the extreme irregularity of experience; it was that which presents and reveals itself as the continually recurring question in life, death and in memory. Thus he transformed the Hegelian theme of the end of self-consciousness into one of repeated interrogation. But because it consisted in repetition, this philosophy did not lie beyond concepts; its task was not that of abstraction, it was, rather, to maintain a certain reticence, to break with acquired generalisations and continually to reestablish contact with the nonphilosophical; it was to draw as close as possible, not to its final fulfillment, but to that which precedes it, that which has not yet stirred its uncertainty. (A 236)

I would like to emphasize what Foucault calls the "endless task" of philosophy, its continuous recommencement in the continually recurring question in life, death, and memory. Rather than revealing itself as the thought of inaccessible totality, philosophy reveals itself as conceptual structures of repeated interrogation. Foucault uses a word in this context that is also important in Heidegger's writings: *reticence*. The turn in post-Hegelian thought from a teleology of fulfillment to a question of origins is marked by a "certain reticence" that arises in the question of the very conditions for philosophical thought.

Temporal conditioning and historical relativism are no more the primary occasion for this reticence than is an inaccessible totality. Reticence in thought arises from its own questionableness, its own self-disclosure without a distant or imminent presence that defines it and gives it a future of self-actualization. It is not the reticence of a fallen agency that has appropriated its distance from a conditioning and sustaining power. It is rather the reticence of an occurrence that belongs to incompletion, question, and the *aporia* of mortal disclosures. By this turn Hyppolite prepared his students for the thought that neither the perceived world nor subjectivity nor another absolute provided a law of system and presence that gives rise to thinking. Thought arises in the question of being that takes place in Hegel's magnificent and unreticent attempt to eliminate that very animating question.

I would like to punctuate these remarks about the turn in our philosophical lineage on the part of these French philosophers by noting that as they reread their predecessors they were also overturning the priority that subjectivity, intentionality, and to a certain extent epistemology had exercised in philosophy on the Continent. But they did not follow primarily the question of being that occasioned the ontological turn in Heidegger's work. Multiple influences played major roles in their thought, forces that are muted in Heidegger's. The logic of dialectic, the cruelties and contradictions of war, the experiences of social, moral, and religious oppression, experiences no longer formed by religious symbols and affections, replacement of monarchial imagery by a different imagery of democracy, the import of historicism on knowledge, the growth and decline of Marxism, the divisions and distributions of knowledges without an ideal of epistemic unity, the conception of an unconscious, linguistic basis for conscious structures, and the emergence of the human sciences, their formation, their discoveries in linguistics, their divisions of knowledge, their production of humanism, and above all their emerging replacement by genealogy, grammatology, ethnology, and a new psychoanalysis: these occurrences gave the broad Kantian and Husserlian problematics as well as the traditions within Western metaphysics to fade in significance. These French thinkers, for the most part, did not develop further, for example, a project like Cassirer's, of showing the historical development of the a priori structures of perception and understanding, or like Schleiermacher's and Dilthey's groundbreaking studies of hermeneutics. They did not advance the work of historical relativism or existentialism. They turned, as they reworked the canonical texts of the Western tradition, to seemingly nonphilosophical domains that bordered the discipline of philosophy but did not constitute it. Saussure, Lévi-Strauss, Mallarmé, Propp, and Jackobson accompanied Plato, Aristotle, Descartes, Rousseau, Hegel, and Marx in their studies. These nonphilosophers indicate a turn away from ideas and self-conscious logics in their attempts to understand the memories and connections that are hidden in the thoughts and styles that dominate Western reflection. And rather than develop an ideology of historical relativity, they put in question the ideas of history and its discipline to such an extent that the assumptions that supported traditional historical relativism crumbled. Neither a priori subjectivity nor its relativization allowed the reticence or the questionability that now appeared to pervade the self-disclosure of thought.

Loss rather than presence gave rise to this questionability and reticence, specifically loss of transcendence. The emerging thought in the language of "Paris" as the title of this discussion states it, from Bataille and Blanchot through Foucault and Derrida, and including in an interesting manner Levinas, is that transcendent presence is an inadequate idea by which to think of the excess that escapes at the perimeters of human control and experience. *Transcendence* in our philosophical lineage suggests—perhaps demands—presence. *Presence* in this context means something that grounds or causes or allows. Presence yields presence. But the experience that gives rise to thought in Paris is that loss of transcendent presence yields both presence and language.

I shall divide this broad claim into two parts. First, an ontological claim for which Heidegger is indispensable. In *Being and Time* he showed that mortal temporality is the so-called grounds for human beings and that while *mortal temporality* names the presencing or disclosing of our being, it does not name anything that is present. Even the a priori structure of mortal temporality belongs to a kind of event that exceeds the thought of presence. The awkwardness and misleading nature of this central term—a priori structure—in *Being and Time* led Heidegger to give up talk of the a priori and conditions for the possibility of existence. But the thought that revolutionized his work and had an inestimable bearing on contemporary French thought is that the ground of dasein is an event that is at once coming to presence and losing presence, one that withdraws from presence as it occasions presence. Dasein's occurrence is disclosure without grounding presence. Its being is in question in its occurrence. Far from an existentialized version of transcendental subjectivity, *Being and Time* gave an account of human being whose occurrence and unity are found in temporality without the temporal presence of human nature or identity. The thought of transcendence turned inside out as Heidegger followed his seminal insight into the passage of mortal time, and that turning is one of *Being and Time*'s primary accomplishments.

Heidegger turned the inherited ontology of the Platonic, Aristotelian, and Kantian traditions away from the organizing power of transcendental presence in any form, and much of his work after *Being and Time* rethought and restated this turn outside of transcendence as he showed that, far from original with him, it is found in the thought that is originary for our heritage. He found himself recovering something that had been both preserved and overlaid by the idea of transcendent being.

But the French on whom we are focusing did not directly pick up Heidegger's ontological claim about the loss of presence in the coming of presence. They read him in the richly different contexts of war, oppression, democracy, linguistics, Marx, and Freud, to which I have referred, in an ethos in which the power of the Platonic and Aristotelian traditions had undergone a far more radical—if implicit—questioning than in Heidegger's world, and in a context in which a finitized and radicalized Hegel ignited a Nietzsche far more radical than even Heidegger's remarkable anti-Nazi rereading of Nietzsche could allow. Or perhaps a turn to Nietzsche ignited a far more radical Hegel than Heidegger's careful work on the near completion of nihilism in Hegel could allow. In either case, Heidegger's ontological claims opened a field of loss in which, for these Parisians, language found its origin in a flow of tropes, perversity, negation, power, contradiction, and above all limitation that made the language of transcendence suspect until it turned on itself and discovered in its intentionality a denial of its own fragile, insistent, aporetic occurrence. Some in Paris found that in language transcendental presence is lost even when it is the object of disciplined knowledge.

But why? Why this radicalization?—and this is the second part that elaborates Paris's thought that loss of transcendent presence yields presence and language—that gives rise to an image of possible victimizing that is reflected in our title, "What Is Paris Doing to Us?" What kind of determination gives their thought a radical turn? Why would transcendent presence *need* to fall into question to such an extent that even authorial transcendence is subverted? Consider one instance, that of Jacques Derrida. He has stated (*Derrida and Differance*, "Interview") that the intersection in his own life of radical anti-Semitism (often covert and masked behind its seeming opposite), a collapse of cultural security, the disclosure of danger *in* the cultural order that accompanied the collapse of security as well as accompanied persecution, the multiple and often *contradictory* dimensions that occurred within the order, the destructive banality of state-controlled culture, the enormity of deceit that accompanies formal relations of power, the violence and fear that flow through the textures of ordinary life: he found that such things in his culture gave him to know that *disconfirming* and undoing our bonds of hierarchy and meaning have a *revealing* power, that such de-structuring projects need not originate in negative or even hostile emotions but can originate in affirmations and a thorough sense of commitment to the importance of politics and ethics. He, like so many in Paris, wanted to address the dangers in our values and communities, particularly the dangers that are invisible to us outside of crises that shake and threaten our common lives. When dangers are found in what binds us together as a people or as a specific society, their address can call into question our deepest bondings. And this is "not to renounce ethical affirmations or politics, but on the contrary, to ensure their very future."[1]

Derrida, like his compatriots in Paris, finds such danger in the structures and practices that constitute our communal lives. His early work, for example, which puts in question a silent prioritizing of voice that is definitive in linguistics and semiotics, not only shows that an uncritical, perhaps even naive, assumption about privileged access to a transcendental signified operates in many traditional interpretations of sign. It also shows that *within* our dominant knowledges of language a silent conflict takes place that turns us toward writing and a loss of the transcendental signifier. The account that Derrida gives in *Of Grammatology* shows that in a significant body of traditional knowledge the meaning of transcendental reference is both unconsidered and silently contested in the body of that knowledge. Transcendental presence, with the confidence and totalizing appropriation that accompany it, needs to fall into question because of the dangers and unconsidered values that constitute its thought and its effect.

You can see that the turning of thought in Paris is a turning of the figuration of thinking. The easiest way for me to mistakenly think that I am in Paris when in fact I am in an early twentieth-century house in the United States is to place, say, Foucault or Derrida or Blanchot or Levinas in a problematic that arises from an Americanized Hegel or from Dewey or Quine. Such an appropriation is entirely appropriate if one wants to remain within the boundaries of their established lineages. But Paris becomes lively and original only as one undergoes a fundamental transfiguration in the movements, exchanges, and values that define the manner in which thinking goes on.

The importance of the transformation of the thinker is as old as Socrates' insistence that true philosophizing depends on a conversion of the soul to love of the good. The Parisian turn on the claim to transformation that is most germane for us is found, perhaps ironically, in the thought of two Germans: Nietzsche and Heidegger. I note that for Nietzsche the movement of withdrawal from the rewards of moral and religious obedience through the explorations, suffering, and solitude of free spiritedness, *toward* a way of being that is no longer under the sway of our lineage's unconscious fear, resentment, and cruelty—a way of being that is beyond our forms of life and is articulated by a myth that he called 'the overman'—this movement is one whereby language, custom, and thought are transformed in human recognition and synthesis, in knowledges and conceptual formulations. Nietzsche's work is designed to constitute a transformation of human life in the form of an experimental discourse, one that is embodied in transformations of style, perception, and judgment. Without such transformation our thought is controlled by traditional inevitabilities that are beyond intentional control.

As Heidegger's thought developed on what in *Being and Time* he called *Eigentlichkeit*—an open allowance of one's being in the manner in which one relates to one's being—he probed with increasing intensity the necessity, as he saw it, that a change in our relationship to the question of being take place if the occurrence of our language and thought is to be appropriate to their own disclo-siveness. I shall leave aside what such claims mean in order to limit myself to noting that the first intention of his first critical and de-structuring work is to facilitate a beginning for a fundamental transformation in all of our relations to people and things. Such a fundamental transformation will happen only if the force of axiomatic meanings, beliefs, and values is broken. And that break-ing can occur only by the slow and disciplined turning of language and thought through its defining structures to formations that develop in the turn-ing process.

I suspect that such processes of transformation within the work of Nietzsche and Heidegger incite many people to strong emotions and encourage them to reabsorb Nietzsche and Heidegger into terrains of thought where *their* turning does not take place. I mean that by putting them into our familiar prob-lematics and axiomatic structures, we both cleanse them of their originality and make them safely interesting to us. Paris, however, followed the turning in these senses: axioms of thought, practice, and value must be loosened in their force upon us; we must undergo the radical uncertainty that accompanies the trans-formation of our lives' axioms; and we must learn how to think with disciplined care in their turning and its accompanying loss.

This turning can be given focus when we consider the inevitability of re-presentation in our thinking. The work of self-overcoming in Nietzsche's thought, Heidegger's contrast to representation by what he calls *thinking*, the transvaluation of the modern subject of representative knowledge in Foucault's *Order of Things*, the 'ethics' of Levinas, the question of authorship in Blanchot, and Derrida's transformation of writing have in common the perceptions that representation can now be in a process of transformation for people who think and that we can begin to discover the dangerous values that have been hidden by the hegemony of re-presentation for our disciplines of knowledge and reflec-tion. I have been engaged in representational thought throughout these re-marks, and if our Parisian colleagues are accurate in what they say about rep-resentation, one cannot avoid it when one thinks and speaks. But something else might also go on. We might look to what happens in thought, for example, that is other to representation. We might look for nonrepresentational dimen-sions in signifier-signified relations or in the formation of our disciplines of knowledge or in the moods that accompany axiomatic values or in the disclo-siveness that accompanies processes of objectification and designation. We might question the range of power that is exercised by the assumption of sub-jectivity in the formation of intelligent perception. We might, in a word, read the Parisians in the *question* of certainty that unsettles each of our and their val-ues and attempt to find the limits of representation that inhabit the stance of the thinker and the position of what is thought. I believe that this is what they are "doing" to us: they are placing so radically in question *their own* values and manner of thinking, with a sense of the danger and destruction that inhabits our lives when our lives seem to be at their best, and they are opening *their* thought to a future given in this transformation that they—the Parisians— make us feel threatened where they too feel a threat at the center of the Western traditions that give us to hope, think, and worship with an unquestioned sense of rightness. If that looks like madness, it is a madness bred of a sense of both danger and a different future, the perception that our sanity has madness in it, and that the only way around it is through it. We could all name the figurations of madness that our sanity presents: sterilization in thought in quests for clarity, violent attacks on violences different from our own, destruction of cultures in the name of saving them, oppression in the pursuit of just societies, technologi- cal destruction in the pursuit of human standards of life, and so much more. It is not a matter primarily of being right or wrong, as Foucault remarked. It is rather that danger seems to accompany our ideals, clarity, and affirmations. It might well be the case that when we forget the questions that accompany our discoveries of what seems right—when our thought does not move in the ele- ment of question—and when we assume that correct representation is the form of thought at its best, something essential in our being alive is dangerously ob- scured. Paris is thinking in the element of question; paradoxically, we in this democracy may be reminded that in looking for accuracy of knowledge or for Truth, we overlook the likelihood that thinking in our lineage happens in the generation of questions, a generation that belongs to the questionableness of be- ing alive and one that shows our need of questions if we are to survive.

So Paris thinks and speaks differently from our accustomed philosophical normalcy. And this difference arises in repeated encounters with our traditional texts and practices. Those of us who expect to understand the Parisians without learning their unrelenting discipline of transformation, the rigor of their gene- alogies and deconstructions, their styles of transvaluation, their careful lan- guage that is designed for saying what is not quite sayable in our canonized patterns of thought and speech—without learning such things that might well break our expectations for philosophy, we will not understand them and their originality. And those of us who attempt to understand them without learning to reread the texts of our lineage in their different way, without learning how to put in question the approaches that have defined the texts of our tradition, the assumed truths of interpretation, and the patterns of representation that hold in the thrall of modern knowledge those thinkers who have inadequately questioned the axioms of modernity—those of us who read quickly will lack the discipline of thought that marks Paris at its best.

Paris, I believe, is open to us for dialogue but not for amalgamation, for respect but not for easy dismissal: for the hard work of respectful encounter but not for either use toward our own ends or reverential discipleship. Encounter but not use. Paris has a singularity that escapes, I believe, some of our categories of familiarity. It gives to us difference and dignity that require the hard work that something singular and other usually requires. Otherwise, in its forces of originality, it seems unresponsibly to reject our orders of knowledge, to be something bad or evil before our goods, something to be overcome without being thought.

In the work that I have done on the writings of Paris I have felt very little need to agree or disagree with these writings. I have largely experienced in them freedom from the dominance of judgment and found, rather, the priority of developing a range of highly variant kinds of perceptiveness—ways of seeing and hearing—that invite their own reversal and multiplication. I have found it necessary to question a silent inclination toward totalization in my own language and thought. I have found the canonized philosophies of my heritage open to an uncertainty that belongs to their apparent confidence, to the experimental dimension of their 'systems', to the desires that upset their seeming serenity and clarity, to the questions that give them to think and that are unavailable for resolution, and to possibility that breaks the hegemonies of meaning and presence. I have experienced danger where I had expected to find obvious universality. I have found rigorous, disciplined engagements with what we might broadly call technology. I have found a singular affirmation of thought and knowledge, of active, political concern for the suffering that we and our social systems inflict on ourselves, affirmation of human life with its creations, dangers, and injustices. I have found a politics of thought that addresses and interrupts the axioms of largely unconscious practices. Paris constitutes a remarkable event, an unusual surge of creative energy in both critique and insight. It arises from our Western traditions, from turning movements within them, and from a turning through them toward what has been excluded or unsaid by them. The issue is not one of subjection or victory. The issue is rather one of engagement with a different thought from the ones with which I have been most familiar, engagement with ways of thinking that give both a different past and a future different from what I have expected and known.

8 | Self-Fragmentation
The Danger to Ethics

If you mean by ethics a code which would tell us how to act, then of course *The History of Sexuality* is not an ethics. But if by ethics you mean the relationship you have to yourself when you act, then I would say that it intends to be an ethics, or at least to show what could be an ethics of sexual behavior. It would be one which would not be dominated by the problem of the deep truth of the reality of our sex life. The relationship I think we need to have with ourselves when we have sex is an ethics of pleasure, of intensification of pleasure.

—Michel Foucault, *Politics, Philosophy, Culture*

An Ethos of Critical Thinking

What can the ethics of an intellectual be . . . if not this: to make oneself permanently capable of detaching oneself from oneself (which is the opposite of the attitude of conversion)?

—Michel Foucault, *Politics, Philosophy, Culture*

OUR QUESTION IS, why does Foucault's genealogy of the formation of the ethical subject not lead to a new normative ethics? There is *in* Foucault's work an ethos, a self-relation that is constituted by a complex historical inheritance, but it is one without a normative ethics. It is an ethos based on the observation that one is able always to detach oneself from oneself by virtue of the fragmented elements that constitute it. This ethos is operative in genealogical studies that use what Foucault calls critical thought in the context of following the lineage of capacities and institutions that constitute our lives. On Foucault's terms critical thought is a constellation of powers; it constantly checks the necessities in our lives by reference to marginalized options. Critical thought, we shall see, means that an individual extracts himself or herself from the power of subjectivity. Foucault calls it an experimental process whereby one is put at a distance from the behaviors that subject one to dominating powers, but it is a process that attunes one to a nonrepresentable nonnecessity that seems to run through—in the sense of a run in a stocking—the controlling, subjecting powers that define our identities as citizens and persons. This nonnecessity, which I will elaborate in discussions of liberty and freedom, is found in the fragmentation of things—particularly, for our purposes, in the fragmentation of ethical subjectivity. At this point I want only to note that the process of constantly checking is an *attunement to fragmentation,* that something happens to an individual in this process that is distinct to *subjection,* and that constantly checking forecasts a way of being that might be different from what we ordinarily call subjectivity and selfhood. This issue will return later and provide one of our primary questions: is there an option to what we ordinarily call subjectivity and selfhood that emerges *with* Foucault's thought?

Foucault violates our intuitions when he says in effect that subjects and selves do not belong to themselves, and by this observation he takes away the privilege of self-constitution in his account of subjectivity. Subjects and selves belong to circulations of powers and to a destiny of not belonging to anything at all. When we make ourselves permanently capable of detaching ourselves from ourselves by constantly checking the powers that make up our relations to each other and to ourselves, we affirm our nonbelonging in the midst of everything that makes us live as we do. The direction of his thought is not toward converting people to a better kind of communal life. He is neither a polemicist nor the leader of a concerted movement to establish a new consensus. Rather, Foucault's thought interrupts not only our conventions but also the operations of our agencies of coherence and our uncritical senses of belonging to inherent or primordial ways of being. By approaching every state of being in terms of a genealogy of unstable power formations, Foucault makes possible a critical dismemberment of everything that makes us to be as we are. We belong to—we *are*—formations of powers, and when critical thought interrupts those formations, another kind of power comes into play. This is a power that loosens the hold of other powers and opens us, as we shall see, to no power at all—to a kind of nonbelonging that leads nowhere but allows us to stand less solidly, less staked, less persuaded in the values that direct us and that give us to direct others.

I find Foucault's hardest and most important claim to be that domination, totalization (i.e., incipient fascism), and subjection are inevitable in our traditions of conservative, liberal, and radical usages of power. That means that these dangers inhere in ethical subjects and their normative values. His studies that developed this claim most clearly are those of cultural powers and their genealogies of self-formation in Western culture. For his own part, he is attempting, he says, "apart from *any totalization* . . . to open up problems that are as *concrete* and *general* as possible, problems that approach politics from behind and cut across societies on the diagonal, problems that are at once constituent of our history and constituted by that history: for example, the problem of the relation between sanity and insanity; the question of illness and crime, of sexuality" (FR 375–376). We will find that his word *problematization* refers to a process of simultaneously attempting to solve fundamental problems within an ethos *and* making other fundamental problems by the constructed solutions. Problematizations form in the clashes of constituting values and asymmetrical relations and develop largely without awareness in the knowledges and practices of a particular locale. By genealogically and critically following processes of problematization, he cuts through and interrupts the power formations that define political and ethical subjects—he cuts through to the problems that a society finds in its own ways of living and to new forms of interaction that are constructed as people meet resistances to what they want for themselves. By this process of interruption and discovery he hopes to make optional the totalization and domination that our culture has constructed for itself. His thought is thus intended to stand both inside and outside of its own governing social conditions and at the same time to avoid reconstructing better truths and solutions. "Stay within the dangers and problems" is his maxim. In this way, thinking and knowledge might escape the largely unconscious passions for truth, certainty, and right that ignore their own problematic and dangerous histories. A way of being—an ethos—that is not founded on subjectivity might emerge in this thought, something emerging from fragmentation that does not avoid fragmentation but affirms it and thereby qualifies our traditional drift to totalization. Foucault is looking toward a management of liberty that is not based on the subject or the self that our history of problematizations has produced but that comes from self-detachment, one of whose practices is critical thought. When we think of subjects and selves we thus need experimentally to think of something made over a course of time by a complex interplay of power relations that presents individuals to themselves and to each other in describable ways. Our subjectivity has been formed in processes of "subjectivation" in which we have come to relate to ourselves by values which overlook our own fragmented histories and thereby carry a largely unconscious inclination toward totalization and fascism.

Instead of thinking of him as uncommitted and, by thinking this way, holding our thought within the framework of what he calls the attitude of conversion, of the committed or uncommitted subject, we can think of *attunement* to something that is not fixable within the boundaries of subjects and representations. I do not know how to speak of something so out of the bounds of representation and subjectivity. We are familiar with attempts to think in accord with radical alterity (Levinas), the withdrawal of being (Heidegger), or unspeakable deferral and differencing (Derrida). Such thinking may diminish itself in the process of asserting itself; it may cultivate reticence in the space where judgment or certainty are traditionally appropriate; it may lead to an ekstasis of self-transcendence; it may give priority to its own self-overcoming; or it may make inevitable its own deconstruction. Whatever the strategy, an effort is going on to rethink thinking by reference to 'something' unfitted to the language of power, subject, judgment, assertion, or self-constitution. Surprisingly, Foucault's thought with regard to fragmentation is part of this attempt to rethink thinking in such a way that something different takes place from a re-aligned ethics or a rededication of the self within inherited structures of power. When *all* confederations of power are constantly in question, the possibility for thinking without reassertion of the subjected subject might take place, and that would be a new thought, one in which another totalization might not be able to grow in the name of yet another, better morality or a new cooperative endeavor. This is a fledgling thought without wings for flying, much less for soaring, and I will have to hop with it from branch to branch without knowing either its element or its possibilities—other than the possibility for opening problems up and providing a new memory for the powers that form us and give us a sense of belonging to ourselves. In Foucault, it is a way of thinking that opens us in the fragmentation that runs us through and that has been marginalized to the point of invisibility.

We shall ask whether thought from the outside of specific political and ethical commitments can provide a space of exposure of the subjection that produced our selves and our citizenship. Or is thinking completely circumscribed by selves? Shall we entertain the possibility that our just causes are configurations of powers that tend to move toward totalization and exclusion? And can that entertainment stand outside the purview of our just causes? Does Foucault address that narcissism which gives satisfaction in 'being on the right side' and 'knowing better than the others'? Can his thought avoid such narcissism? How much prominence can we give to questioning that is at odds with its own normative interests? In Foucault's thought we might have an ethos of differences without a normative ethics, and we surely have a way of thinking that is repelled by its own movement toward certainty into outer dark as it discerns the problems that it makes for itself. Were we to follow Foucault's thought, I believe that we would undergo the seduction of a chance movement in our culture which promises—and we can trust this promise—surprise, passion, and death without a hint of a sovereign hero to draw our passions from us or the hint of a cause that reveals to us a full meaning for surprise and death.

The Sense of Ascending Transcendence and the Space of Fragmentation

I wish to underscore Foucault's point of departure when he speaks of powers. He does not begin with a theory of power, neither his own theory nor someone else's. His thought does not emerge from theoretical unity. Nor does he begin with an ancient event that plays itself out in a complex body of determinations and inevitabilities. We will find that his genealogy of Western ethical subjectivity does not follow the metaphor of either dispersion or a destiny that comes to us from the future. We will see that his genealogy of the moral subject does follow a line of development that privileges the past, even if that line, as a form of knowledge, is threatened by the knowledge that the genealogy produces. In the instance of powers, however, Foucault begins with the recent destabilization of theoretical knowledge in favor of what he calls 'local research' and 'local knowledges'. Out of the cultural criticisms provided by Marxism and psychoanalytic theory, for example, has come a "noncentralized kind of theoretical production, one that is to say whose validity is not dependent on the approval of the established regimes of thought" (PK 81). In this decentralizing process, knowledges that have not been subjected by dominating theories and beliefs come to the fore as viable options, and these knowledges, alert as they are to their own fragmentation and the powers which have dominated them, may be especially attuned to the protean and historical manner in which normalizing federations of powers develop their hegemonies.

Subjection can take place in the form of theoretical disguise: given the operative systems of dogmatic thought of the time and the functional organization of the asylum, for example, the conflicts and invested interests that produced the asylum in the seventeenth century were disguised by theories that gave a veneer of normalcy and good sense to the oppression, marginalization, and forced conformity that run through the administration of the asylum's life. Knowledge of these subjecting elements—subjecting because they produce the subjectivity of the 'healed' insane—became possible because of the more recent, critical dismantling of unifying theories concerning reason and benevolence. Further, the knowledge of the patient was viewed as unimportant and was disqualified and silenced by the powers that governed commitment, administration, and 'healing' of the insane. Such disqualified or disguised voices and knowledges have reemerged to influence language and thought regarding the asylum in the wake of destructuring the power of the once dominating theories and practices that subjected the insane to silenced alienation in the institutions that identified them.

These emerging knowledges of the previously disinherited are regional in the sense that they have claim to their own circumstances and have no purchase on the whole of society or on the world or on another ethos. By affirming their own fragmentation they may renounce the traditional claim to sovereignty that accompanies traditional ethical standards as well as accompanies the knowledge that holds certainty and truth as ideals.

Foucault thus begins his reflections on powers in the contemporary collapse of unifying theories, in the emergence of multiple, fractured voices and knowledges, and in the critical recovery of disguised and marginalized bodies of experience that were lost to view. The breaking apart of globalizing discourse is as necessary for Foucault's genealogies of power formations as the fracturing of theistic belief was necessary for Nietzsche's genealogies. In this deterioration of globalizing discourse, the sense of ascending transcendence is altered. Foucault begins to think in an interdiction of rational transcendence vis-à-vis traditional problematizations and constellations of powers. All events refer to

other events in lineages of formations. The space of reference is a surface of occurrences, not a region of ascent and descent. Knowledge within a context of
ascending transcendence, by contrast, gives powers to ascend or descend beyond themselves to primordial sources of which they are expressions. Contingent powers ecstatically exceed both their instances and their experiences. In
Foucault's discourse, as the self detaches from itself, we shall find the remain-
ders of a sense of ascending transcendence in the distance that the self establishes for itself before pleasure and desire and in the distance of differences that
traverse our fragmented knowledges and practices. But these quasi-transcen-
dences do not ascend. They flatten out in a broad but limited volume of space,
spread out like spacing in and in between organizations and domains. They
are composed of distances that cross over into different regions of discourse and
space. In Foucault's self-detachment the remains of the sense of ascending transcendence is thus found in his sense of *limited* distances and differences, and
we shall pay attention specifically to the way he establishes the self's distance
to pleasure in its mastery of pleasure and to the way he finds liberty not in a
human capacity or natural quality but in the spaces that divide the composite
elements that make up the fragile unities of the agencies whereby we know and
conduct ourselves. Marginalized knowledges and types of people, for example,
transcend the organization that holds them to the established truths and normalcy that make them to be marginalized.

We can also see the remainder of the sense of ascending transcendence in
Foucault's development of critical knowledge. This knowledge does not originate in a transcendental capacity or in something given with human nature.
Critical knowledge develops as he undergoes the impact of marginalized and
rejected knowledges on the body of certainty that constitutes his intellectual
inheritance. Their recognized and accepted differences modify and condition
the knowledges and conducts that have marginalized and rejected them. *Their*
impacts in their differences, in the decline of globalizing theories, and not the
activity of an autonomous self, produce critical knowledge. The quasi-transcen-
dence necessary for critical knowledge is thus found in the fragmenting impact
of differences out of their distance within established hierarchies, methods,
rules, and structures of cultural life. It is found in the movement of self-detachment which does not lead to a whole, but to a lineage of subjection by which a
self forms that *must* know its truth.

There are times when I read Foucault on power that I wish he would whis-
per to me that there is much that cannot be said, that behind the criticism and
scholarship there is something momentous that in its silence waits not to be
said but for reticent attentiveness, that he and I could listen together in an ekstasis of quietness and speak indirectly in and of transcending movement beyond a surface of differences that connects and divides all that we experience.
I find myself wishing that in his language something like 'mysterious being'

would surprise me, like the distant shape of a great fish breaking for a moment on the horizon of water and sky, to let me know that below the surface something beyond even the traditional sense of mystery unspeakably moves, promising both catastrophe and hope and a sense of *beyond*. But that is exactly what Foucault will not do. As we enter his discourse we find a loss of transcendence, a *loss* that radically *opens* powers to their own variances without even an erased trace of unspeakable difference or of Gods and divine madness, without the lightness of being's self-concealing, without a sign of eternal return. We begin rather in a series of contemporary fractures that open to histories of conspiracy, largely unconscious problem-solving, and anxious totalization that have produced our capacities for discrimination and social and ethical judgment. In his discipline, which he calls an *ascesis*, history harbors no secrets, the knowledge of which would elevate or deepen us, but holds at a distance both processes that formed established patterns of truth, practice, and knowledge *and* the overlooked, maimed, marginalized, and silenced themes, the knowledge of which will give us to realize that our normal will to be true is an optional play of powers and that our hope for ascending transcendence of any kind has no ontological privilege, is no more true than it is a lie. Our wills—the force of our wills—and our hopes are bred on the surface of conflicts and struggles and are maintained by repetitions that are required by mutations of powers that give us ourselves and that were themselves sprung from other conflicts. Yet Foucault takes joy in this. Few contemporary writers are as affirming as he of the changes in the histories that we must live, and we shall keep in mind his unembittered laughter as we follow his engagement with voices that will overturn him. I believe that in spite of great differences he is not far in mood from Rilke's lines at the end of the Tenth *Elegy*:

> And yet, were they waking a symbol within
> us, the endless dead,
> look, they'd be pointing, perhaps to the
> catkins, hanging
> from empty hazels, or else
> to the rain downfalling on dark soil-bed in
> early spring.—

> And we, who think of happiness
> *ascending*, then would feel
> the emotion that almost startles
> when something happy falls.

As we read Foucault on powers, his turn away from his early lyrical style and his relentlessly checking the powers and sources of our culture's happiness—the senses of ascending transcendence, for example, that in relation to power and history has given so much satisfaction—we find him renouncing privilege to the emotions of ascending, flattening out our sense of wonder to fit the surface of human engagements, and leading us to think in the startling probability that the fall of the sense of ascending transcendence is where our knowledge now is to begin. We are left to chance necessities found in circulations of powers and perhaps will find in their play attraction to lives in their multiple fragments. We can see that Foucault's attentiveness to fragmented, circulating powers incorporates thorough loss of the sense of ascending transcendence, that fragmentation does not call for healing in his discourse, and that the sense of ascending transcendence is closely affiliated with the *loss* of that liberty by which we can trace the lineages of the problems that beset us. Fragments without ascension give us the space among them into which we may fall and come to think outside of the forces that happen to define our senses of belonging and the secured desires of our selves. This space among fragments is one without selfhood. By attunement in and to this space of fragmentation and by critical attentiveness to projects of universalization and totalization, Foucault finds the emergence of a way of thinking that re-members the canons of our lives, a way of thinking that runs counter to the normalcies of our time by following the run of disinherited experiences which, as he says, cut diagonally across the patterns of established thought and speech.

I speculate that Foucault's lyricism shifted to a flatter prose as the effects of thought without a sense of ascension worked on his style. Even though I quoted Rilke to bring us to the descending mood of nonascendence, I wonder if lyricism itself is not in question, at least for the moment, as ekstatic ascension comes into question. The lineage of a multistoried world with spiritual beings appropriate to each of its dimensions dies as Foucault writes, and there is no call to language to ascend, to take us beyond the spiritual poverty of living in concern for things and their histories to higher and truer being. In this sense I believe that his style strikes at the heart of what he calls our subjection: he holds us on the surface to the relations of powers and does not affirm the deepest desires of our *selves* to find a primordial relation that is simple and true and to which we ontologically belong. That sense of primordial relationship and power is at the core of the subjection that he traces. Is it correct to say that lyrical ascension, no matter the telos, has within it the seeds of hierarchical exclusiveness that forecasts totalization and destructive control of individuals? Does it arise from a process of subjection and with the sense of ekstasis throw us under the power of an authorizing agency? Must we put in question our history of ekstasis and find it—ekstasis and its lyricism—to be a problem for us? Perhaps an exaggerated distance between the self and desire is at the core of our sense of self-transcendence and the lyrical ecstasy that can accompany it.

Blanchot says that from Foucault there "emerges a discourse entirely surface and shimmering, but bereft of mirages." Do we find an alternative to the ascending quality of lyricism in Foucault's surface, shimmering prose, a language not built on symbolization and imaginative flight, but one that finds itself outside of a contrast between the real and the imaginary, and one that lets the insufficiency of our language emerge from the circulations and fissures of its heritages, one that finds its horizon *in* its insufficiency? This language takes pleasure without regret in its shimmering and constant withdrawal into its transience. Perhaps *this* pleasure in Foucault's prose makes us ready for pleasure that has escaped bonding with both a sense of ascending transcendence and the distance that is woven into self-relation; perhaps in this shimmering, surface prose we meet our mortality more sharply than any language of transcendence will allow. Shimmering without ascension. Is this the turn from a religious and philosophical heritage that strategically reinstates itself in all ecstatic attempts to depart from it?

Problematization and a Genealogy of Sexual Subjectivity

> There are times in life when the question of knowing if one can think differently than one thinks, and perceive differently than one sees, is absolutely necessary if one is to go on looking and reflecting at all. . . . In what does [philosophical activity] consist, if not in the endeavor to know how and to what extent it might be possible to think differently, instead of legitimating what is already known?
>
> Philosophy is still what it was in times past, i.e., an ascesis, *askésis*, an exercise of oneself in the activity of thought.
>
> —Michel Foucault, *History of Sexuality*, vol. II

Foucault's genealogical study of sexuality is a study of "the modes according to which individuals are given to *recognize* themselves as sexual *subjects*" (HS II, 5, emphasis added). This is not a conceptual analysis but an account of "the *practices* by which individuals were *led* to *focus* their attention on themselves . . . as subjects of *desire*, bringing into play between themselves . . . a certain *relationship* that allows them to discover, in *desire, the truth of their being*, be it natural or fallen" (HS II, 5, emphasis added). The practices in question provide focus for individuals. That focus is on themselves. *Subjects* of desire are not found in desiring, but in *relationships to* desire. Desire, then, is at a distance from the subject of desire, and this distance includes many relations of power of which Foucault will give a genealogy. The subjectivity of desire is found in the relationships to desire that developed in our lineage; desire, in its distance to the subjects who were to govern it, was recognized as the truth of our being. Hence, truth, desire, power, and a certain fragmentation among them are all implicated in his study of the formation of sexual subjectivity. We thus note at the beginning that the *subject* of desire, i.e., a specific way in which an individual relates to himself or herself, is not structured primarily by desire or a force of will but by a circulation of powers that emerges as individuals are formed relative to desire within given cultural circumstances. The subject takes its form of movement from cultural problems that have to be faced because of the values and purposes that are found in the relations at hand.

The areas of circulations of powers will be found in the relationships, foci, recognitions, discernments, and practices that make up subjectivity in relation to desire. The subject in its manner of relating to desire leads us to its lineage and not to an ascending movement of energy. Practices give attentiveness; attentiveness defines a certain manner in relating to one's body and those of other peoples; and the relation produces a body of knowledge of truth. In *The History of Sexuality* Foucault calls this particular complex of practices, attentiveness, relation, knowledge, and truth 'sexuality', and we will see that sexuality composes a moral subjectivity, that the moral subject is a way of relating to the body's desires.

Given Foucault's statements about transforming structures of philosophy, we can expect that his genealogy of the subject of desire will be part of a process that will make uncertain what he knows about sexuality as he finds it and lives it and will place him at a distance from his own subjectivity, which formed without the impact and resistance of genealogy. His genealogy questions knowledges and produces a type of knowledge that interrupts the subject's recognition of truth and hence the subject's sense of being. Whose truth and being? Foucault's, for one. His genealogy is itself a subject's action regarding itself. In one sense it is a way a self cares for itself, but now in a form of interruption and questioning. If I am right that his genealogy is an address out of and to problems that inhere in our being selves and subjects, we will want to see how this care of self departs from and carries out the ascetic care of self that he describes in volume III of *The History of Sexuality*. In his words, one goal in his genealogy of the sexual subject "was to learn to what extent the effort to think one's own history can free thought from what it silently thinks, and so enable it to think differently" (HS II, 9). On Foucault's terms that is a self-detaching endeavor that does not lead to a normative ethics, but to a type of vigilance. An ethos without a normative ethics? We shall have to see.

Not only does Foucault not begin his work with theoretical structures; he also does not begin his work on sexuality and the self with repressions or interdictions of sexual desire. Such an approach would universalize sexuality and attend to cultural and social ways whereby something universal and natural for all people is denied or diverted. Rather, he makes problematizations his center of attention in order to give accessibility to the historical character of sexuality. The emergence, formation, and development of sexuality can be traced in our complex lineage. When we keep in mind that sexuality is a relation *to* desire in the form of practices and knowledges, this strategy does not appear to be radical. Foucault's perception is that sexuality began to develop out of individuals' concerns in ancient culture for the health of their bodies. Problematization—confronting problems and developing practices to address those problems in a complex flow of powers—and not repression is thus his point of emphasis as he gives a genealogy of individuals' concern for health in Greek and Roman culture. His concept of power as a circulation of assertions and resistances in cultural and social relations, rather than power as an essence that takes a variety of forms—that concept of circulations in relationships is central to his genealogical project. These relations are fluid and continuously encountering their own limits before changing circumstances: subjects are always in crisis because of flows of events that are not unlike a river's multiple, fluid projectories. We are unsteady creatures in our identities, not because we repress our true natures and not because we have our true natures repressed for us by our parents, our leaders, or our culture. We are unsteady in our selves because we are relational in who we are and our relations are formed in lineages of problems whose transformations have produced other problems as well as identities made in relation to problematizations. Our selves are questionable not because we have fallen from something pristine, essential, and preestablished but because lived questions and answers that raise other lived questions give us to be as we are.

Foucault's work is a genealogy of the formation of ethical subjectivity, for example, as he traces the movement from public constraint to inner constraint in the changing, Hellenic ethos. Careful fulfillment of external social roles was replaced by inner discipline, by a self of discipline. His long-range intention is to show the transformation from an external, social discipline to an identity of self-constraint for the sake, first, of self-health, then for the sake of the goal of salvation, then for the sake of forming normal modern subjects by state governance. By working on problematizations—confronting problems and developing responding practices—Foucault is working on our self-determinations in a lineage that transcends itself by a distance for removal from desire and by the accidents and limits that push people to change their ways of living.

A note on the function of the Greek ethos for us now. Foucault is clear that he is not describing an ideal to which we should return. The Greek and Roman projects of care for self responded to problems which are different from our problems now. He finds no clarity now regarding either pleasure or desire, and one of his intentions, I believe, is to clear a space for asking what pleasure and desire might *now* be and how we might speak regarding them. The problems that we face arise from the subjection that resulted from the processes of division from desire that he follows genealogically in our cultural lineage. If he can find some of the problems and in the process put in question a knowledge of pleasure and desire, he will have done much of what he hoped to do. His knowledge and practices, and ours, will be in question, will come to be at a certain distance from our nongenealogical certainties; our values will be uncovered in their multiple and fragmented strands, and by virtue of genealogy's excess of our values, practices, and knowledges, we will be, in his discourse, to a certain extent outside of the selves that we are given to be. We will be without a clear model for relating to our desire, and we might have a sense of danger that excites energy to ask more and to assert less. Our certainty and our uncertainty will be problems before which we stand, now mute, but wondering how to address them in the absence of an historical lesson, a general theory, or an ideology that would produce clarity and a sense of identity to which we belong by right.

Foucault says that freedom is found in the ability to reverse or to resist a situation. In his introduction to volume II of *The History of Sexuality* he spends a surprising amount of time on the process he followed in coming to the approach that he took in that volume and its successor. He notes that he broke with the broad conviction that sexuality is a constant and with the privilege given to repression as the primary form of power relating to sexuality and culture. He had to dislodge from his own discourse the notion of a desiring subject which was formed around the principle of desiring man instead of around the processes whereby people came to *recognize* themselves as subjects of desire. He had to move from *theories* of power to accounts of relationships that exercised power. He returned to *relations* to self rather than to a broad concept of the self in order to see how the individual constitutes and recognizes himself as a subject and how, in this play of self regarding self, games of truth take place *in* the play of self-regard. What, he asked, was the interplay of truth and error that gave shape to experiences of desire? All of this led Foucault into territory that was new to him. He moved out of the seventeenth and eighteenth centuries, where his work had been concentrated, to classical and late classical culture and to the two centuries after the beginning of the Christian era. In this process he lost his original project as he had projected it and threw out more than one manuscript. He found himself uncomfortably reliant on secondary texts at first and found himself at the beginning of his research a novice instead of an expert in the necessary scholarship. He lacked that Wagnerian confidence whereby anything around him could be dominated by myth and force of will, by the charismatic power of extraordinary vitality combined with unshakable conviction. He was on a long detour of risks that resulted from a strategy that blocked the authority of those knowledges that functioned axiomatically in the present day. The boundaries of what he knew shifted as he worked on his genealogy of "desiring man," his style of writing and conception changed, and he found himself with fragments of documents and pieces of evidence in the absence of unifying theories as he established the trajectory of his research.

I believe that his experience in coming to a knowledge that reverses some knowledges of subjectivity gives expression to the freedom about which he writes, that it exposes the ethos of liberation of which he speaks tantalizingly and nondefinitively. This is an exposure of the ethos of genealogy in which he finds an ability to reverse approaches to texts and to resist certain inevitabilities in the inherited knowledges. The arts of existence, he says, "are those intentional and voluntary actions by which men not only set themselves rules of conduct, but also seek to transform themselves, to change themselves in their singular being, and to make their life into an *oeuvre* that carries certain aesthetic values and meets certain stylistic criteria" (HS II, 10–11). In the case of genealogical work, Foucault underwent a similar process. The problem he faced was that the canonized knowledge of desire did not account for its own history: it excluded the process by which an ethical self formed in a division from desire, a division that produced both the knowledge and the canonizing tendency. This knowledge depended on concepts of sexuality and power that gave them the status of nonhistorical essences and that lost the dynamic relational processes of power. The thought of an interdicting authority that stops or diverts a natural process, that ignorantly prohibits the expression of something given and right— such a thought transmits a venerable metaphysics of paternal authority which goes awry in relation to a preestablished and universal truth of being: a metaphysics of a misguided father in relation to a higher paternal authority. He found that the *subject* of desire did not account for its distance from the desire of which it was subject, and that the subject did not account for its own ability to *recognize* both itself and desire in multiple, historically produced ways.

Foucault's effort to follow the emergence and development of the subject of desire exposed a freedom that puts the inherited truths and knowledges in question. It is not a freedom that comes from one's falling from something essential and being unable to find the dangerous way back. Nor is it a freedom of disclosive openness in the withdrawal of being. It is rather a surface freedom that accompanies the fragmentations that run through our historically produced selves, the freedom of being also on the margins as well as in the center of the dominate relationships and truths that give us the ability to recognize ourselves. Not being the unities that we sometimes project ourselves rightfully to be, we are liberated from the governing necessities by the silenced voices in our self-constituting lineage, by the patchwork quality of our axioms, and by the separations that divide us from ourselves. Foucault found freedom manifested in the shortcomings of his own approach and in the problems that state-of-the-art relationships and thoughts presented. As he revamped his approach, squirmed and threw out sheets of paper, and hypothesized with different questions, he found emerging a knowledge of another kind of relation to his body and to himself as a subject of knowledge that did not forecast a true self but that offered care for the self in the form of knowing the self to be dangerous to itself and to others.

Is this really in the lineage of care for self, this thought from outside the control of subjectivity, this vigilance concerning the dangers that inhere in our avoidance of other dangers, this disinheritance of the self from its discourse of transcendent paternity? We could take a quasi-essentialist approach and say that Foucault is putting us in touch with the way we *really* are, that his thought makes possible a true knowledge of our selves and takes care in that way. But Foucault's rigor is found in holding to a focus on the lineages of knowledges and relations of power which in effect puts selves in question without taking up arguments for or against their ontological status. Within his work we do not speak of what selves *are*. We can speak of this or that kind of self that is formed in this or that lineage of subjection, but we stand outside of the reality question concerning selves as we follow the lineages that have produced the range of the 'who's' that we can be. Still, the lineage for the care of self remains as we follow the development of regulations, practices, and truths that make self-regulations possible and as we discern what our bodies have become for us, how our pleasures take place, how, indeed, much that has been pleasurable has been made unspeakable and unknowable, how we imprison our bodies, discipline our desires, insure our souls, exclude other bodies, and empower our knowledges. As we encounter ourselves belonging to a lineage of subjection, and as we make that encounter in a genealogical ethos that comes to knowledge of itself by accounts of its own lineage, as we encounter our selves in an ethos of fragmented freedom, we both care for our selves and problematize the caring that regulates us. We problematize care for the selves that have come in question by following this lineage.

We are dealing with a freedom of fragmentation, a freedom that comes from individuals' not belonging *essentially* to anything, a freedom that comes from not being *essentially* any one, a freedom that accompanies the differences that constitute a lineage of loose alliances, relations of resistance and mastery, and confederations of fluid interests—a freedom that accompanies the lineages that give us to be *as* we are. This freedom of fragmentation transverses the problems that arise from transformations out of other problems—it is the element of problematization. It names people's ability that arises in specific circulations of powers to look again, say yes or no, experience danger in the midst of security, and hold in question the firmest of principles and established practices. It allows knowledges and practices to fall apart or to mutate with other knowledges and practices. Although this freedom is not anything in particular, cannot be used or directly addressed, and does not belong to subjects, on Foucault's terms it enables genealogy to be done, and genealogical knowledge privileges the freedom of fragmentation that is a largely overlooked part of our lineage. It is, Foucault says, "that in a thing that makes possible its valuation and distinction." Genealogy cannot belong to the freedom of fragmentation—such freedom cannot possess anything. Genealogy cannot embody freedom and make freedom work for it, although we can say that this freedom is the concern of genealogy and in that sense belongs to genealogy, crosses it and interrupts it. Among other things, we are dealing with a fragmentation that allows us to recognize ourselves and other things in fragmented ways when we speak in this discourse, and in that context knowledge of the freedom of fragmentation, which Foucault also calls liberty, allows knowledge of individuals without appeal to essences, substances, heights, or depths. Its knowledge provides the possibility of recognizing dangers and for continuing vigilance. On its own terms knowledge of the freedom of fragmentation constitutes a danger, generates problems, as this knowledge develops and accrues powers in relation to other discourses.

This knowledge of freedom sticks to the surface of events. Even the factors of which it speaks and the local pleasures that it permits lack a knowledge of incandescence, mystical infusion, or participation in emptiness. It is not transcendent or transcendental, this freedom. It is not exactly a capacity or a vapor, not a ghost or trace of something. It is merely nonconnection among connected things that means nonbelonging—nonbelonging to which we cannot belong: a broken, unpossessable surface of circulations in which individuals are at a distance with themselves and with all other things. Neither love nor strife are its meaning. It has no face and no nature.

In his care, Foucault isolates four problems relating to sex in ancient culture: the body, wives, boys, and truth (or the relation between abstention and access to truth). In these practical and discursive areas problems were confronted, such as sexual disease, corruption through pleasure, exclusion of women from moral precepts, loss of masculinity, and the unavailability of truth to those who experience excessive pleasure. In encountering these problems in classical Western culture an individual morality—a practice of pleasure—with public control began to emerge. It was from these *problems*, not from the repressive interdiction, that the subject of desire had its origins; that is, a describable circulation of restraint, discipline, and knowledge developed out of encountering problems in relation to sexual conduct. Not repression, but individual discipline based on private worries set in motion the ascetic powers of moral experience and an austerity in the practice of pleasure.

The Self That Came of Care

> We must also reverse the philosophical approaches of ascending toward a constituting subject who is asked to account for every possible object of knowledge in general. On the contrary we must descend to the study of the concrete practices through which the subject is constituted within a field of knowledge.

> The goal [of a history of sexuality] is to analyze 'sexuality' as a historically specific mode of experience in which the subject is objectified by himself and for others through certain precise procedures of 'government'.
>
> —Michel Foucault, "Autobiography," *Dictionnaire de philosophes*

The subjection process—the process of making moral subjects—with which we have been dealing is complex. On the one hand, the word *subjection*, in the context of Foucault's work, refers to the emergence and unfolding of the subject who measures, regulates, and knows desire. On the other, the word suggests mastery, compelling, and obligating, and it is by subjection that the ethical subject has come to be. We have seen, however, that subjection in this context does not mean repression or interdiction by a higher authority. It refers rather to a process of discipline by which individuals gave themselves a particular self-relation. Out of this at first largely individual *ascesis*, later religious, governmental, and institutional regulations and methods of normalization developed in the context of cultural questions that emerged in other societies. We have also seen that the powers of subjection are found exclusively as relations of self to self and self to others. What are some of the relations that empowered the emergence of the subject of desire—the ethical subject—that has come through multiple moral mutations to be ourselves?

In his discussion of *aphrodisia*—of the "act, gestures, and contacts that produced certain forces of pleasure"—Foucault identifies a dynamic relation of desire, acts, and pleasure that form the "texture" of ethical experience in the late classical period. It is not concupiscence or the inherent evil of desire. *Aphrodisia* names a texture that is both natural and, because of the pleasure's intensity and acuteness, subject to excess. *Excess* means elevation of a pleasurable force above more important things, such as the soul's 'highest' activities or the responsibilities of citizenship.

In addition to the problem of excess, there are the problems generated by the sexual roles played by individuals. In the Greek context, role is identified in terms of activity and passivity. Activity is relegated to men and is closely associated with being a free citizen as distinct to being a slave or a woman. Passivity was associated with women and slaves. This means that the formation of moral subjectivity emerged *within* an active-passive polarity in which the active male's privilege is complete. Passivity meant being an object of activity, and this created problems not only regarding women's pleasure but also regarding the identity of the receptive male. Within the classical context, the passive object was an occasion of pleasure for whom the experience of pleasure was not a primary concern. This is an issue to which we will return.

Within this context of aphrodisia, which Foucault identifies as the substance of ethics in the late classical period and as the interplay of 'natural' forces that became unnatural by virtue of their power and pleasure, I will note the three areas of problematization that he raises and then turn to the care of self in order to focus on the emerging form of the early ethical subject that established the paternity for Western ethical subjectivity.

First, the use or *chrésis* of pleasure. *Chrésis* names the styles of using pleasure. Use is not a matter of what is permitted or forbidden but a matter of prudence, reflection, and calculation in the way one distributed and controlled his acts. It is a question of strategy—use should be based on natural need. It should be controlled by moderation. It should be characterized by no excess: the right use at the right time in the right amount. One region of problems for classical men concerned the use of pleasure, and we shall see that self-mastery is closely tied to the question of how pleasure was to be used.

Enkrateia: self-mastery, self-control. *Enkrateia* names the attitude in relation to oneself that is necessary to an ethics of pleasure and which is manifested through the proper use of pleasures. The word designates the domination of oneself by oneself as well as the effort this domination demands. Self-mastery establishes an attunement with one's need for balance and moderation in an effort to avoid ill health and suffering and to bring to realization the unique nature and beauty of the human soul. *Self-mastery* indicates an agonistic relation in which one fights against many pleasures and desires and cultivates a combative attitude toward pleasures. One must subdue the temptation to excess on the part of 'inferior' appetites (*inferior* means appetites shared with animals). This is a struggle against enslavement by inferior passions. It is not that they are bad in themselves, but their ascendancy and dominion is destructive of the best part of a man. Ethical conduct thus includes a battle for superior powers.

In this battle against the domination of inferior desires, one does battle with oneself. The enemy is one's body. One's body, not an alien power, is the object to be mastered. One sought victory by oneself over oneself *in* the body's desires. Self-rule, self-mastery, and not self-renunciation or purification or integrity were the goals.

Self-mastery is like a governance of the soul, an internal state that is organized by the authority of right principles. Training and discipline are necessary and provide the structure of *askésis* that will enable an individual to subject all that is inferior to whatever is superior. One had to know the dangers, attend carefully to himself, and transform himself. The goal is to face privations without suffering and to reduce every physical pleasure to nothing more than satisfaction of needs: a natural economy that would produce a life of proper satisfaction. We should note that governing oneself and governing others have the same form. Self-governance leads to civic leadership. There is a transfer of power from the governed self to the governed other. But this transfer comes naturally from the right measure of self-governance. Self-mastery was an end in itself; its means were its goal. There was no distinction between the act of self and the ethical conduct.

Freedom and truth. *Sophrosyne* (moderation and prudence) is made possible by *enkrateia*. It is characterized by freedom, not by purity or innocence. Freedom by self-mastery and self-domination is the classical goal. The opposite to freedom is enslavement of the self. One sought, for example, freedom from the force of pleasures. Freedom thus meant power over oneself: "a power that one brought to bear on oneself in the power that one exercised over others." If one were under the control of others, one would not find *sophrosyne* in himself or herself. In that case one simply obeyed. But if one achieved self-mastery, one could make moderation and prudence the measure of one's relation to those under his authority. The test of this virtue comes when one curbs his appetite in relation to those over whom he has power. Such a person was truly free.

This active freedom was known as "virile." The truly free individual commanded what needed commanding, coerced what was not capable of self-direction, and imposed reason on whatever was wanting in reason. This kind of activity was definitive of a free man's proper relation to himself and others. Domination, hierarchy, and masculine authority were thus aspects of a free man's proper measure. Although a woman could be in a certain sense free, she would need to be like a man in that freedom, and such freedom could not be found on the basis of her own resources. To have strength of character, she would need dependence on male virility and hence on a man. And immoderation was known then to derive from a passivity that relates it to femininity and was thus unsuited to males. The independence needed for self-virtue and the virility necessary to attractive males were thus problems for this ethos, because women were indeed independent in household economies and young men were often passive in relation to older, dominate men. Out of these problems different relationships between husbands and wives and men and boys developed.

Sophrosyne necessarily accompanies a certain form of knowledge: *"one could not form oneself as an ethical subject in the use of pleasures without forming oneself at the same time as a subject of knowledge"* (HS II, 86, my emphasis). *Logos* must have supremacy and regulate behavior, and the individual must have a sense for proper timing and measure in the application of rules and principles. The individual must know himself in such a way that his essential relation to what is true is clear to him. Such truth—the truth of *logos*—however, is outside of his own being and selfhood. There was no inclination to turn to the self to know the truth of the self: " . . . it is important to note that this relation to truth never took the form of a decipherment of the self by the self, never that of a hermeneutics of desire. . . . the relation to truth was a structural, instrumental, and ontological condition for establishing the individual as a moderate subject leading a life of moderation; it was not an epistemological [or interpretive] condition enabling the individual to recognize himself in his singularity as a desiring subject and to purify himself of the desire that was thus brought to life" (HS II, 89).

The conditions for a genealogy of the subject of desire would have to wait eighteen hundred years for a time in which the subject's truth might be suspected to exist in the subject's history, a history that was to some degree constitutive of the subject. Ethical subjectivity was born in a power relation in which truth was known to exist outside of the self's relation to itself: the ethical self was formed in a virile, hierarchical structure in which the truth of proper dominion was recognized as existing in a realm as free of the subject's history as the proper subject was free of unnatural pleasure. The principles controlling the use of pleasures was formed nonhistorically, and the ethical subject must know how to distribute them, set limits by them, and establish a hierarchy governed by them. An ontological order was to be established by self-mastery in the self's relation to itself, and its hard task was to maintain this order against the disorder that threatened it from within. Foucault comments that the attraction of this project was the 'beauty of soul' that it promised, that this was an *aesthetic* order controlled by principles that were timeless, outside of the self, and accessible to the free self. The free man must engage with severe discipline in a battle in order to create a beautiful thing that was himself.

One of the implications of this account is that within the inherited structures of the ethical subject there is a privileging of assertiveness and virility that radically privileges males in Western culture. A question that I can raise but not answer is whether ethical subjectivity continues to downplay nonactive values, the values of touch for the sake of touch, hearing without assertion, the gentle qualities of animality such as nonjudgmental nurturance, nestling, gathering, licking, grace of movement, and quiet compatibility with an environment. Does our need for dominance, predisposition to competition, and drive for self-protective selfhood at the heart of ethical subjectivity continue, even after centuries of transformations, such that efforts for goodness and justice, silently, almost unthinkably, cultivate the traditionally male characteristic of assertive virility? Is the ekstasis of victory, that elevation and exhilaration that come with overcoming obstacles and bringing to completion a project of domination, part of what ethical conduct must mean? Does the activity of ethical conduct include a translation of ancient male conduct? In ethics, do we demean a side of our lives that has been branded passive and thus given to enslavement by the elevation of mastering activity as an excellence in self-fulfillment?

We have seen that care for self was focused on self-mastery. The issue is not whether one experienced desires that were bad and needed to be purged. Care for self did not have the purpose of eliminating bad desires or desire as such but had, rather, the purpose of controlling excessive pleasures. Foucault calls his genealogical study of the subject an ethical study, and as his work progressed from volume II to volume III he became clearer that the manner of self-relation and not the content of moral codes was his primary interest. The difference of desire from self-relation means that we need to hold our attention on self-relation, not on desire, as we follow Foucault's account of the formation of the subject of desire. Ethical selves were formed by a self-relation the truth of which was known to exist outside of the self and the known telos of which was a well-measured administration that followed principles which existed totally independently of the self. This means that desire remains on the periphery of Foucault's study of ethical subjectivity since in *his* knowledge of the formation of ethical selfhood desire is not its truth.

I stress the growing importance of the distinction in Foucault's work between moral codes and acts on one hand and ethics on the other. *Ethics* refers to self-relation. *Moral codes* refers to a body of prescriptions and rules, and *moral acts* refers to specific practices of caring for the self by moral codes. *The Care of Self* is part of a genealogy of ethics, and the self-relation studied in that book is a personal mode of caring for the self that had a form of governance as its telos and a body of truth the knowledge of which made freedom from self-enslavement possible. When Foucault gives an account of the care of self he is thus giving an account of the emergence of a different way of being in Greco-Roman ethos: the emergence of a self that is formed in relating to itself by caring for itself. The structures of this way of being are fateful for us in the sense that a capacity for internal reference is coming to be that makes itself its objectifying project. From this capacity we may expect a lineage in which the self is a problem to itself, the *governance* of selves is extremely important, mastery and a high degree of assertiveness are primary values, knowledge of the self's desires and pleasures is necessary for good conduct, care and control are closely associated, and truth, control, privilege, and knowledge are affiliated. Most important of all, perhaps, is that the subject who knows and judges Foucault's work is in this lineage, that both the authorship and the readership of this genealogical claim are of the studied lineage. In developing genealogical knowledge and in being a part of this lineage, we need not only find that we are not connected to something outside of our history to which we are bound by desire and by the truth of our self-relations. We as genealogical knowers also find that we are not the selves that nongenealogically we know ourselves to be. In referring to itself genealogically, the self refers to a lineage that is not like the selves we know in our modern truths, and yet the genealogical knowledge that interrupts traditional self-knowledge is also *in* the lineage of care for self, for as we have seen, resistance to totalization and domination are strong motives in Foucault's work, and self-objectification is a part of his genealogical project.

This is a strange situation. In the form of caring for itself in genealogical knowledge, the self—the subject of ethical knowledge as well as the subject of moral practices—finds itself to be other than the moral principles that it follows and other than the desire that it regulates. It finds itself also to be other to itself. In the tradition of the majesty—Foucault says the *glory*—that the moral self classically assigned to itself as the moderate subject of self-knowledge, it—the self— now finds, by genealogical knowledge, that it is a product of complicated processes of subjection behind which there is no selfhood to be realized and no locale of nonhistorical truth to give it ontological support. In its structure of power the self does not even belong to the force of desire and thus often finds self-satisfaction in the denial of desire and pleasure. But it also knows that it is harmed by totalization, that it is not made for enslavement, and that the liberty that it seeks is without a model or a generative form. Formless freedom. A fragmented self. Care, now without a home for nurturance or a guide for truth. A self whose dreams of a transcendent guide and of a propriety that opens to truth and freedom now finds that such dreams come of circulations of powers that mask a structure of dissymmetrical control. It isn't bad, remember. But it *is* dangerous, and the danger is to itself as well as to others.

So while the changes in moral codes that Foucault describes often attract our attention, these changes do not form the substance of Foucault's history of sexuality. *That* substance is the formation of self-relation on the basis of aphrodisia. His is the remarkable claim that the acts, restraints, and disciplines that produced certain forces of pleasures (aphrodisia) have led to the formation of a self-relation that has dominated Western culture in many forms and has made possible not only genealogical knowledge but our suspicions concerning it. The problem facing Foucault is to show how we are to be selves in the ethos of genealogy while we also stand outside of ourselves in circulations of powers that, without being a self, produce selves. In showing this he must also address the question: how are we to know about our selves without falling prey totally to the history of subjection?

Before turning directly to this problem and question, I wish to follow part of Foucault's account in HS III, *The Care of the Self* (the discipline of self-centering and self-intensification), in order to clarify an aspect of subjection to which, in our scholarly work, we are most likely to fall prey.

The ascetic ideal which plays so obvious a part in the formation of the ethical self is found in Foucault's account in a mistrust of pleasures in the late classical period. They can abuse the body and the soul and must be contained by a *well-disciplined regulator* and by *practices of containment*: Foucault emphasizes specifically marriage and disaffection with the spiritual meaning of love for boys. Pleasures can weaken the body, distract the soul, disperse the body's and soul's interaction. 'Containment' indicates strengthening and is paired against 'dissolution'. The development of an obsession with unity and unfragmented wholeness for the self is clearly anticipated by the emerging ideal of desire controlled by truth and administered by an agent of vigilant self-knowledge. The most dangerous of pleasures were found in sex. Orgasm was associated with epilepsy by Galen, for example. A dark humor congests the ventricles of the testicles and this humor mixes with sperm and results in a dangerous spasm, like a seizure, when it is expelled in its agitation. Retained sperm can also obstruct the vessels of the uterus and cause it to enlarge with hysterical consequences. Further, too frequent expulsions of sperm can dry out the nerves and cause tension. The man must confront this dangerous, problematic region of aphrodisia and become the subject of his acts of desire under the guidance of reason and truth. Good health defined in terms of a balance of soul and body is associated with salvation as much as it is with good health, and both health and salvation have as one of their foundations a mistrust of pleasures.

Given the dangers of pleasures to individuals, one must take care of oneself by *developing an art of existence*. There was, of course, already a body of teaching stemming from many sources—Socrates is primary among them—that prescribed ways to care for the self and that were adapted, elaborated, and applied in relation to aphrodisia. One finds in the writings of Albinus, Apuleius, the Epicureans, and Epictetus, among many others, injunctions to care for and cultivate the self with the aim of perfecting one's life, avoiding suffering, and giving reason power over both the body and itself.

To develop the art of existence a person must *actively develop a group of careful practices*. One must pick times for meditation and "retreating into oneself" (Marcus Aurelius), for physical exercise, for careful, exploratory conversations. People seek out friends of like mind and form more or less structured communities, recognize the more and less wise, seek council, and establish customs and obligations that encourage the care of self. Shared experience was important, so letters, exchanged treatises, and soulish conversations were highly valued. "Soul service," Foucault says, "includes the possibility of a round of exchanges with the other and a system of reciprocal obligations" (HS III, 54). The development of this art thus transformed slowly from a private endeavor to increasingly structured communities.

The diagnosis and cure of souls was *closely associated with the practice of medicine*. Indeed, the lines between treating problems of character and problems of the body were not clearly drawn in classical Greece. And we should not be surprised since the relation of control between the soul and body was so important to the self-relation that was developing. Epictetus described his school as a "dispensary for the soul" and compared it to a physician's consulting room. People new to the techniques of self-cultivation were like sick people who needed treatment. They were in a pathological state. The first step is to recognize that one is like a sick person, feeble in soul and body, ignorant and fragile. Then the proper medications and exercises can be prescribed. These are combinations worth noting as we think of the formation of the ethical self: bodies and souls, ignorance and sickness, doctors and philosophers, lostness and salvation, psyche and medicine, reason and health. We must keep in mind that at this early time *an individual's* self-relation is at stake in contrast to a city of citizens who are governed by externally enforced proprieties, laws, roles, and appearance, and that small communities of concern developed around the problem of self-relation, communities that exercised maximum vigilance over the self of the individual and taught him *self*-governance by the governance and knowledge that they provided. And all of this is in the context of sickness, cure, health, and salvation. Care of self was coming to mean an achievement of good health in both soul and body by means of an actively employed and true self-knowledge in the form of self-mastery.

When we combine the social and community-forming aspects with those having to do with health, knowledge, reason, and salvation and hold in mind that self-relation rather than a social role is developing, we can see that a man's subjecting his pleasures to the dominance of this structure of care enmeshes his privacy in a social structure and an authoritarian knowledge which at this time had no power of official sanction, but could with time and changed public policy come to have that power. Foucault's claim is that there is, on the one hand, a move inward to self-relation in contrast to proper citizenship in the *polis* and, on the other, communities formed that were focused on this emerging emphasis. When we recognize that self-knowledge is interwoven with knowledge that infinitely and perfectly transcends the self and offers the possibility of physical and psychical well-being, we can hear the overtones of mystery and transcendence of individuals in the very knowledge that guided proper self-care. When care of selves later becomes a public obligation, whether on the part of the church or the state, the dynamics of self-relation, based as it is on self-knowledge, demand either that the self be known and transparent to the caring authority or is so formed by the authority that it is already known and transparent when it takes individual shape. Confession or social normalization by education and punishment are two possible means of creating the degree of knowledge and transparency necessary for proper care. Further, masculine dominance is both a problem and a defining element in this self-relation, and one can expect an elaboration of the privileging of distinctly male aggressiveness and virility in the way in which the ethical self most properly conducts itself. A remarkable mixture takes place, like a chamber of powers, in which transcendence, truth, masculine privilege, and the capacity to become hale and whole as a human circulate with each other and create an affectional and reflective attitude regarding desire that will have enormous ramifications.

The making of self-relation vis-à-vis desire required *specific practices* whereby habits and identity are formed. These practices *produced* a self-knowledge which was lived as an identity. One needed regularly to test himself to see if he could do without unnecessary things and remain constant and independent in himself. The Epicureans, for example, carried out disciplines of abstinence to show how a more stable satisfaction could be found when one needed only the most elemental things. The Stoics, on the other hand, prepared for privation without disturbance by absenting themselves from all attachments.

Practices of self-examination accompanied the disciplines of abstinence. A man looked into himself, reviewed his actions and words, sifted through the day's moments, scrutinized and judged what he had done and not done. Learning honest and true self-judgment was an important part of caring for oneself, and to find satisfaction not in experienced pleasures but *in the process* of self-examination was crucial to becoming a true self. One learned how to conduct oneself and which rules to follow when one became a critical spectator of oneself. The goal was not to reject oneself or to cultivate guilt but to become a serene judge of what is best to do by coming to know oneself by thorough and complete self disclosure in reference to reason and transcendent truths.

A third practice is one of *thinking about what one thinks*. The individual "steadily screens representations, examines them, monitors them, and sorts them out. One is like a night watchman, in the words of Epictetus, 'who checks the entries at the gates of cities or houses'." This is a practice of attitude whereby all thoughts and representations are examined and evaluated. One wants to find which are valid and which are untrue. Nothing should be privileged that is shallow or misleading. Looking behind the scenes of thought for their basis and merit is necessary if one is to care for oneself. Only what is consonant with the self's freedom and rationality may be entertained, and thinking about one's thoughts in practical self-reflection is an important discipline. Thought's self-objectification is part of the cure for wayward people who do not know who they rightfully are to be in the world. We note again in this study of subjectivation the movement into the primacy of the self in order to know oneself properly in relation to others.

Foucault calls the general principle for these practices *conversion to self* (as distinct to detaching oneself from oneself, or the discipline of genealogical critical thought). (*Epistrophé eis heauton*: attention paid to a person or thing, regard, wheeling about, reaction, twisting-turning about: turning to self with regard to the self.) This turn demands attention to what does not enslave one to what is untrue and passing. It expects freedom from the everyday, from curiosity, momentary absorption, and hence from the body's search for momentary intense and engrossing pleasure. "The soul stands on unassailable grounds, if it has abandoned external things; it is independent in its own fortress; and every weapon that is hurled falls short of the mark. Fortune has not the long reach with which we credit her; she can seize none except him that clings to her. Let us then recoil from her as far as we are able," says Seneca (quoted in HS III, 65). One is to "belong to himself" in the sense of possess oneself by self-mastery, i.e., one is to be one's own slave and master according to true knowledge. One answers to oneself and is free from the preoccupations of the external world. In conversion to self one possesses oneself without anxiety, fear, or hope. Self-possession is an end in itself. This is the change the development of which Foucault wants to follow in antiquity: the self forms itself as an ethical subject that replaces, as far as ethics is concerned, all authorities in the world and comes to its identity as it knows and brings to bear universal principles of nature or reason. Because the self is frail and subject to disease and dispersion, self-knowledge grows in importance: "The task of testing oneself, examining oneself, monitoring oneself in a series of clearly defined exercises, makes the question of truth—the truth concerning what one is, what one does, and what one is capable of doing—central to the formation of the ethical subject. . . . the end result of this elaboration is still and always defined by the rule of the individual over himself. But this rule broadens into an experience in which the relation to self takes the form not only of a domination but also of an enjoyment without desire and without disturbance" (HS III, 68).

An Excursus on Pleasure

An absence of pleasure is at the core of self-conversion by uses of pleasure. A distance of pleasure and desire is not meant by the word *jouissance*, although it means 'use' as well as 'enjoyment', 'possessing pleasure', and 'being in the possession of pleasure'. *Jouissance* has the sense of simultaneous sexual, spiritual, bodily, and mental involvement as pleasure. The word refers us to a body of pleasure, an earthy inclusion without an implied mysticism. *Jouissance* is not without meaning—indeed it is saturated with meaning in the sense of having pleasure and mind together at once. But it lacks the sense of having meaning *in* a regard for something that stands outside of the meaning's structure. *Jouissance* does not occur as representation or as object of use or possession. This immediacy, this fullness of pleasure, is lost in the distance of the self's usage. *Subjection* means a loss of pleasure by a mastery of pleasure. By subjecting pleasure and desire to the interests of a discipline of good health, the subject of desire gains their determination and loses that indeterminateness that occurs in *jouissance*. The subject of desire comes to possess pleasure and desire, thereby losing them by mediating them. This self gives pleasure a space that is not of pleasure but is of an ascesis that has its own space and time. The body's space and time of pleasure is determined by the space and time of a mastering agency. The body might know pleasure in a way that gives its own words and sounds as it bodies itself toward its own absence. It might undergo pleasure's pleasing in a heightened mortality, a fragile passing, an intense and deathly movement which brings together living and dying without a clear division, providing a passage that comes of itself as it leaves itself, enriching and sickening, without practical foresight, threatening disaster as it touches the deepest flow of life, giving everything and losing it in the gift, leaving behind exhaustion and only a possibility of return. Unsecured vibrations of touch, febrile flesh without the transcendence of self-projection, without the anxiety of the self's time.

The subject of desire knows of such fullness in a movement of abandonment. In order to preserve pleasure it abandons the region of *jouissance*. *Jouissance* 'uses' in the sense of 'engages fully and indulges'. The subject of desire 'uses' in the sense of 'converts pleasure to the service of something that is outside of pleasure'. When we recall that the antonyms of pleasure are anger, pain, injury, and displeasure, we can see that Foucault is showing, in an elaboration of Nietzschean "resentment", that the ethical self emerges in a movement that takes pleasure away from itself, a movement that angers and hurts while it fulfills a different body of intentions. The ethical self finds *its* satisfaction in a loss of pleasure. I believe that this movement shows one of the dangers embedded in ethical subjectivity: it is made in a nonverbal antagonism between itself and the force of pleasure, a structurally dictated suspicion of *jouissance* that not only makes a language of *jouissance* impossible but also constructs a disinclination regarding pleasure's pleasing and an inclination toward satisfaction in the severance of body from proper meaning and value. Does this mean that the tendency to universalize and totalize has as part of its destiny a demeaning of the body in the self's 'highest' interests and pursuits? Does an angry and antagonized body find revenge in selves that are twisted from their own bodies and the bodies of others in the pursuit of conquests and control? Does the distanced body angrily give suffering in the self's pursuit of a proper measure? Would we have a different compassion if we were free of the control of those values that find satisfaction in victory at the expense of pleasure's pleasing, values that seek to overcome the death that lets pleasure be?

The problem that Foucault is uncovering is that the ethical subject may well displease the body in satisfying itself, that it angers its life in attempting to satisfy its life, and that it endangers its life by the offense that it makes as it attempts to give itself a proper life. This danger is at the core of his suspicion that radical insensitivity to the body and cruelty indwell the best intentions of ethical responsibility.

The Ethos of Genealogy

> At this point, I would say that Foucault, who once defiantly declared himself a "happy optimist," was a man in danger, who, without making a display of it, had an acute sense of the perils to which we are exposed, and sought to know which ones are the most threatening and with which it is possible to compromise. Thus, the importance for him of the notion of strategy, and, thus, also his toying with the thought that he might have been, had fate so decided, a statesman (a political advisor) as well as a writer—a term he always rejected with more or less vehemence and sincerity—or a pure philosopher.
>
> —M. Blanchot, in *Foucault/Blanchot*

I have highlighted the process of subjection in the formation of the ethical subject: the emergence of this subject includes self-attentiveness—the making of inwardness—by means of strategies of self-mastery. The object of mastery by practices and knowledges was the forces of pleasure, or aphrodisia. Excess is to be avoided; proper measure by governance according to ascendant truths is to be achieved. A certain male virility, conceived within an active-passive polarity, is privileged. The ethical self forms in a highly governed use of pleasure. Governance in this context means self-control. Freedom in this context means the privilege of self-activation as distinct to being governed by others. A man achieves freedom by means of an autonomy that he creates by transcending the forces of pleasure in self-mastery. Both pleasure and self could be properly known only in the propriety achieved by a well governed self: self-control and domination of the forces of pleasure are necessary conditions for true knowledge. Health, virility, mastery, domination, control, transcendence, governance, knowledge, and truth circulate together in the ethical self's emergence. This self was formed in a hierarchial play of powers in which the truth of proper dominion was recognized as existing in a realm as free of the subject's history as the proper subject was free of unnatural pleasure. Freedom, elevated truth, and transcendence of whatever is ordinary and contingent give the emerging ethical self an early oblivion to the problematized history of its own necessities.

By the powers of genealogical knowledge we have found ethical normativity turning in Foucault's discourse to a practice of critical interruption. Reflectivity has become in his work a process of constantly checking the imperatives and roles that are given to us—checking in the senses of hindering the exercise of normative discursive powers, impeding their reflective and cultural force, and verifying their lineage. His genealogy thus provides a checking knowledge of social, cultural, and discursive relationships. Its positive cut occurs as it creates a new relation of restraint in connection to other ways of knowing and doing. Its resistance to totalization is found in its making no demands to replace authoritatively other discourses. It is designed for encounter and interruption, not for providing a new style and language that will supplant other, less adequate discourses. It does not destroy so much as it plays a role of the new kid on the block. Foucault's work eliminates options much less than it creates tension with other knowledges, makes demands on them, and casts doubt on many discourses. He has no desire to create a new ethics. But he does intend to alter power games by adding new elements to the cultural milieu. That is the movement he wants in the circulation of powers that he encounters. We, of course, want to totalize him negatively by asking about completions that he has no intention of establishing. What about our human need for myths, transcendence, and ideology? Can we live together without axiomatic and authoritative beliefs? What if our society loses its ideals and goals? We ask these questions because we naturally look for something reasonably complete, reasonably limited by an origin and a telos, and reasonably thorough in its suggested solutions to problems. Foucault, however, primarily intends to make problems, to unsettle, to look again at axioms of knowledge and behavior, and to affirm the incompleteness that we may wish to eliminate by seeking conclusive answers to such questions.

I have organized this discussion around four problem areas: problematizations or regions of transformation, the sense of ascending transcendence, totalization or the tendency toward fascism, and power as relational circulation. I believe that some of Foucault's most unsatisfying limits occur in these problem areas. (In a moment we must ask, unsatisfying to whom?) In the absence of totalization we lack teleologies by which to make sense of the world and our lives as a whole. The absence of totalization means fragmentation in the absence of a unifying system of belief, speculation, and myth. Without a sense of transcendence we find ourselves leveled to a space of lineage that holds no resonance for something more splendid, more terrible, more beautiful than these fragmentated lines of knowledges and powers. We wonder, in the affirmation of the loss of a sense of ascending transcendence, if we can have loftiness of spirit and visions of mystery. When power is conceived in terms of relational circulations, the possibility is removed that we can see problems as the consequences of repression of something natural and, for all practical purposes, timeless. Foucault finds our problems within relationships that have been innovative and creative. He puts in doubt our creative efforts by attaching innovation to the relations that oppress and destroy. We have in Foucault the expectation that in the fragmented, various powers that constitute our identities lie possibilities for resistance and modification, that relations of powers are crossed and double-crossed by differences and counterplays by virtue of the margins, differences, and hierarchies that the relations create. In his knowledge there are no unproblemed axioms, nothing to be reverenced, nothing that is internally stable.

In a 1980 interview conducted in San Francisco by Michael Bess the following exchange took place.

Question: I have to admit, I find myself a bit lost, without points of orientation, in your world—because there's too much openness.
Foucault: Listen, listen.... How difficult it is! I'm not a prophet; I'm not an organizer; I don't want to tell people what they should do. I'm not going to tell them, "This is good for you, this is bad for you!"
I try to analyze a real situation in its various complexities, with the goal of allowing refusal, and curiosity, and innovation.

Question: And as regards your own personal life, that's something different...
Foucault: But that's nobody's business!
I think that at the heart of all this, there's a misunderstanding about the function of philosophy, of the intellectual, of knowledge in general: and that is, that it's up to them to tell us what is good.
Well, no! No, no, no! That's not their role. They already have far too much of a tendency to play that role, as it is. For two thousand years they've been telling us what is good, with the catastrophic consequences that this has implied.
There's a terrible game here, a game which conceals a trap, in which the intellectuals tend to say what is good, and people ask nothing better than to

be told what is good—and it would be better if they started yelling, "How bad it is!"

Good, well, let's change the game. Let's say that the intellectuals will no longer have the role of saying what is good. Then it will be up to people themselves, basing their judgment on the various analyses of reality that are offered to them, to work or to behave spontaneously, so that they can define for themselves what is good for them.

What is good, is something that comes through innovation. The good does not exist, like that, in an atemporal sky, with people who would be like the Astrologers of the Good, whose job is to determine what is the favorable nature of the stars. The good is defined by us, it is practiced, it is invented. And this is a collective work.

Is it clearer, now? (*History of the Present*, no. 4, Spring 1988)

Many of us have felt ourselves afloat, like Michel Foucault's interviewer. And Foucault responds in the absence of anything off of which the wise, the pure, the well-disciplined and knowledgeable can read what is good for us. Here is perhaps where we can feel most clearly the impact of the loss of a sense of ascending transcendence: the intellectual loses his or her privilege of reason and insight to aspire to tell us what is to be normative. The stark absence in Foucault's work of the traditional poet's quasi-religious role to speak in and to a universal human spirit, the absence not only of charismatic Wagnerian self-seriousness but also of the philosopher's privilege to speak wisely and clearly of matters that can tell us how we should be—the philosopher as either a surrogate for the seer or the person of rational truth—such consequences of thought and knowledge without transcendence leave Foucault, on his own terms, with a morality of refusal, curiosity, and innovation: he refuses to accept any proposal as self-evident; he needs to know how knowledge and subjects of knowledge come to be as they are; and he seeks out in our reflection those things that have never been thought or imagined. Further, he is unwilling to normalize this genealogical ethos beyond its local context. Instead of working with things or the representation of things, he works with the formation of subjects who recognize, represent, and objectify themselves and other people and things in describable ways. His field for research and thought is made up of forms of subjectivity, relations of powers, and the formations of truths. Deviation is as informative for him as spiritual truth. The historically concatenated and unrecognized components of subjects who have made major contributions to the formation of Western humanism are as arresting from him as the "games of truth" that constitute our humanism. I find in him no nostalgia for departed Gods, no hope for a saving power, no regret that both theism and humanism have lost their creative edge, no obsession over the powers of metaphysical thought to turn us back, despite our best efforts, to the meanings that have perennially determined us. I note in his work an absence of that suffering peculiar to sensitive souls in our tradition. His ambitions are local. He wrote in a short autobiography under a pseudonym that

> it is undoubtedly too early to appreciate fully the rupture that Michel Foucault, Professor at the Collège de France (Chair of the History of Systems of Thought since 1970) introduced in a philosophical landscape heretofore dominated by Sartre and by what the latter termed the unsurpassable philosophy of our time: Marxism. From the very start, *Madness and Civilization* (1961), Michel Foucault has been elsewhere. His task is no longer one of founding philosophy on a new *cogito*, nor of systematizing things previously hidden from view. Rather it is to interrogate that enigmatic gesture, perhaps characteristic of Western societies, by which true discourses (including philosophy) are constituted with the power we know them to have. (*History of the Present*, no. 4, Spring 1988, p. 13)

He wanted to make an impact in our culture by critically and genealogically taking apart the certainties of our lives, by tracing the lineages of their component parts and of the agencies that hold them in power. He sees himself in the *critical* tradition of Kant, sans pure reason, transcendental structures, the desire of reason, the transcendental unity of apperception, necessary beliefs, or moral imperative: critique and intelligence on the surface of history, so contingent that even the rules and structures of contingency do not open to mystery or to the possibility of proper, serene attunement to Being in its revealing concealing difference from everything namable or experienceable. He is relaxed about using such metaphysical words as principle, history, reflection, freedom, power, and subjectivity because he finds them already so eroded in his genealogical context that they can inspire at best only vigilance, resistance and uncertainty. On his own terms his genealogies make a small interruption in the flow of our knowledges and institutions. But he is not a spokesman for Being or other momentous things. To be a prophet or a moralist or an ontologist would be to lose his local perspective and to lose the register of the minute work demanded by genealogy.

Foucault asks at the end of the quotation I gave earlier, "Is it clearer now?" and the answer is no. It is not clearer now, and it is not clearer because there is no clarity concerning what is good and bad. The generation of what is harmful out of solutions to other harms seems to be pervasive. There are moments of clarity within given knowledges and values. But on the whole we have no idea what individuals will do with the knowledge generated by genealogy or how goods might shift under the impact of genealogical knowledge. When we look at the actions of ethical subjects genealogically we find a mess of contradictions. In ethical subjectivity we find cruelty and mania for power over others; we find destructiveness at the core of ethical agency; and if we are intellectuals, we who do genealogical studies, as we look for causes and motivations behind practices and institutions, will try to synthesize, regulate, and institute. On Foucault's account we *must* do such things as ethical, knowing beings. And as genealogists we will know that we are determined in this in being the subjects that we are. And we will look further, curious about our own danger as we say yes and no. Shall we despair in this or be energized, give up or affirm the mess and our desire to clear things up? Is it possible for us to be moral and not to universalize, to be moral and local at the same time, to be moral and to affirm our fragmentation as selves and as peoples?

If I ask these questions in a moral persona, I feel discouraged in Foucault's legacy. I feel a terrible lack of the arising, ecstatic spirit. I feel the pain of small gains and large defeats before injustices and unspeakable suffering. I feel the threat of bestiality, of the cat's quiet eyes as it cracks the wren's skull, of the tyranny of the strongest when reason fails. I want to feel the inspiration that breeds hope by the force of knowing that a greater cause is served, that from ashes the human spirit rises with new energy coming from an unquenchable source. I want that meaning that is promised in being the ethical subject that I am given to be: the meaning of truth and beauty and mystery that gives Apollo to shine, God to love, and the human spirit to soar. In this persona I know the powers that have collected in the lineage of the care of self. I know that fragmentation and a life given to pleasure are the elements of sickness, enslavement, and disaster. I desire to be guilty when I violate principles of truth and right. I need to release my violation, to confess, to renew myself, and to turn again to what is good, lasting, and right.

But in the genealogical persona I wonder if pleasure that is associated with the body's desire can be well known by the ethical subject. Is that pleasure now so connected to the ethical subject that it is found usually at a distance from the experiencing self, as though one *possessed* his or her pleasures, as though pleasures belonged to one in that sense, as though pleasure were an adjunct to the self, like a property that can be possessed and transformed—spiritualized, humanized—because it is external to the self's reality? Pleasure in this relation is a concern—'to concern' is one of the overtones in the word *belong*—and the body's difference to the self is meant in this kind of concern. I suspect that the self's satisfactions arise out of successful mastery, as when one gives the body its due at appropriate times and places. By the accomplishment of propriety in the distance that we give to pleasure, the self's distance from the body is reflected in the depth and in the spiritual quality of this satisfaction that is so different from the body's happy gratification.

Within the persona of genealogical ethos I also suspect that the very height and depth of the self's satisfactions constitute a fragility. This subject that is made of disciplines designed to overcome all that is trivial, mean, and enslaving has its ascetic substance—its self-forming disciplines—to rely on. It can take pride in its activity even when that activity sacrifices the self in favor of a higher truth. In this lineage sacrifice, wounding, and self-formation are closely connected. The self's withdrawal from nonselflike attachments provides the space for those powers that free one to truth and self-discovery. But the fear of enslavement and everydayness has in its aversion a barely controlled fear of what comes *only* to pass away with no claim to universality or ultimate truth and meaning. The ethical subject is made to need to know what fills the spaces of fragmentation, spaces that offer no resonance of continuity beyond repetition, collection, and reflection. The ethical subject is not made to know what Foucault calls freedom and liberation. It is made to master itself and others in a power of life and truth that masters it. The living form of ethical self-relation is made to belong to itself in a transcendental world to which it belongs. It is made to resist the triviality of locales of knowledge that resist their own drift toward universalization. This subject finds its satisfaction in its difference from body by virtue of a sense of superiority that invests its own spiritual movement. I suspect that its pleasure means not only mastering and subjection, but also protection from the mortality of the body's pleasures. Perhaps it is fear of that mortality—and a trivial mortality at that—that provides sufficient anxiety to prefer to 'mean well' than to let the body pass away in the pleasures of its touch and the totality of its movements when only its pleasure pleases.

The point has little to do with abandoning the self to pursuits of physical pleasures. It has to do with knowledge of those pleasures. Must they be at the distance of possession to be known? Is this not a question of intimacy *in* the self with the body, a question of what the self-with-body can be without mastery or domination? Is that not almost unthinkable for us: self with body without ascesis? How can the self resist *itself* in open curiosity with the body and in allowance for an innovation, for the emergence of something different in the body's draw and force? The unspeakableness of the body's pleasure has become a problem in Foucault's interruption of the authority of the ethical subject. Is pleasure in its pleasing something not subject to mastery? Is its unspeakableness witness to what is lost to the ethical subject? Is its unspeakableness what the cogito cannot know except by losing itself? Is this unspeakableness a mask of the body's mortality, a mortality that the ethical subject in its many phases is designed to eliminate as the self learns and relearns how to be responsible to itself?

9 | "Not to Be Trapped by Abuse . . . "
Genealogy and a Child's Pain

> How lovely it is that there are words and sounds! Are not words and
> sounds rainbows and illusive bridges between things that are eternally
> apart?
>
> —Nietzsche, *Thus Spoke Zarathustra*

WHAT MIGHT THE child have to do with genealogy and its study of origins
and descents? It is not only innocence and new beginning that we have to recall.
The study of formations of power for the genealogists in our tradition is at once
a study of human capacities within a given lineage. The lineage that Nietzsche
and Foucault submit to interrogation is that of Western humanity, of what our
period has often called *man*. A prominent creation of 'man' is modern humanism, a creation that took its departure from Greek culture, its transformation of
Catholicism. Foucault, for example, traces the formation of such capacities as
conscience, judgment, memory, and sexual attraction and the formation of such
institutions as hospitals, confession, and the family. This tracing is attuned to
power, to the control, for example, of bodies by the value of free male citizenship
in fifth-century Greece and the formations that develop in that control, such as
marriage, an ethics of self-control, and a drift toward asceticism in our Western
values. Such work as that of the genealogist seems out of the child's ken. Unless
we think of the child in connection with its abuse.

Distortion comes of abuse. The abused child learns to forget, to act as
though nothing abusive happened in order to find and accentuate the nurture
that is life-threatening. It learns not to know what happened, to separate itself
from its body and to return when it seems safe to be there again. It learns not
to tell what is accurate and what is not accurate. It learns to lose touch. If the
child is very young, abuse seems to register without judgment, without 'abuse'
but only as something inceptional, as something already there beyond focused,
later memory, to arise in dreams and images that are constitutive of the grasp
that would hold them for understanding, to arise in choking the cat to death or
beating the other child senseless.

Genealogy is born of the observation that our lineage carries in it and is
defined by abuses that produce capacities and institutions of distortion—ca-

pacities and institutions, for example, that are born in the need to forget their determinations and origins. Genealogy is a study intended to take small segments of a lineage apart, to find the power relations, to trace the events that chanced to impact the formation of this or that practice. It looks for abuses that are built into our structures of normalcy and necessity, for the unconscious strategies of distortion and forgetting that are a part of our capacities to know and discern. Various genealogies have shown, for example, a powerful and definitive predisposition in our lineage to find normative presence when withdrawal and lack of normative presence happen—not unlike the inclination of some of those who are abused to see the known abuser as a friend, as someone who loves them, or as a strange and unknown person. Genealogies have shown that in our lineage people who considerably exceed our normal ethos and its mythologies are taken in their abnormality to need correction and regimentation. Pleasure, death, and freedom require in our lineage elaborate strategies of masking and control. We may wonder about the energy expended to regiment and normalize. Is there distortion at work in producing a society of agreement? Is anything being systematically forgotten?

Distortion is a wily event. It can hide itself in the very activity that professes to recognize it. The genealogist is actively a part of the abuse in our lineage, and like the rest of us the genealogist acts within abusive and forgetful structures as he or she engages in the tracing and interrogating activity. It is not a question of standing outside of the lineage that includes abuse or of knowing nonabusively what constitutes abuse. It is a question of transformation, not of avoidance. Perhaps—and I am not sure whether this is true—perhaps a first or early step in such transformation is affective intellectual recognition of the pain and sorrow that are parts of our historic selves and that are continued by our practices.

I will return to this observation. I would like now to recall our image of the abused child in connection with an image of a child without abuse. I have used the image of the abused child as an opening to the abusiveness in our lineage that can be uncovered by genealogical work. And that image also has suggested the element of distortion that can characterize an abused consciousness, distortion that can define a lineage and the genealogist as well. The image of the abused child also suggests another image, that of a well-treated child, one who seems to have nothing to hide, who reaches out to the world with open curiosity, whose emotions are largely unrestrained, and who has not been treated as other than a child, not subjected, for example, to adult sexual acts or overpowering force. Let us allow this image of an abused child and that of a nonabused child to be beside each other, fused into each other. We have now one who is abused and not abused, a very mixed and oblique identity, an image that is not governed by singularity or unity. Each image transfuses the other, and the voice of each invokes the other. This transfusing of abuse and nonabuse is similar to what we as genealogists find in our lineage. We find ways of living, knowing, and valuing that constitute a mix of abuse and nonabusive elements that are not separable from each other, and transfusion that does not allow for anything in our culture to be thoroughly nonabusive or thoroughly abusive. This is a situation that requires caution because our goods are also dangerous and our bads are also structured by values that we identify as good. It is something like Milton's presentation of Satan. Not only is Satan the most drawing figure in *Paradise Lost*, but he also bears a major part in the poem's beauty of presentation and constellates the poem's life and movement.

This fusion of the abused and nonabused child is also something like the experience of some survivors of abuse. One survivor said to me that what makes a person crazy is "to stand holding both the experience of abuse and of being a nonabused child, holding apart the experiences of abuse from those that seem normal and everyday." She added: "The survivor has to bring them together so that nothing in her life is free of abuse and nothing is pure abuse. Even your understanding of your own abuse is subject to the abuse that you come to understand. Sometimes you get caught in the examination of the abuse and go round and round, examining it and reexamining it, over and over again. Then you do not break through the abuse. You just repeat it. There is no one in me untainted by abuse. When I look for that kind of pure model I just get trapped, then. Like there is part of me that is removed from my history of abuse. I have to go through it without knowing where I will come out. Not to be trapped by abuse, you have to know all of yourself as affected by abuse."

Caution is one word that names a proper response to such a divided, mixed, and dangerous situation, which is so like that of our lineage: the one who has faced his or her emotions toward abuse of others. Abuse does not hang upon us like clothes. It is lived as a surprising enjoyment of abusing others, as sometimes an eruption in an otherwise nonabusive life, as a dark, often subterranean predisposition to cruelty, and as a divided sense of identity that gives a strange and macabre sense in world relations. Consider what it is like not to be sure whether one's memories are accurate, not to know if one's knowledge is worthy of trust, to be unclear whether one's truths are lies, whether one's emotions are to be trusted, whether those around one are who they say they are, to feel that intimacy is an opening to pain and loss of life. To live a life consequent to abuse is often at once to be drawn to what one hates and simultaneously to be repelled by those one loves or wants to love. How could one not be cautious when one is in touch with the pain and sorrow of an abused life?

If Foucault and Nietzsche are right in their claims that our lineage is one of abuse mixed thoroughly without best and highest values and knowledge, then our image of the adult life that is produced by the abused child is not far off the mark when we think about our own ethos. Presumably we are most prone to a kind of craziness produced by images of purity that are split off from the abuses indigenous to our lineages and to repeat cruelties when we are unalert or unconcerned about the cruelties that constitute the fabric of our abilities to know and value and produce images. It is not a matter of goods and evils, pure rightnesses and pure badnesses. It is a question of dangers in the structures and movements of images, values and knowledges that are most intimately a part of who we are.

The image of the nonabused child is also powerful within our lineage. It is the one who takes delight in the life of things, even when it scatters them or smashes them or puts them in its mouth. The nonabused child is drawn to things in their appearances, in their color and variety. It plays with even the dangerous dog next door or the pretty bottle with poison in it. It explores freely, gets into everything, sleeps when it is sleepy and cries over frustrations, hunger, and all other discomforts. Its fingers are uninhibited. It explores, inhales the world, as it were, through its body, and enjoys all pleasures. It knows by moving, touching, turning upside down, and taking things apart. Its life is like one of repeated inceptions that are unrestrained by mores.

This is an image, of course, and one that over-distills the unabused child in us that functions in genealogical work. In an important sense, the unabused child does not know abuse and does not recognize the abused child. This inceptive innocence is in the lineage too, always contaminated, never a singular perspective, but powerful nonetheless in giving direction additional to the hurt seriousness of the abused one. I have seen a slapped child pause before its shocked scream, pause to feel the sting, the rush of blood, the pop of its neck, the radical change of moments. And then while crying, reach out to the one who injured it to find comfort and erasure of the shock of pain and confusion. Even *in* its abuse, the abused child gave expression to something unabused and opened to the life of that moment. I have seen an abuser grab the hurt child and hold it close and comfort it in a radical change of emotions that will indeed comfort the child and also help to produce a lifetime of distortion in the consciousness now being formed.

Let me begin a process of bringing these images into closer proximity to each other in their connection to genealogy by returning to the importance of recognizing the pain and sorrow that constitute an abused life. Revenge is always a possible response, and we should have little to say to those who adopt revenge against their abusers and others like them—except to note how much under the control of abuse they are and how close they (and we) are to abuse's abusive perpetuation. In addition to revenge we might also clearly determine and define the reality of abuse—and I believe that Nietzsche is right, that such analysis, interrogation, and determination is a form of abuse, in this case an abuse of an abuse, but abusive nonetheless—we might determine and define the occurrences of abuse so clearly that what is not this abuse comes to greater clarity. I suspect that the primary way to the reality of abuse is our pain and sorrow.

I suspect too that our pain and sorrow are hard to clarify because they will play a role in their own determination. I am thinking of the pain and sorrow in such normalcies as humility, philosophical thought, worship, and clear honesty, that is, the pain and sorrow that are distorted into happiness and a sense of well-being. But regardless of the difficulty and counterintuitiveness involved, by pain and sorrow perhaps we find a way to the abusive aspect of our lineage. And in them, perhaps, we find an option to revenge and in which option we see, perhaps, alternatives to the abuse that moves us.

I have been cautious about this suggestion because I am suggesting something that *might* happen in an interruption of the abusive. I do not know whether such an interruption is always possible, and I do not know whether any options to abuse would occur in any given interruption. I do know that my hopes and beliefs at this point are inevitably informed by the lineage whose interruption I am exploring. I believe that any suggestion of an abuse-free utopia is itself a kind of cruelty bred of distortion and denial. I am clear that pain and sorrow, while pervasive, are subtle and elusive in their many self-affirming occurrences. But by interruption we might give rise to other options, as I believe that this language of interruption itself arose from interruptions of the lineage of ascetic ideals and a dominance of the image of presence.

A basis for my hope might be found in the image of the unabused child that contaminates that of the abused child. In this image we might find an option to pain and sorrow that accompanies pain and sorrow, an open unpained interest in pain and sorrow, a playful exploratory disposition to the contortions and deceptions of an abused life. This child is equally arrested by the distortion of itself that returns to it in the mirror of pain and sorrow. It can laugh at the image and touch its cruel exterior and turn away from it to something else that arouses its pleasure or its interest. It is an image of inception that is excessive to the contamination of its ethea and lineages and that also arises in our ethea and lineages. Is this image itself a distorted memory? Or a memory that alleviates distortion? Quite without divinity this child sticks its finger in a cat's eye without abusing it. It quietly watches the other crying child without caring, or it cries with the other one without concern for it. It seems to be an image of something before abuse, enslavement, normalization, and goodness. Not before pain, but before pain and sorrow in their combination. I can hope cautiously that the unabused child—much less than an angel and certainly different from a God—gives an image of inceptions before abuses, one that offers differences within cultural interruptions, not ends and goals, but different beginnings.

But caution also rules at this point. Within a genealogical experience there is no pure image that is unaffected by the interests of the lineages that dominate and subject and that have an interest in tradition's forgetting its own contingent powers. Purity itself is such a value, purity that subjects and dominates the value of contamination, the sensuous flow of juices, the contradictions that define identities, and the impossibility of pure simplicity beyond the conflicts of power. Would it not be nice to have the pure child?

In order to consider further this caution before the hope that I have expressed, I turn to one of Foucault's more controversial examples of the production of sexuality in a situation that looks repressive. It is a situation that today we would describe as abusive.

> One day in 1867, a farm hand from the village of Lapcourt, who was somewhat simple-minded, employed here then there, depending on the season, living hand-to-mouth from a little charity or in exchange for the worst sort of labor, sleeping in barns and stables, was turned in to the authorities. At the border of a field, he had obtained a few caresses from a little girl, just as he had done before and seen done by the village urchins round about him; for, at the edge of the wood, or in the ditch by the road leading to Saint Nicolas, they would play the familiar game called "curdled milk." So he was pointed out by the girl's parents to the mayor of the village, reported by the mayor to the gendarmes, led by the gendarmes to the judge, who indicted him and turned him over first to a doctor, then to two other experts who not only wrote their report but also had it published. What is the significant thing about this story? The pettiness of it all; the fact that this everyday occurrence in the life of village sexuality, these inconsequential bucolic pleasures, could become, from a certain time, the object not only of a collective intolerance but of a judicial action, a medical intervention, a careful clinical examination, and an entire theoretical elaboration. The thing to note is that they went so far as to measure the brainpan, study the facial bone structure, and inspect for possible signs of degenerescence the anatomy of this personage who up to that moment had been an integral part of village life; that they made him talk; that they questioned him concerning his thoughts, inclinations, habits, sensations, and opinions. And then, acquitting him of any crime, they decided finally to make him into a pure object of medicine and knowledge—an object to be shut away till the end of his life in the hospital at Maréville, but also one to be made known to the world of learning through a detailed analysis. One can be fairly certain that during this same period the Lapcourt schoolmaster was instructing the little villagers to mind their language and not talk about all these things aloud. But this was undoubtedly one of the conditions enabling the institutions of knowledge and power to overlay this everyday bit of theater with their solemn discourse. So it was that our society—and it was doubtless the first in history to take such measures—assembled around these simple-minded adults and alert children, a whole machinery for speechifying, analyzing, and investigating. (HS I, 31–32)

Foucault is showing an instance in which the danger of sex is intensified and defined at a local level with the effect of contributing to the formation of a normative knowledge about sex and its proper regulation, the production of what Foucault calls 'sexuality'. In this instance from 1867, the retarded man's sexual play with a girl was in a twilight zone in which impropriety and what we now call abuse was in a process of being defined by means of a developing sensibility and a body of regulations. The man himself became an object of scientific investigation within an unconscious articulation of an atmosphere that was driven by interest in the formation and control of sexual pleasure. In this instance the control of bodies by regulation of sexual acts contributed to the formation of knowledges and attitudes that produced abuse and criminality out of "petty" and "inconsequential bucolic pleasures." *We* know that that was an abusive situation. Then, such knowledge was not fully in place. The retarded man's own abuse and that of thousands of other people by the authorities and medical scientists are part of the lineage of our knowledge and experience of sexual abuse. The transformation of such pleasures into guilt-producing and life-destroying trauma seems also to be a part of our knowledge of abuse.

The image of the abused child is itself within a lineage of knowledge and experience that suggests considerable caution, for the value and definition of abuse are complex and far from simple and pure. In this lineage of the formation of abuse there appears to be a questionable subjugation and domination of pleasure. Perhaps my image of the abused child invokes a lineage that has produced the meaning of *abuse* in such a way as to generate guilt and trauma in situations that have not always required such pain and sorrow. Perhaps it is within a lineage that facilitates a distortion that marks also abused awareness.

10 | Responsibility and Danger

I CONTINUE THE questioning of responsibility and danger because of the like-lihood that being responsible inevitably includes 'something' unresponsible, as well as a concentric movement of will that excludes what is unresponsible and gives increasing power to the forces of will and subjectivity. The subject is strengthened in responsible action. The movement of subjectivity is toward it-self as it acts with regard to something other to itself to which it gives itself. It draws itself toward itself as it draws toward the other. In responsibly choosing to belong to something—be that something a God, another person, a commu-nity, or an ideal—the individual is given intensity, a strengthened sense of the future and past, and above all a sense of worldly coherence and meaning. These are good things, and they seem to be excellent things if that to which we are responsible has unqualified worth. Such values are not denied when responsi-bility is put in question. Further, the question of responsibility's danger does not ask about that to which we are responsible. It asks about the value of re-sponsibility. If we protect responsibility by giving it unquestioned or hardly questioned value, the subject too will continue to enjoy a virtually unqualified value in our thought and action, and we will ignore or denigrate an absence of responsibility that is borne by responsibility. But when responsibility occurs as a question in our thinking, its own movement will be checked in our thought. Perhaps something unresponsible will take place, and perhaps the unresponsi-ble will expose a danger in responsibility, namely that it excludes something vital for the way of being that is to be served by responsibility, something that is lost to responsibility, something that is not some *thing* at all, but is other to the range of experience that is available to the responsible subject.

Our approach to the question of responsibility and danger will be from Nietzsche's thought of will to power. In both instances we will find that respon-sibility is a way of belonging to beings that closes out not only other ways of being but also the occurrence of unresponsibility. The issue is not whether we should be responsible but how responsibility is limited in its active power.

To what do we belong that gives us to be responsible? In asking this ques-tion I have in mind first Nietzsche's genealogy of morals in which he shows that in our values we have a dual heritage. On the one hand we belong to a lineage of effort to establish a meaningful conjunction of value and being. In this lineage both our thought and our ethics manifest unconsciously a deep terror before a completely nonhuman life force, a terror that turns us away from it. On the other hand, this is our 'own' movement of life. People's lives turn with a sense of life that has been formed by domination and suffering. A hopeless lack of meaning and will threatens that life. Nietzsche's genealogy shows that our response to this terror is definitive of our responsibility: moral responsibility, as it occurs in a turning away from the excessive energy and of nonhuman life, is a phenomenon of anxious willpower in the face of our force of life that has no regard for weakness and neediness. But this response is also part of the life force that belongs to us. It is part of a creative endeavor to establish a place of life, meaning, and power for frightened and disinherited people. This region of safety for disinherited people developed, as Nietzsche's genealogy has it, into what we can broadly call 'responsible humanity'. Humanity, in both theistic and nontheistic humanism, names in part the agency of our responsibility. In terror before the power of life we have become morally responsible, according to Nietzsche's genealogy. As humans we belong to this response of terror, which gives us our traditional morals and our traditional sense of moral responsibility.

That is one part of our moral heritage. Another part is shown by the work of Nietzsche's genealogy. It responds to the power of life and its lack of intrinsic meaning by attempting to redetermine within the heritage of responsibility the thought and language by which we speak and think responsibly. By showing that moral responsibility as such has within it a deep, unconscious, and inevitable hostility and fear regarding the way our lives move in their vitality, he puts moral responsibility in question. Moreover, by thinking *in* the *question* of responsibility, he responds to the urge to be which lacks moral responsibility. This responsibility of Nietzsche to unresponsible vitality includes the claim that another kind of affirmation can develop in which an individual, in undergoing the terror at the heart of our moral heritage, may also undergo the overturning and self-overcoming that are the hallmarks of vitality. One may come to a very different responsibility, a responsibility that probably will outgrow its own value, thought, and language in ways that we need not now even attempt to imagine. Nietzsche's responsibility is to this self-overcoming and is not to the creation of another construction that he knows will, at this time, repeat the formations that he holds in question. His responsibility is to think in the question and to be alert to all of the question's metaphysical dissatisfactions. Hence, for Nietzsche, thinking responsibly is an attempt to both describe and affirm responsibility's own self-overcoming.

A third part of his work is found in his recognition that moral responsibility is itself an expression of energy that falls outside of moral responsibility. The *creative* work of building a morally responsible culture considerably exceeds in its energy its own formation and the authority of its value and meaning. In his phrasing, value appears to derive from absence of value. In our phrasing, moral responsibility belongs to its own lack of moral responsibility. Or, to return to Nietzsche's phrasing, the creative work of moral responsibility manifests the will to conquer and to overpower its own responsible morality. There is something suicidal and deathly in the dynamics of Western moral responsibility: it overpowers in the name of self-disciplined release to life; it conquers in the name of freedom; it constricts and delimits in projects of expansive self-creation. In recognizing this danger, which comes to expression in multiple systems of social order, Nietzsche is responsible to the vital unresponsibility of moral responsibility. The danger of responsibility—its vital suppression of its own vitality—reveals also the will to be which is deranged in our lineage and which gives new life as responsibility is allowed to undergo a self-overcoming process.

We can see the degree of Nietzsche's involvement in the mainstream of our heritage when we recall that moral responsibility has often been presented as radically insufficient for those who would be faithful to God. The knowledge of God, as conceived, for example, by Jacob Böhme or Martin Luther, turns our moral accomplishments and their values into works of pride, because those works and the standards of their judgment derive from the interests of human life. Those interests are no less fallen than their immoral opposites, and their trajectory is toward a society of ignorance and recalcitrance before the creator that gives all life. Such ignorance is not benign. Its meaning is found in human suffering, anxiety, and lostness, which are preserved and advanced by the full range of responsibilities by which people attempt to live well together. Only in a radical suspension of the human-given meanings and values that govern our lives, a suspension that can rightfully occur only with obedience to God's self-disclosure, will human beings find the values that are proper to human living.

Nietzsche's thought does not surreptitiously make the will to power into God, but there is a spatial similarity in this sense: a region of otherness to every interpretation and creation, an otherness to which the vitality of our values and meanings belongs, vastly exceeds everything we can think, say, or value. This excess is like an abyss in the sense that no human capacity can bridge it. The excess bridges itself—discloses itself—and remains in its coming incomprehensible. Our appropriate response to the vast other takes a form of self-overcoming: only by renouncing the authority of what we create and our powers to grasp, understand, and structure, vis-à-vis alterity, do we take the first step toward affirmation of the otherness in question. This renunciation in Nietzsche's thought includes a self-overcoming movement that does not validate meanings and reasons; it is a movement that allows them to transform through their own creative power. And in that self-overcoming movement one is affiliated with—attuned to—the abysmal difference to human values and meanings. Life-movement then gives way to itself and leads beyond the structures that define it. In such an affirmation one belongs to self-overcoming. *This* belonging means that the individual's subjectivity, language, and thought are thoroughly in question by virtue of the vitality that animates the individual.

His own mission, Nietzsche says in *The Genealogy of Morals*, is given in the coming of his ideas, and those ideas do not arise from anything capricious or sporadic but from "a common root, from a *fundamental will* of knowledge" (GM, Preface, 2). Finding and speaking solely from an originary source is what is "fitting for a philosopher" (ibid.). The true philosopher has "no right to *isolated* acts of any kind: we may not make isolated errors or hit upon isolated truths." Our ideas, affirmations, rejections, doubts and qualifications "grow out of us with the necessity with which a tree bears fruit—related and each with an affinity to each, an evidence of *one* will, *one* health, *one* soil, *one* sun" (ibid.). After such a rousing call to responsibility to a single and original source of thought, and after such brave clarity regarding the impropriety of isolation in thought, he begins the next section of the preface with the phrase "because of a scruple peculiar to me." He confesses that his project of coming to know the origin of good and evil came to him when he was a boy of thirteen and that that project, as it grew, separated him from other philosophers. He found "his own country" for thought that was "like a secret garden the existence of which no one suspected." He is not saying that the origin of his thought is in himself, but he is saying that only by way of withdrawal from the pervasive understanding of morality could his knowledge of the origin and lineage of good and evil flourish. His responsibility to something fundamental and singular that came with the ideas he inherited—to the will to knowledge as distinct to the content of that knowledge—required withdrawal from the traditional community of thought. In the context of giving a genealogy of the ascetic ideal, for example, Nietzsche's own withdrawal and his many metaphors of the desert suggest that his allegiance to this question about good and evil and the question itself required his departure from the commonweal of philosophy. Indeed, he says that he must know how to keep silent in his secret garden if he is to reach the depths that his description requires. The note of withdrawal from common understanding is one to which we will be attuned. Presently this withdrawal appears to be in the service of reaching something singular and fundamental, not God in this case but will to knowledge. We hold open the questions whether the will to knowledge will discover itself to be something singular and one, or whether the discovered will withdraws from such language, whether the language of singularity is part of the lineage from which Nietzsche withdrew and in which moral responsibility has unquestioned priority. We are presently following a double movement. On the one hand, there is Nietzsche's process of discovery that moral responsibility secretly includes radical fear of the inhumanity of life and a cruel self-destructiveness that forms out of this fear. On the other hand, this process of discovery arises from Nietzsche's responsiveness to the danger and to the silence of the danger in practical and theoretical responsibility, a responsiveness that requires his withdrawal from the lineage that gives commonality and unity for philosophical thought.

What gives Nietzsche to be responsible in his undertaking? Not a community. Not the truths of a tradition. Not loyalty to anything shared openly with others. But rather a *"fundamental will* of knowledge" that he finds as he thinks philosophically and that draws him away from traditional communication in which that will is embedded. He was not drawn by a cause or by a specific social or political need. His thought did not belong to a specific good or even to a specific group of values, as we shall see, but to his fundamental will to knowledge which is not good or evil, not good or bad, which he links to philosophy, and which he also finds takes him away from philosophy. Do we catch a whiff of irresponsibility here in the middle of his responsiveness to the will of knowledge? Or do we sense unresponsibility—something neither responsible nor irresponsible—that comes with responsibility? We shall have to see.

Nietzsche speaks of possibly replacing one error with another when he reflects on his overturning of *The Origin of Moral Sentiments* by Paul Rée. This is what the "positive spirit" is willing to do: "to replace the improbable with the more probable," which may be no more than replacing one error with another. His larger project of putting in question the value of morality may be taken as part of his responsibility and also as possibly replacing one error with another. Nietzsche regularly puts in question his strongest certainties: that is part of his responsibility to the will to knowledge. It is not a matter of responsibly replacing an error with a truth or replacing a wrong with a right. Nietzsche's responsibility leads him to replace one error with possibly another error. So getting it right for the first time is not Nietzsche's responsibility. It is rather a matter of double questioning: questioning both the given intelligence and the replacement of that intelligence. Something other than goodness, truth, and correctness is fundamental for Nietzsche's responsibility, and this other comes with the will to knowledge that has moved Western thought without acknowledgment.

In section 5 of the preface Nietzsche says that Schopenhauer's thought taught him to be suspicious of the *value* of morality. His lesson did not arise positively from Schopenhauer's thought but from Schopenhauer's blind and, for Nietzsche, stupid articulation of the value of self-sacrifice. This gave Nietzsche a clue to the instinctive movement of Western morality. It moves out of a simple rejection of the egoistic and toward a systematic valuation that replaces the ego's life with something that exists only as an ideal projection. On the one hand, Nietzsche has withdrawn by the power of will to knowledge from the mainstream of philosophical endeavor and from the benefits of deep communal sharing, withdrawn to something like a spiritual desert in order to draw closer to the fundamental *will* to knowledge that is beyond good and evil, good and bad. On the other, this seemingly ascetic strategy is in the service of deny-ing the value of the anti-egoistic and of strengthening the value of the ego's *life*. This life manifests the will to knowledge. But are we on the way to quasi-relig-ious thought in which God is replaced by a subject that is no less absolute but only different in its identity? Are we learning to attune ourselves to a different voice, whose demands are no less taxing and lead to no less a piety of practice than those found in the heritage that Nietzsche intends to overturn? We are clear that he wants to identify and make optional the will's turning against its own life. Such turning is, for Nietzsche, the great danger of morality that exists silently in the value of morality. We are clear that by identifying this danger Nietzsche finds opened before him "a tremendous new prospect," "a new pos-sibility," and a "*new demand*" for a "*critique* of moral values" (GM, Preface, 6). We are also clear that in this new prospect a different kind of being from human being becomes imaginable, a way of being that opens to a future of affirmation that eliminates the dangerous cruelty of morality and gives way to the creative, self-overcoming intensity of life's movement. This new opening comes from re-sponsibility to the unresponsibility of the will to knowledge, from affirmation to the Dionysian of knowing that has been deeply hidden by "responsible" knowledge. This responsibility to unresponsibility creates a tension in his writ-ing that both accentuates the danger of responsibility and leaves open the pos-sibility that something quite different from moral responsibility might develop out of this tension.

In section 7 Nietzsche says that his plan for a genealogy of morals arose from the new prospect that opened for him when he saw the problem of the value of morality. This plan presupposes his withdrawal from the broad com-munity of moral persuasion: it comes from the *question* of morality. The question leads to a descriptive undertaking, which we know could be yet another error and the fundamental goal of which is an exercise of the will to knowledge that includes responsibility to unresponsibility. We can be sure that whatever knowl-edge is produced by this study, that knowledge will be for the sake of an exer-cise of will, and that that exercise will tell us more about responsibility than the knowledge that is given to us.

I interrupt this discussion, this responsibility to Nietzsche's text. I have been attempting to hear what is written. I am in a silent dialogue with other interpreters as well as with my own past readings of Nietzsche. It is a complex situation of transmissions and translations. I hear something that speaks si-lently as I read it. But there is also incoherence between the writing, which says nothing, and my hearing it by means of reading it. At times I hear it in German, its native language but not mine, at other times, in English, which is foreign to Nietzsche's text, but native to my hearing. This difference silently pervades the reading. My own work with Nietzsche constantly speaks through this writing without articulating itself in sounds or specific directives. There is a continuous play of subtle forces in this writing, such as the near canonization of Nietzsche's work, a pervasive recoiling from German national socialism, and an anxious retrenchment behind the continued priority of responsible selfhood and hope for a human future. The linguistic and institutional strands are gathered and interwoven in this writing and its reading. They take place without anyone doing the gathering. The divisions, exchanges, and couplings are not made by what I do or even by how I do what I do. I am responsible to the text and for what I say, but there is an excess of responsibility, more than responsibility, that takes place in the interpreting, writing, and speaking. There is, as Blanchot uses the word, something *unavowable* in the gathering of so many things, something that cannot be stated directly, subjectively produced, or openly acknowledged. My open response to the text—this interpretation, this experiment—leaves unspoken something that is unresponsible. Not irresponsible or responsible, but something that does not respond in the responding. Do I cover over the unresponsible as I work responsibly? What would I do were I responsible to the unresponsible? It is not a question of becoming irresponsible, and it is not a question of not responding. It is more like hearing something that is silent and that responsibility obscures, something that withdraws in responsibility. Does the unresponsible that accompanies my responsibility allow an opening to the thought that responsibility is dangerous?

To what do we belong that gives us to be responsible? Nietzsche answers this question first by giving a genealogical account of the lineage of "good" and "evil," "good" and "bad." We are interested, however, not only in his answer, but also in *his* responsibility as he carries out his genealogical work.

The English psychologists had given in Nietzsche's time the only histories of the origin of morality. Those responsible studies lack interest, Nietzsche says. The authors, however, *are* interesting. While they propose to show the evolution of human consciousness and sensibility from mean and primitive awareness to a summit of moral civilization, namely to European and specifically English morality, they are driven in fact to expose a deep *passivity* in human beings that has functioned paradoxically as human moral *agency*. In their will to know they expose considerably more than they can think or affirm. Our traditional moral agency is found in the inertia of habit, in "something purely passive, automatic, reflexive, molecular, and thoroughly stupid" (GM, I.1). While they acted responsibly within their moral context and advanced the highest morality they could conceive, operating within the English moralists was probably an unconscious instinct to belittle humanity, an equally unconscious suspicion that arose from resentment against the life that they wanted responsibly to justify. Perhaps embedded within their drive to understand themselves and their culture was hostility toward the very tradition to which they responsibly gave fully their conscious support. Perhaps they unconsciously, in the will to knowledge that moved them, took delight—hence the energy of their efforts—in the grotesque, paradoxical, questionable, and absurd quality of their very project, this project of elevating their kind above the unconscious motivations and primitive incompleteness of those people who were closer to animals than to Englishmen. Perhaps their own pinched and precious rituals of self-adulation showed a will to knowledge and a will to pleasure the very hint of which would have shaken their confident moral bearing. Perhaps they revealed more than they could responsibly allow.

While Nietzsche builds his case, which is possibly true, that *good* did not originate in unegoistic actions and *evil* did not originate in forgetting the benefits of such actions, and while he shows that *good* originated in the egoism of powerful and self-assertive nobility and *evil* originated in the self-protective interests of weaker and less bold kinds of people, he shows throughout that interplaying with the will to knowledge is will to power, which moves in the constructions of good and evil, good and bad. There is an interplay between will to knowledge and will to power in the sense that will to knowledge traditionally seeks both to dominate and to be free from what it dominates and what dominates it. It seeks always to overcome freedom. The will to knowledge finds pleasure in uncovering and exposing whatever it creates. It takes delight in every absurd, fanciful incongruity, such as that of converting no truth into truth and the unknowable into knowledge. The will to knowledge is a will to conquer, grasp, shape, and misshape. Above all, the will to knowledge seeks to intensify its own life, and in addition to its pieties and canons it loves the contradictions and stupidity which hide in the good sense that it produces and which in a hidden way save it from the easy satisfactions of normal observation. The origin of good in that egoism that gambles everything for love of chance and struggle and the origin of evil in the fear of the power of confident self-assertion as well as in fear of the power of life show why will to knowledge must pervert itself to find itself: its responsibility to goodness, truth, correctness, usefulness, and wisdom has developed out of the mean desire to protect weakness of spirit from the movement of life energy that animates all of its creations and to protect as well people for whom the affirmation of life can come only in forms of life-denial.

The *will* to knowledge undercuts and perverts the morality that forms it because it loves self-assertion and thus loves turning what appears as error in the context of responsible knowledge to constructions of truth and vice. Its perverseness is its return to its own life, its movement away from the responsibility that fear of life has given it. Further, the idea that universal subjectivity causes whatever takes place and seems to be the condition for the possibility of both knowledge and morality comes from the resentment of the weak and downtrodden. Nietzsche asserts with possible truth that will "is nothing other than . . .

driving, willing, effecting, and only owing to the seduction of language (and of the fundamental errors of reason that are petrified in it) [which conceives and misconceives] all effects as conditioned by something that causes effects, by a 'subject'." "Morality . . . separates strength from expressions of strength, as if there were a neutral substratum behind the strong man, which was *free* to express strength or not to do so. But there is no such substratum; there is no 'being' behind doing, effecting, becoming; . . . the deed is everything" (GM, I.13). The given subjectivity as distinct from the specific actions of individuals preserves the passivity and fear of those who are unable to be alone in their striving and choosing. The linkage of responsibility to a shared nature perpetuates the appearance of a universal community whose hidden interest is to make us responsible to something protected from chance, error, and the mutational development of values.

The unresponsible in the activity of responsibly thinking, reading, and speaking appears to have this in common with the will to power which is the life of responsible action: neither is defined by responsibility or the agency of responsibility. We have seen that Dionysian will to power is located in the self-overcoming movement of all structural events. Thus it cannot be adequately thought by the concept—the subjective structure—of will to power. Will to power is unresponsible, both in the claims that Nietzsche makes regarding it and in its self-overcoming nontruth. How are we to think responsibly with something that lacks definitive structure, something that disperses and scatters all fixations and prescriptive activity? How can Nietzsche be responsible with the unresponsibility of will to power? Apparently only by engaging affirmatively in self-overcoming movement that disseminates everything, gives no privilege to responsibility, and puts in question its own conception.

What is at stake, then, when we speak of the unresponsibility of will to power? Instead of a higher responsibility to something infinite and absolute, we find ourselves with nothing to do, with nothing to bring to realization as we experience the excess of will to power in our responsible thought. We are not commanded to withdraw from responsibility. There is no suggestion that we are to become like will to power or that our nature, which seeks self-realization, is the will to power. If we remain alert within will to power's withdrawal from responsible action and thought as well as from its own authority to name something transcendent and real, we are at least able to undergo the unresponsibility of responsibility, to see the limits of responsibility, to forgo the temptation to close the world by responsible projections and expectations. But where does that lead us?

To say that Nietzsche's thought originates in will to power would be to give that will a substantive position and fail to see that it is a construction that arises from a lineage of struggle, creation, and submission. The genealogy of Nietzsche's thought of will to power is not different from the genealogy of resentment and the ascetic ideal: it too is the child of a monstrous creation. The difference is found in part in an absence of the seriousness that accompanies resentment and asceticism. "To be incapable of taking one's enemies, one's accidents, even one's misdeeds seriously for very long—that is the sign of strong, full natures in whom there is an excess of the power to form, to mold, to recuperate and to forget" (GM, I.10). This lack of seriousness arises from an excess of power that traditionally is turned back on the individual as he/she harbors and preserves what befalls him/her: " . . . 'the enemy' as the man of *ressentiment* conceives him—and here precisely is his deed, his creation: he has conceived 'the evil enemy', *'the Evil One,'* and this in fact is his basic concept, from which he then evolves, as an afterthought and pendant, a 'good one'—himself" (GM, I.10). The 'good one' keeps and preserves the powers that assail him by the formation of evil: evil is like a receptacle that receives and nourishes whatever threatens, injures, or daunts, particularly whatever threatens the constructions of God or human universality through which individuals find life hopeful and fundamentally meaningful. Releasing the seriousness that maintains such creations is an attunement to the creative power that is in excess of the creations. Nonseriousness in these matters *is* the excess at work. To say that this nonseriousness is done by an individual is to say too little. Even to say that nonseriousness is the result of an individual's act of will is misleading. Nonseriousness, rather, is more like one's release of a demand and, in consequence of that release, undergoing a loss. It is more like ceasing to belong to the demands of a construction to which one belongs. In that sense, it is like letting a part of one's life die in its effective presence and finding that energy in excess of the construction's self-maintaining energy drives beyond the construction and its value. Nietzsche wishes to think and speak in the flow of that drive.

The dialogical imagery that accompanies the language of responsibility is limited in its appropriateness. Nietzsche is not responding to an other in his work. He is not responding *to* will to power. Rather, will to power is itself a construction that comes out of energy both carried by and excessive to traditional morality and faith. Neither is he responding to this energy in the sense of conforming his ideas to it. He finds no formation to conform to. To say that the excess speaks to him would be to overpersonalize it, to return to the dominance of subjectivity. To say that Nietzsche is in the hearing of this imagery, that he in some sense belongs to it, loses the excess and locates it nonexcessively. One cannot belong to or perceive such excess. In Nietzsche's thought one may affirm and assent excessively. One may allow for the excess's draft as one goes beyond—is sucked beyond—the given boundaries in willing to know. One constructs, creates, destroys. One can affirm the excess in transformatively affirming the construction. We can say that we are responsible to our values nonseriously when we are not primarily responsible to ourselves or even to the force of life. Affirmation of will to know and will to be, for example, includes affirmation of their self-overcoming and an excess of the constructions' values. We are serious in our responsibility but nonserious in allowing the excessive unresponsibility that vacantly moves the construction to which we belong.

I use the word *unresponsibility* in order to set Nietzsche's account of will to power apart from irresponsibility and to name an absence of responsibility that appears in the formation and life of responsibility. Although the word is attached to responsibility, it indicates that the value of responsibility is qualified in the process of Nietzsche's thinking. We are left to be responsible to many things—to causes and identities, to any cluster of values that might arise. But the value of responsibility is in question, given our heritage, in the absence of any responsible foundation for it. If we hurry to politics, for example, in order to check our greatest dangers to ourselves, and if we thereby reinvest responsibility with unquestioned value, we, in Nietzsche's thought, continue to carry out a still greater danger in a tradition that is formed in blind perversion of the excess of valuation and subjectivity. When the value of responsibility is put in question by its genealogy we are given to know that nothing originates our responsibility other than the constructions to which it belongs in its formation and that its danger, given its lineage, may be addressed by genealogical accounts that are given responsibly without responsible seriousness.

These thoughts emerge: responsibility's danger may be what we need to be responsible to; in that move the value of responsibility is put in question; responsibility's danger and the possibility of thinking it have to do with nonresponsibility in responsibility. I turn now to Heidegger's "Question concerning Technology" in order to raise again, given the way we have come so far, this question: to what do we belong that gives us to be responsible?

Heidegger's questioning in this essay is intended to give us a relationship to technology that is not technological. That beginning on Heidegger's part is probably the most difficult aspect of this work, because a nontechnological relationship with technology is no less difficult to think than is an unresponsible relationship to responsibility. In fact, as we shall see, these two relationships— one to technology and the other to responsibility—cannot be separated.

If in our attempt to think nontechnologically regarding technology we make technology the object of our thought, we will not be nontechnologically related to it. Rather, we must find an accord (*Entsprechen*) with the essence of technology because technology cannot free us from technology. The essence of technology is not technological. It cannot be thought technologically, but it might give a nontechnological way of thinking regarding technology. A different way of thinking and being is required of us if we respond nontechnologically with our being technological. Our freedom from technology is necessary if we are not to be overcome by it. This thought is similar to Nietzsche's, that in addition to being morally responsible creatures we must be free of moral responsibility by thinking unresponsibly if we are not to be overcome by the cruel suppressions that deeply and silently compose moral responsibility. Our temptation is to say that we should be responsible but now to something essential and true. Nietzsche's and Heidegger's thought, however, places in question the value of responsibility and not only the values to which we are responsible. If we treat technology responsibly and make it a thing to put in proper order, we will be under the sway of technology no matter how lofty the values are by which we give a proper place to technology. We *are* responsible beings, according to Nietzsche, and as responsible beings we *are* technological beings, according to Heidegger. Hence we find ourselves faced with the necessity of thinking and living in a way that counters the way we as humans have come to be. This means that responsibility and technology must come to their completion, their end, in our being if we are to put them in question. Far from being antiresponsible or antitechnological, we are faced with the possibility of being responsible and technological as we think in their completion and ending and thus find ourselves in the sway of being unresponsible and nontechnological. For Nietzsche this possibility arises in a self-overcoming movement of will to power. For Heidegger it comes in technology as the nontechnological essence of technology. We shall return to this issue of completion and ending after we consider the part 'cause' plays in being responsible.

In our tradition a being belongs to what causes it. Causes indwell a being and give it to be as it is. An efficient cause, for example, gives a being a specific movement, and the being is indebted to the cause for its movement in its movement. A formal cause gives a being its definitive limit. A final cause gives a being its telos within its form and movement. Technology, for example, is definitively limited by instrumentation. Its telos of human well-being incites a process of putting things in order by humans for the sake of ends that they establish for themselves. When *this* boundedness and purposiveness is exceeded, technology ceases. It comes to its end. Its form and telos, which are at once its confinement, are parts of its occurrence. Technology belongs to the circumscription that gives it definition and specificity and in that sense is indebted to them. In this context Heidegger uses the word *verschulden* to say that a being is indebted to—and, in that sense, responsible to—what causes it. Within this way of thinking we are indebted to whatever causes us to be as we are: to our common nature, for example, or to the purposes of human existence or to technology.

To the extent, however, that all causes are thought of as bringing something about and effecting a result, they all have an instrumental, primarily efficient dimension, and the dominating thought of cause would thus seem to lead to the dominance of technology. Heidegger asks, however, whether causes themselves are effects of other causes in an unbroken causal chain or whether there is 'something' noneffectual in causation to which causes belong? Do causes belong to something noncausal? The occurrence of indebtedness is Heidegger's clue to an alternative to the priority of causal productiveness. In *Verschuldung* (indebtedness) we find a way of belonging that does not find its expression in bringing about an effect.

Heidegger interprets indebtedness not in a lineage of revenge and enjoyment of revenge, as Nietzsche does, but in the radically different thought of "owes thanks to." That to which we are indebted is that thanks to which we are as we are. William Lovitt often translates *verschulden* as "responsible for": a cause is responsible *for* something, and the caused being is responsible *to* the cause. But in Heidegger's account we are answerable in the way of thanks as we come to be in excess of causation. We are in a *claim* (*Anspruch*) *to be* as we experience ourselves as caused. *This is a noneffective claim to noneffectiveness.* We are in the claim *to be in thanks* to the giving of being in the giving of cause.

What does this mean? So-called causes allow something to come forth in coming to pass ("Sie lassen es in das An-wesen vorkommen") (VA 14). They let something arrive, come into presence. They give something to be. 'Causes' bring forth into presence out of nonpresence. This is different from an efficient action of striking something and thereby giving it a direction or forming something or giving a purpose to something. Heidegger is redetermining the language of causation by speaking of bringing into presence without the action of a quasi agent or purposiveness of will. He is speaking of an uprising of presence and appearance. Causes are ways of bringing something forth into being out of concealment into open unconcealment. The four causes have in common the revealing of something out of nonrevelation, the appearing of something out of nonappearance. *In being caused we belong to noncause and are in thanks to our coming to be.*

We have come this far: the ordinary sense of responsibility assumes that something causes us to be as we are and gives us to be answerable to the demands placed on us by what causes us. When we discover, for example, that our community causes us to be mutually dependent on each other for our very existence as well as our well-being, we are aware that we are responsible to the community to act in community-supportive ways. And when we discover that we are formed essentially alike in our fundamental humanity, we are aware that we are under an obligation to conform to our shared essence that causes us to be essentially as we are. To belong to a community or to a shared essence is to be obliged to enact ourselves in certain ways in conformity with the common cause. In Heidegger's thought, however, we, in being caused, are more than caused: we are given to be. Given to be is different from caused to be, because in this case no cause acts or effectively enacts itself. The claim that indwells our given-to-be is thus excessive in relation to our responsibility; we are not only made to be in a determinate way in our given-to-be. This excess is not in opposition to the claims of specific ways of life but is quite other to them. Being indebted and in thanks to our coming to be is not like ordinary responsibility: we can do nothing that is both appropriate *and* effective or efficient or instrumental with regard to it. We can be, however, unresponsible when we have in mind the usual sense of responsibility, viz., being a moral agent and accountable for our actions with regard to what essentially causes us to be as we are. I will say later that one way of being both responsible and unresponsible is found in attending to the danger of responsibility. But we need to ask first about the danger of technology in order to see how the danger of technology puts responsibility in question and reveals, in spite of itself, noncausal unresponsibility.

Technology is a way of bringing things forth that is oblivious to its bringing things forth. In its absorption with effectiveness in achieving goals, a technological way of being is thoroughly out of touch with its own nontechnical dimension, which Heidegger calls its essence (*Wesen*; I shall translate the word as coming to pass): its bringing beings forth out of concealment into unconcealment. Such talk itself, in its nontechnological language concerning the nontechnological, is an irritant to the technologically trained ear. *Technology* is nonetheless a region of bringing things into existence as specific kinds of beings. It "is a mode of revealing. Technology comes to presence in the realm where revealing and unconcealment take place, where *alétheia*, truth, happens" (BW 319). Its way of bringing things to presence is to order things by imposing values on them. Out of human interest technology pays little attention to the way beings are, except with regard to their instrumentality and useability in light of goals and values. It extracts and stores and manipulates as it produces goods and energy. Instead of attending to things in their disclosiveness it intrudes upon them with timing and interest that take them into a region foreign to their own way of appearing. The demands of technology are like forms of defiance, like an individual's making use of a child to suit a project that is alien to the child's rhythm of life and expression. Its manner of bringing things forth is forceful and intrusive, blind to the fragile and vulnerable lives that are disclosed to it. The truth of technology, its letting ways of being come to be, is violent in its pursuit of human well-being, and this strange countervalence in technology's truth is as destructive as the recoiling cruelty that Nietzsche found in moral responsibility: it wrenches beings from their lives and wrenches its own truth from itself as it discloses beings and itself stupidly in the guise of not disclosing anything, but of merely producing what humans need. Technology gropes and squeezes the life out of beings as it converts them to valuable purposes that it justifies by appeal to human need. Its calling things forth into being is at once a demand that discloses things by transforming them into objects of power and that transforms its own disclosure into a willful process of single-minded instrumentation.

Technology's coming to pass is thus hidden in its bringing things forth and placing and ordering them and preserving them in their effective placement. It comes to pass in gathering things together by producing and presenting them. In its gathering and bringing forth, the essence of technology—coming to pass—is neither technological nor human. Something other than human action takes place with human action: humans do not make gathering or disclosing. Rather, humans too are gathered and disclosed as they act technologically. They appear as produced by their culture and as gathered by the forcing, enframing process that brings them to their common identity. Humans too are technological, and their disclosure, their truth, occurs with an obscuring of the technologies coming to pass in the appearance of things. Indeed, humans are this concealment of their own truth.

The danger of technology is thus found in its revealing and concealing. In technology we find the sending of being in the coming to be of technological things. In it takes place the coming to be and passing away of beings. A history of coming to presence itself comes to presence in technology. As definitive of the present time in the history of being's coming to presence, technology constitutes at once the possibility for life and the possibility for the destruction of life. Its greatest danger is that technology gives humans a way of revealing that blocks them from the nondestructive truth of technology. Coming to life technologically brings with it the greatest danger to life. In technology, coming to be recoils on itself with a fixing efficiency that cannot listen to its own being. In it, coming to be is at catastrophic odds with itself as it obscures and loses itself in its own process. Thus when we who are technologically disclosed are obliged to anything, we are circumscribed by technology, as when we are obliged to our communities or to our shared identities as humans. In our responsibility within a technological world we are caught thoroughly in this danger. We order ourselves in stances, reserves of values, and preestablished patterns of productive exchange. Responsibility to the environment, for example, comes in the form of developing procedures for using the environment in such a manner that cherished things will not be disastrously contaminated or used up. We have preserves set aside, areas reserved for nonuse, natural resources treated for purification. *Technology* sets to work to clean up technological excesses. We set up smoke-free regions, no-hunting months; some streams are set aside to be kept clean. Impurities are removed from the air and dumped in less hazardous spaces. But these helpful technologies perpetuate the technological world. Things are placed, arranged, and kept according to values that serve us better than uncontrolled growth and pollution. We remain oblivious to both the danger of technological disclosure and to the nontechnological coming to presence of technology.

Heidegger's language countervails technology in the very process of showing the danger of technology. He is giving word to 'something' that he cannot produce or place in reserve when he names the essence of technology. In showing how technology comes to pass he is saying more than he can mean or grasp within the region of technology; in excess of technology's domain. Technology in this sense has come to its end, its limit, in his thinking in spite of his not grasping the essence that he names. Heidegger is responding to 'something' both unresponsible and nontechnological that is outside of technology's boundaries and outside of his own ability to make it work efficiently in his thought.

The word he uses for his response to the coming to pass of technology is *entsprechen* (to answer, to be in accord with), not *verantworten* (to be responsible or accountable). He understands his thought to be in accord with the way technology comes to be—in thanks to it—not in a relation of duty or accountability with it. The coming to presence of beings technologically is not like a demand, obligation, or the action of a free agent, not at all like a cause that makes obligation. Heidegger thinks without responsibility when he thinks in the coming to pass of technology. Why?

The short answer is: the coming to presence of beings is not 'something' to which we can be responsible, although it is 'something' to which we belong.

Revealing—coming to presence—is not something that we can avoid. We belong to it and in it, but we are not caused by it in belonging to it. Our thought and language—the coming to be of beings in our lives—began in the *question* of coming to presence and passing away. The issue for Heidegger is *how* things come to presence in a given time in the wake of this originary question—how, for example, beings were speakable and thinkable as representations of a higher being that appears to eliminate the question that moves it, or as relative parts of a linear history that fixes time calculatively, or as is the case now, how beings come to be and pass away enframed in a pervasive demand for functional, technological usefulness that has no time for the upsurge of beings in a life of passing away. The technological enframing of beings is the way they and we are given—sent—to speech and thought in the draw of the heavily obscured question of being's coming to pass. There are two moments in this account that I want to highlight. On the one hand, we—and most especially Heidegger's language and thought—cannot avoid a technological way of being. It defines *our* particular capacity to communicate with each other and to live together communicably. On the other hand, this present inevitability of technology is alterable by virtue of its own obscured essence, its own coming to be as a way of giving unconcealment. The sending or coming to pass of technology does not compel or constitute a demand that places us in an order of responsibility. Its obscured essence can grant us freedom from the compelling and composing order of technology: we belong to the sending of disclosure, and we are truly free only insofar as we belong to the realm of sending and become people who listen, but do not simply obey. (This is a paraphrase of a sentence in BW 330.) We are within the hearing of, i.e., we belong to, the coming to presence of beings in the midst of technology's compulsions and fixations. In the midst of the seemingly overwhelming power of volition and human subjectivity, human beings belong to the giving of presence, a giving that is without will, human value, or subjectivity. Rather than being produced or efficiently caused by this giving, our indebtedness calls for listening, hearing what we cannot enframe with obedience, projects, or good world-order. It comes, Heidegger says, unexpectedly as a freeing claim. That is a sending that breaks the sway of the way beings presently have to come to be.

The danger of technology is thus the danger of responsibility. When we think and speak responsibly in our common humanity we inevitably enframe ourselves and other beings in values that serve our common needs and common causes. The value of these values and the agency of responsibility are both in question when we find the danger of technology. As we think and speak attuned to the danger we are attuned to the unresponsibility of coming to presence. This attunement is different from the value of envisioning a better world and ways of attaining it. Human happiness and liberation into a more efficient and effective world are not within the purview of this attunement. But this difference is an attunement that exceeds the dangers of human agency and human ideals. It gives us to know that our best values have a life-threatening danger *in* their value, that *self*-fulfillment may not be a timeless goal for human life, and that uncertainty regarding the value of responsibility might give us options for thinking and speaking that open to unresponsibility. That is not irresponsible. When we are responsible to the danger of technology, when we think with the likelihood that technology gives us now to be responsible and that this giving gives us to be unresponsible, we are able to hear more than we can responsibly say or do, and that recoil opens us to something other than responsibility. This opening with the anxiety that accompanies it might not give us much to hope for. We may well doubt that it is the saving power that Heidegger calls it. But without his prediction of salvation, we can nonetheless expect to expose responsibly the danger of responsibility for humans who, as humans in a time of technology, are made to overlook the destructive compulsion of being answerable in an agency of subjective effectiveness.

11 | A People's Witness beyond Politics

But to hear a God not contaminated by Being is a human possibility.
—Emmanuel Levinas, *Otherwise than Being*

"OH HEAR, Israel, the Lord our God, one God." This prayer and affirmation without a copula permeates Levinas's writing. It is not a statement about pervasive sameness in reality or immediate presence. It is not a statement about a divine nature in which all people are participant. It recalls that God is the One who called a people, gave them to be Israel in a covenant that preceded their identity, freed them from slavery by a bonding they could not choose, and gave them in their lives a law of life. It is a prayerful saying by a people of God who do not have God before them. It is an affirmation by a people who came to be a people in the call, who were not before the call, who found themselves in a call that was there when they knew who they were. In it God is not a being but is nonetheless—God, so other that nothing they say or know grasps or conceives this one God, this Other who gave them to be. As a people they are witness to this Other who is never an object, not even in prayer, and who gave them to be in a call beyond consciousness, to be hearers of God's word before all people, to be God's testament to the entire world. This awful responsibility—which is at once a gift of persecution, "a deafening trauma" (OTB 111), and a destiny, which is alien, beyond Western identity, and yet something to which a people of the West belongs and to which European civilization belongs—this awful responsibility is the call to which Levinas gives answer in his writing. He thinks in response to an Other-beyond-presence, to an Other-beyond-consciousness, to an Other-beyond-human-origination as he calls into question the lineage of *Lógos*, *Theós*, the Hellenistic Christ, the lineage of *Geist*, the self-presenting intentional subject, the divine condition for the possibility of rational truth, and human nature as the seat of responsibility. Levinas's thought and the ethics that he discovers answer the Singular Other of Israel who, One beyond Oneness, (is) the Only One who called this people and gave its individuals to know that what God gives is beyond conscious value. Levinas knows that individual life in its flesh may not be taken by humans without violating the Singular One. He knows that God gives singular lives beyond understanding, and our hope is not in understanding but in obedience to the covenant. It is a people's hope. It is a covenant that requires an embodiment of responsibility to the flesh of others, to that flesh that is struck by death but, being able always to die, does not age as flesh and blood (OTB 106). His writing is permeated by this affirmation, which has its bearing in impossible situations of death, persecution, exile, and suffering when a people knows that before God, *Theós* and immediate presence are lost, that God—the Singular One—is heard as Israel remembers its name.

"In the form of an ego, anachronously *delayed*," Levinas says, "behind its present moment, and unable to recuperate this delay—that is, in the form of an ego unable to conceive what is 'touching' it, the ascendancy of the other is exercised upon the same to the point of interrupting it, leaving it speechless" (OTB 101). We are turned by him to the other, not to a divine presence, as he turns to hear God beyond the contamination of human responsibility. The Other beyond contamination commands our first attention. The movement begins in a people who, as a people, has already heard God, and in this beginning our attention is turned not to divine presence but to the other who is proximal to us in our having been already called. That this "us" is in some sense Israel is an issue that will recur. For the moment, I note that instead of invoking a category of universality, Levinas suggests—always indirectly and subtly—that we Westerners, we Europeans, are already of Israel and that Israel is of us. It is not a question of human universality. It is a question of a people already covenanted by God without choosing the commission or necessarily knowing about it. In this condition, we have an opportunity to discover ourselves as a people in confronting a responsibility that precedes our intentions and theories. We who are of the Greeks are more of the Hebrews than we may know.

In this thinking we must assume a contour of consciousness as described in broad idealistic and Husserlian terms: consciousness as a structure and movement that is a priori and before the presented object. The neighbor's coming, however, is not described by consciousness. He or she is not, in this coming, consciously ordered. The neighbor's proximity is neither spatial nor temporal nor present in a conscious presentation. The neighbor does not originate in any intentional synthesis. The neighbor's coming is not part of a social history. He or she does not occur first with a social definition as poor or powerful or strong or deprived or victim or gendered or child or attractive or authoritative or curly-headed. The neighbor does not come temporally as young or passing away or finite or changeless. The neighbor does not come spatially as here or there or present or absent. He or she is not contexted by any conscious order. The neighbor comes singularly but anarchically, not as part of a stated whole. The neighbor is not part of a nation or race or culture. His or her proximal but unpresent touch obsesses and persecutes consciousness in refusing the interrogation that the neighbor incites and in escaping the reach for which the neighbor calls. An act of consciousness is delayed in its self-enactment before the neighbor who,

being without a who or consciousness, is timelessly before the act of consciousness that unavoidably bestows time and presence on the neighbor. The neighbor
is before the before, unlost before being lost, utterly unpolitical before its political beginning and consciousness. The neighbor renders us speechless in giving
us to speech. It denies consciousness the identity of its self-enactment in giving
its identity. It breaks the truth of consciousness, its self-disclosure. Foundering
in its struggle for recuperation, consciousness, which is always political, finds
itself without the authority necessary to found an order for the neighbor and
loses the neighbor in recognizing the neighbor. Whatever consciousness does
regarding the neighbor, it contaminates by order the neighbor's coming: by orders of respect and benevolence, by orders of generosity, greeting, concern, protection, and nurturance. No politics will reinstate the neighbor's touch. No
grammar will move the neighbor to renewed life. No gesture will designate the
neighbor without contamination. No thought of excess will restore the neighbor
to the integrity of its ownness. In this persecution of consciousness, this cease-
less cutting into the texture of consciousness' body, we must turn without
authority to oppression and suffering to find the vacuum of our words and values. We are lost before we began. Our community is severed. *Homo politicus*
finds its home in the neighbor's loss.

This incommensurability of the other and consciousness resonates with the
incommensurability of God and Israel. Proximal and yet absent in presence, be-
spoken and yet unbridgeably different, the other is lost to its naming and placement. "A responsibility stronger than death," Levinas says (OTB 195).

I wish to emphasize the importance of the notation that social history does
not constitute *ipseity*. One might be tempted to hear the echo of transcendental
thought in this anarchy. With ipseity we are not before transcendental consciousness. Rather we face the transcendence of an unreachable Other whose
call or covenant is already in effect in our recognition of ourselves, a call or covenant that does not constitute an a priori element in our identity but rather interrupts our identity in giving identity, a proximity that obsesses us in holding
us to something impossible for us, one that sets us apart from ourselves and
from *our* history and gives another impossible history in which we are without
initiative and in which we are always beginning in loss before proximity. We
face not transcendental identity but transcendent loss of our identity in the bestowal of our identity. Levinas chooses well the word *exile* in this thought. We
are already—i.e., transcendently—exiled.

This thought is so very nongenealogical, so very non-Nietzschean. We
might give genealogies of our limits and possibilities as a people. But even here
Levinas appears to be willing to give the idealists the day in their accounts of
consciousness. The problem is that the language of Levinas, its *abusive* quality
in his terms, is an abuse that is not inclined to find its capacity to signify in its
lineage. Something proximate and other to its lineage is so privileged as to es-

cape the history of abuse and exile. We could say that proximity is historical *before* any history or that it is political before any politics. And yet Levinas pits a Hebrew lineage against a Greek lineage even as he joins them, pits a midrashic thinking against a thinking of *lógos*, a lineage of persecution against one of aesthetic satisfaction and self-contemplation. He speaks as though the neighbor were there before determinant time and history, as though being were broken prior to being, as though responsibility were always unsaid, as though passivity has always already interrupted spontaneity, as though we were already called to the abuse of language before the enstated orders of *lógos* and self-relation.

This context of Levinas's thought is one of departure from the priority of consciousness and subjectivity in transcendental idealism, particularly its nineteenth-century legacy in Hegelian thought and classical phenomenology. He sees—accurately, I believe—that when the other is found in movements of self-presenting consciousness, the other is dying, that when God is the object of belief because of subjective necessity, God is dead, that when consciousness is founded in its own self-positing and self-recuperating movements, alterity is lost in the sameness of this reflexive movement. Through Levinas I hear in transcendental philosophy a certain blind cleansing of the other's otherness, a reduction of the other to the sameness of consciousness, a subtle and demonic attack on whatever takes consciousness from itself. And Levinas hears as well in transcendental thought an atheism in its theism that is far more severe than his own atheism in the name of God's otherness. The transcendental placement of God, the demand that God be for the sake of world order, loses God's continual misplacement, God's infinity, God's specificity, which displaces all conscious acts that would find God, name God, or know that God *is*. The other, rather, comes in a specific proximity and call, not hidden as a thing behind or beyond the phenomenon but as a proximity so real that I have no choice but to respond, so real that I am responding as I find myself to be. And I—I am in response to the other before the other is a phenomenon, before I intend the other in any way, before I am conscious of the other.

This context is not only one of departure from mainstream Western thought and experience. It is also one of hearing *in* Western consciousness an obsession that interrupts it. I shall return to this interruption, but I note now that we are not leaving Western thought in this departure. We are finding in Western thought a departure that it has ignored. This departure from consciousness occurs in Western consciousness. In Levinas's work we hear something of our lives that has been lost to our dominant values and theories.

The moment of maximum interest for us is not found in the theoretical sparring with transcendental thought in which Levinas engages with skill and subtlety. One *could* become dazzled by the ways in which Levinas uses the language of condition for the possibility of consciousness in order to overturn the transcendental conditions for alterity. Or one could develop and extend Levinas's thought of consciousness as assassination, language as abuse, and the other as persecutor. But *the* moment of interest occurs when thought comes to an end and one, in the silencing of reflection, hears and responds to an other— hears and responds not as a philosopher or priest or rabbi but as only this one who belongs to the other's proximity and who responds out of a passivity and a covenant that originates in the other's call or cry. I then do something in the interruption of originary spontaneity. I might do my best to redress the killing appropriation of my recognition of other, hear the other in a call that escapes my intentionality, and *take* responsibility in the responsibility that the other has already bestowed on me. I would then respond in my responsiveness.

This nodal point is beyond undecidability. Up to this moment nothing is decisive. Whether there is a God, whether the other is really there and outside of conscious appropriation, whether I am constituted by responsibility beyond spontaneity and the freedom of autonomy: all that is undecidable. Although Levinas makes his descriptive claims with the intention of accuracy, and although he means that his account is more accurate than other accounts, he has already required undecidability by his claim, which he thinks is accurate, that language and consciousness, in their meanings and syntax, are murderous distortions of the other. We know, in this discourse, that the other is before meaning and before the stated ethics that befall the other. We know that we must use language abusively in order to break its sense of essence and the dominance of its requirements. We know that the other is beyond the 'is' that identifies and places the other. *Hence* what we know and recognize in Levinas's language is undecidable even if it is by the canons of descriptive discipline accurate and convincing. Only in the contortions of Levinas's language, contortions that give it its poetic effect, does the trace of something other to subject and object and beyond description cut the reminder that our covenant with the other is not produced, posited, or formed by anything that can be meant or signified. In its meaning and by its own account, Levinas's thought requires suspicion of *what* it says.

But this undecidability is broken when I respond to the other in a division from consciousness as I answer the other. I may answer in hatred or love or concern. But the answer in its language and recognition is also before language and before recognition of the other by name and status. Then it is the other and I before we are ranked in our positions of designation. I may pull the trigger, offer solace, turn my back, give food, or say yes in sorrow over my inability to be fully one for the other. In such "words" before there is language I am this one for this one, and life is real, concrete, decided. Nothing is derived from nature or rights. That moment is derived from proximity in call before there is selfhood and otherness.

I want to concentrate on this moment. It appears to me to be constituted by values for which Levinas does not fully account. It appears to me to be the appearance of a tradition that is before the other. And the bearing of this tradition, as it disappears in Levinas's account, is what I find most telling, most important, and what I shall call the crisis, the turning, and the before-politics of the other.

I shall turn for a moment from this most interesting point of movement from thought and theory to the other in order to raise an issue that will bring us back to this point. The singularity of our values and traditions usually defines our local practices. We know from long experience that when a locale or a people universalizes its peculiar values and turn the tribal into an encompassing, universal expectation for all people, justification for conquest, colonialism, and oppression is a small step away. German tribalism and German National Socialism, for example, are not separable. Claims to racial superiority and claims to cultural superiority are often mutually dependent. Such experience gives us caution before any elevation of spontaneity and appropriative assertion over reticence, reserve, and kindness regarding the differences that separate us. We are well aware today of the dangers of local and tribal formations as we face the fragmentation, nationalism, and war that arise as various peoples reassert their ancient tribal and national identities. Such assertiveness is, I believe, among the dangers that Levinas's thought invokes as he turns the priority of consciousness and subjectivity in our lineage toward its inevitable assassination of the other.

Although I cannot here fully engage the question of universalization in Levinas's thought, I note that in his language there is—perhaps in spite of himself—a turning from universalization in the very claims to which he seems to give universal meaning. His descriptive claim, for example, that consciousness has as its necessary condition a radical passivity that is other to consciousness, so other that the possibility of dialectical relation between consciousness and other is impossible—this claim finds its crisis in a movement of response to other that is not reflective or syntactic. This most interesting point of contact is both the meaning and the destruction of meaning of Levinas's thought. His claims about possibility and proximity become, in the retrospective of hearing and answering the other, more like a proclamatory language that is closer to prophecy or a kind of prose poetry than it is to a systematic and descriptive account of essence and other to essence. The obsession that accompanies the ego's exile and persecution returns us always to something lost in every 'said', returns us to the unsaid word of the oneself, returns us to the utter and fleshly other-beyond-consciousness. Our thoughtful, universalizing language dies at this turning point, a point to which Levinas's thoughtful and universalizing language brings us.

But this crisis point marks the space where the local and tribal are most in effect, and something like an unspoken universalization is the greatest danger in this turning. The unspoken universalization can happen in the radicalization of particularity as feeling becomes predominant in the other's proximity.

We might call this crucial point of enactment a 'tribal universalization' that occurs when a people's sense of common identity falls out of question in these people's rituals, in their practices of returning into themselves, in their reinvocation of the common ways of dwelling which give them to know who they are *and* when in this movement they find not only themselves but also a feeling of specialness and ascendancy regarding others. This feeling of ascendancy is veiled in Levinas's thought. It takes the form of radical responsibility for the other in which one answers God and confirms the singularity of God's call in a people's most fundamental identity. "Oh hear, Israel, the Lord our God—one God."

Surely Levinas is guarded against such a predominance. Surely passivity beyond passivity and the one for the other are far removed from the control of feeling. And surely the very idea of the priority of feeling is an aspect of the privileging of consciousness that Levinas overturns with remarkable originality. But we are at the point where thoughtful precaution fails, where the overturning of universalizing syntax lapses. We are at the point of concretion and radical singularity of the other with me. We are at the point of my answer before the other, an other who is outside of discourse and the precautions of philosophy. This is the area where identity is most likely to function as a practical absolute, where I am most simply this Jew, this gentile, the one who belongs to this language, these practices, and, above all, to these values. As I turn and find my neighbor in proximity—*in the turning*—who I am most particularly becomes definitive in the proximity as well as in my word of response. In this turning and finding my neighbor to whom I belong, feelings beyond which there seems to be nothing feel the place of my existence. Here is where I will be with God or without God, where I will feel bereft or liberated in a fleeting absence of God. Here is where values feel their value, where the important things of life stand out, where rituals speak in silent, life-giving meaning, where one knows nonreflectively how to live and die.

This concrete turning point is, in a word, the space of greatest ethnic determination. It is where all living things belong to a world, where meanings give syntax far in excess of our grammars and logics. It is the space of relatedness and disrelation, where one feels connected or dispossessed, where one feels one's life to be alive or lost. The determinations of one's life, in their full arbitrariness, are *already* intimate with the world and its things. These determinations give world order. These determinations give the world in its apparent universality. The concreteness of things, of *their* lives, of *their* coalescence, is in their determination, and when things are determined in a call of other, when they exist already in external exposure to the word of God, they, in *this* determination, belong already in their existence to an ethnic God. Far from determination by consciousness, the other, determined by this God, is sedimented outside of the reach of consciousness. The other is identified from the outside, from an outside so removed from conscious origin as to be hidden and revealed by constant interruptions of removal from human intentionality and self-conscious identity. *In this Hebraic determination*, one *must* depart from the ethics of other Western peoples, depart from all that is foreign to the foreign proximity of "a God," depart from any theology that emerges from human familiarity in order to return to the recurrence of the other in its outsideness vis-à-vis human creation and bestowal.

This point of greatest interest, this contact with that which is other that is before ego-identity, is far removed from consciousness and subjectivity, but it is not on that account removed from determination and meaning, from the flow of practices, from the formations of lives, or from the meanings that let a world cohere. Although the other cannot be constituted by conscious intentionality or by the self-positing reflections of subjectivity, the other nonetheless gives passivity to the self. The other withdraws as other from the sameness of consciousness. The other exposes the I and renders naked what is covered by being. The other requires response. The other, that is, is determined as other in its interruptive determination of meaning, and in that interruptive determination an entire history plays, a history of covenant, call, guilt, mission to all people, separation from God, exile by failure before call, persecution by deafness to call, sorrow for lostness before God, and the joy of response to God in which, in the failure of the response ever to capture or see God, one knows obliquely the unspeakable Otherness of the One who does not cease to call because he has promised to be there, utter and apart, but proximate and life-giving.

We can see that 'what' is otherwise than being and beyond essence carries with it, in the language of its lost recognition and the power of its meaning beyond meaning, a tribal tradition, the heritage of a people in exile. And we can also see that what is beyond universalization suggests something more than a universal. It suggests a faith founded in a sense of call beyond consciousness and meaning.

But this is not news to Levinas. Of course the interruptive determinations of the other carry with them a tradition, and of course Levinas's own language is determined by faith and culture. Why else would he be writing in the face of the erosion of this faith in the idealism and empiricism of the nineteenth and twentieth centuries? Although I believe that Levinas's work is moved by the persona of the rabbi who is also a philosopher, the neighbor is not dependent on the rabbi. The rabbi is dependent on the neighbor. More than dependent, the rabbi stands in unceasing indebtedness before the other and, as rabbi, kills what is not to be killed as surely as the nonrabbi kills. And kills in his or her effort to free the other as other. The value of this discourse is not found in its successes or its vitality or its syntax. Its value is found in its abusive turn on its success, vitality, and syntax, in its losses and failures before the other that gives it to be.

The value of this discourse is in the other's recurrence—a recurrence before value—and not in the persistence of the discourse. Only the other's loss, not the other's presence, is to be found in Levinas's discourse.

At this most interesting point of contact with the other, both ontological claims and a tribal faith are interrupted by the other's cut. The other does not happen as it is *said* to happen. But we *can* bear witness to a determination beyond conscious events. We can see that crisis accompanies conscious determination. We can hold clear the obsession that accompanies the other's determinations. And in this we turn toward an ethic beyond the ethics of essentialist persuasion.

I believe that we have come to a still point, a point without ontological or pistic validity. Even the meaning of showing the loss of the other and the priority of the neighbor is in question, because such meaning is saturated by ontological values and the meanings of a tribal faith. The other is valuable in Levinas's discourse by virtue of a series of affirmations: the other withdraws "from the game that being plays in consciousness" (OTB 107); "this withdrawal excludes all spontaneity" (OTB 107). The one for the other is "incommensurable" with consciousness (OTB 100). "Anarchy troubles being" (OTB 101). The "Infinite" comes to pass in "an extreme proximity of the neighbor" (OTB 156). The other is the neighbor. "God" is "the *apex* of vocabulary, admission of the stronger than me in me" (OTB 156). Our most interesting point demands doubt and yet leaves no room for doubt of the infinite importance of the other, whose importance cuts through the determinations that both make it important and foreshorten its importance. "Proximity can remain the signification of the very knowing in which it shows itself" (OTB 157).

So there could *be* no other as Levinas finds it were there no ontological language and tribal faith. Even the other to the other of this language bespeaks a midrashic faith of the other's loss in its determination. And the infinite value of the other speaks in Levinas's recognition of other-beyond-value. A faith turns through itself and rediscovers itself in the withdrawal of what it posits. In this turning an exilic faith loses itself and returns to itself as it marks the other-beyond-determination. This faith finds itself articulated in the proximity and withdrawal of the Other-in-Infinity which it recognizes and before which it gives its fealty. Far from withdrawing us from the tribal, this discourse reestablishes the tribal in an unending movement of removal and rediscovery. Beyond universality, it bears witness to the Infinite in its Infinity.

This return to the tribal out of a contestation of what the tribal establishes takes place in an affirmation of the proximity of the other, in an ethics that vastly exceeds any normative ethics. The movement to note is that of return. Levinas, as we have said, makes many descriptive claims as part of this movement. In such descriptive statements Levinas bears witness to something that is to be "seen." His purpose in *Otherwise than Being* is "*to see* in subjectivity an exception putting out of order the conjunction of essence, entities and the 'difference'; *to catch sight*, in the substantiality of the subject, in the hard core of the 'unique' in me, in my unparallelled identity, of a substitution for the other; *to conceive* of this abnegation prior to the will" (OTB xli-xlii; emphasis added). Levinas writes as a witness who sees more than can be said and who remains faithful to this knowledge of excess. As a witness, in being a witness, he returns to the tribal but now in a way which suggests that the tribal has opened something so determinate and pervasive as to exceed the parochial universality of consciousness. It is a return not unlike that described by Nietzsche in Book III of *The Genealogy of Morals*, in which the ascetic priest brings self-sacrifice full circle to the full meaning of self-sacrifice and to the authority of the one who knows self-sacrificially this meaning most intimately. In this book Nietzsche, in the role of the ascetic priest, sacrifices both the meaning and the self-sacrifice and gives way to a self-overcoming of the moral tribe. Without such self-overcoming, the meaning of tribal prophecy, self-contestation, and cultural identity recur at the tribe's point of contact with what it knows it had lost in the beginning. In the loss it regains what is lost and rediscovers itself full and clear in its impairment.

This movement of departure and return is not entirely dissimilar to that of consciousness as Levinas describes it. Our consciousness is an unending process of self-loss and self-recovery, a *process* that establishes a sameness for all aspects of consciousness. We might call it an obsession with identity in which conscious identity finds itself through an endless process of contamination and conversion. The other obsession that interrupts this conscious obsessive process—the other obsession that Levinas describes—turns us beyond consciousness, crosses all conscious order and quietly gives witness to freedom and responsibility outside of conscious spontaneity, commitment, and normativity. The return that we are tracing in this other obsession, however, is one which directs us by a tribal language, a language which is remarkably sophisticated and well-versed in the languages and practices of adjacent tribes, to what is described as one-for-the-other, proximity beyond conscious constitution, and an ethics of responsibility that is constitutive of our "unparallelled identity" (OTB xli). In this witness we are given to see something that is beyond our common syntax and intention which already identifies us and which is more deeply composed of the syntax of covenant, call, and radical monotheism than any language in the syntax of *logos* and conscious subjectivity can properly say. It appears like a deep and covered-over alertness in our heritage that has accompanied the dominant and dominating discourse of Western awareness and selfhood. It appears as a recovery of the Hebraic experience and meaning that have been submerged in our Greek and modern lineage, as something other than the dominating and complex subjectivity that constitutes an anti-Hebraic force which depends on its Hebraic aspects. In this witness on the part of Levinas many people should find a surprising expansion of their own sense of identity, undergo a discovery of themselves in their Hebraic lineage, and, surprised to find themselves also Jews, experience fearful relief in a rediscovered ethics of God's call. The tribes mixed long before our births, and that mixture has surely given us to desire, deep within ourselves, the dark clarity of God's call in the values which allow us to know ourselves and all others.

In Levinas's writing we may experience a return not to transcendental consciousness but to the transcendent meaning of a covenant with God that calls us preconsciously to be in God's hearing as we name what is good and bad. It is a tribal call, and we probably prefer, like all tribes, to universalize by fundamental values and rights a particularity that gives us our names and values, even when we are otherwise exiled and homeless. As we return to our Jewishness with a renewed sense of rootedness and identity, we make the ancient movement that holds a tribe together: we return to founding meanings, no matter how elusive and terrible, and to a sense of rightness, no matter how interrupted and fragile. This movement of return, which Nietzsche found definitive of the ascetic ideal in our lineage, while it interrupts a language of essence, nonetheless restores an identity in its loss. The tribe makes metaphysicians of us all.

This movement of return in Levinas's thought is before politics when by *politics* we mean a complex conscious structure for actions among peoples. At the beginning of these remarks I recalled that the "Oh hear" affirmation is a prayer that arises from Israel and is addressed to Israel. It is a people's prayer by which these people know themselves in a covenant with a Singular One. It is not addressed directly to God. But it arises from a people that belongs to this Singular One, and it gives expression to Levinas's interruptive thought in the context of Western experience and theory. This belonging is before politics, but it is political in the sense that it gives a people to be *this* people. The "Oh hear" affirmation recalls for a person that he or she belongs to a people called by God when in the greatest of life's extremities as well as in the normal everyday. While this belonging is pretheoretical and prior to any stated value or course of action, it is ethnic in that it both bestows and expresses identity as well as constitutes a direction of destiny in that identity. This belonging is a political dimension in Levinas's thought. It is not theological. But it is constituted as a movement of return in a people's 'God-given' identity, a movement and identity of which Levinas's thought is a part. The saying of this identity begins as a prayer and finds its expression in witness—the witness of responsibility of the one for the other in writing as well as in attitudes and other actions. We have located the danger of this political witness in its return to itself, in the "Oh hear, Israel" by which return we as Jew Greeks find ourselves confirmed before all thought and value in our loss of God's presence as we hear God, who is not contaminated by being and who calls us in Goodness beyond value to be obedient in his call.

12 | Democratic Space

I AM NOT sure whether politics or something other to politics is more important. Maybe neither is more important than the other. When I say 'something other to politics' I mean differences that set us apart from our everyday lives. Some people call the dimension of such difference poetic; others, spiritual; others, aesthetic. I believe that most of us are familiar with this dimension. It happens, for example, when the world around us is transformed by relationships of love and friendship or when we find what is important and unimportant as we confront death. The experience of sheer magnitude can set us outside the parameters of our everyday lives, as when we contemplate the stars or the forty billion or more years that it has taken the light from one of them to reach the range of our present sight or when we consider the tiny fraction of the earth's existence during which our kind of being has been upon it. We might also experience a translation of our experiences into this dimension when we think in thought's difference to our normal, largely imperceptive awareness as we go about our daily lives, or when we take part in something massive and pervasive that seems to move in our language and art and to give meaning and presence far in excess of literal usage and perception.

In such ecstasies we know unpragmatically. The mechanics by which we organize and stabilize our institutional lives might appear to be saturated with boredom. The purposes that move us to become absorbed in work, accumulation, and possessions appear trivial and demeaning. Management of such things on small and large scales—the work of governments, councils, committees, agencies, and parties—strikes us as more like the flailing of a drowning soul than like an environment proper to a human being. Perhaps Dionysus *is* the friendliest God to humans in providing excess to all the structures that define us and that give us, in their repetitions, quiet erosion of creativity and imagination. Perhaps he gives us to know beyond value a dimension that will not work for us, an element of life that is outside of political wisdom and civic virtue.

I have no doubt that each of us must make the case for politics. We can add up the costs of bad politics and political indifference. There are the big words: war, holocaust, famine, overpopulation, and the lesser but no less telling ones: homelessness, abuse, racism, sexism and intolerance. Running through the meaning of these words are qualities of human suffering that so far exceed tabulation as to make quantification obscene. Our Western inheritances make inevitable our desire to bring together intelligent action and right values, and our North American inheritance makes inevitable our hope for an order of justice that belies other convictions concerning the inevitable meanness and foolishness of our lives.

The impact of twentieth-century Continental thought on our North American hope is not decisive. It too is so divided as to create uncertainty over the meaning of *politics*. On the one hand, particularly in the wake of Marx, the Frankfurt School, and critical thought, as well as some interpretations of Hannah Arendt and American pragmatism, we find an obsession with political relevance that is compatible with our desire to make things work for a state of well-managed happiness and justice. On the other, in the thought that is in the lineage of Nietzsche, we find knowledge of the destructiveness inherent in such hope and work when they arise from our absorption in traditional goals, values, and sensitivities. But to make the traditional and everyday our primary concern threatens the loss of the excessive dimension of life without which we become short-sighted and mean in our cherished values. To assume that we know what politics is, to lose the question of politics, is ample evidence of the narrow parameters of our perceptiveness and sensitivity. To live with diminished attunement to the questionableness of our common endeavors is virtually to guarantee on a broad cultural scale the monotony of the ordinary, the bureaucratic, the normally moral, and the usually religious as well as the monotony of political language and seriousness.

In this context of uncertainty concerning politics, concerning its necessity and its danger, and in the additional context of the constitution of the political subject, which we will consider in a moment, I would like to develop the thought that the space of Foucault's thought is democratic and that this space yields something that is political and that holds in suspension political options that usually arise when we consider our responsibilities as citizens.

Politics, the political, and the subject of desire arise strangely in Foucault's work. I say *arise* because he gave voice to an art of recognition that produces knowledge that is different from that of the canonical disciplines. I say *strangely* because this emerging knowledge is interruptive and often counterintuitive. His radical position is in a context of learning, documents, and archives that one expects in conservative scholarship. The political dimension of his writing disturbs the certainty of revolutionary commitments as sharply as it disturbs reactionary passions. He shows that the subject of action is a play of surface powers that excludes transcendental grounding as clearly as it gives responsibility to the individual. I shall address the political importance of these countervailing forces in his thought by an image of space that recurs in his writing to show that the value of democratic space is found in its withdrawal from political determinations, in its surface vacuity, a vacuity that disrupts movements of pervasive self-projection, movements in which subjects and values organize their worlds and environments around themselves. The space of democracy gives no rights—that is, it allows all rights by a liberty that is without guidance and meaning. And yet this emptiness finds determination in Foucault's knowledge and functions in a remarkable way to organize and disorganize at once the value of that knowledge. The knowledge that his work produces allows a relinquishing of determination and allows with this abandonment of the value that Foucault assigns to democratic space an upsurge of political interest that lacks ideology, singularity of direction, and a mythology of origin. This combination of relinquishment of determination in occurrences of determination and an accompanying emergence of political interest will hold our attention as we think about the space of Foucault's writings. We will probably be tempted to give democratic space a negative theological meaning, as though it were some kind of 'there' which, when properly discovered, demands appropriate response. But that kind of meaning will mislead us as we consider a way of knowing that requires the impossibility of a unified space by the manner in which this way of knowing signifies its own organizing values and exchanges of meaning. Political values arising in this continuing process of displacement hold our interest in part because of the power that is now exercised by the belief in communities of solidarity which carry with them a heritage of totalization constitutive of our hope for justifiable political action and for prevention of radical injustice.

I note a *distinction* between an attitude of *espousal* and one of *interested involvement*. Other names could be used for these two attitudes. I have in mind on the one hand an individual's drawing passion—life-energy—from an involvement or a commitment in such a way that he or she knows that life would be threatened if that cause were removed. Other people who strongly disagree appear as opponents, even as life-threatening agents, if they have power in the context of this attitude. We see this kind of intensity among theoreticians and philosophers who know that life would fall apart if 'postmodern' beliefs and language were broadly adopted. It is richly manifested in the abortion debate, in environmental commitments, in the passions elicited by racial and gender commitments, in holocaust discussions, and so forth. On the other hand, there is an attitude of concern that elicits involvement with issues on the basis of commitments, values, and beliefs and that holds these evaluations with an expectation of transformation. One's sense of life in this latter instance belongs to the turning, fragmented, and problematic manner by which things arise and pass away. One is in touch with an excess of life that passes beyond one's configuration of feeling and involvement. Passion is figured by self-aware limits and by the much greater stretch of possibility that enlivens the specific values that move us. One has a sense of possibility that exceeds whatever is present and that can break any given certainty, habit, or commitment. These are different attitudes of involvement. The first requires for its vitality a strong sense of fundamental stability to accompany its sense of rightness. The second makes its claims with a sense of impermanence and absence of definitive origin. The first belongs to traditions that are dominated by images of authoritative, enduring identity. The second belongs to a priority of difference, instability, and what Foucault calls 'liberty.'

Democratic Space in Foucault's Writing

By "democratic space" I mean a surface in Foucault's writing that allows an unlimited range for diverse values and commitments none of which define the space of their occurrence. It is the space of 'the' people in the sense that the multiplicity, divergence, and struggle of individuals is maximized rather than a unity of the principles and values that regulate people and make them to appear as 'one'. By acting and thinking in reference to such space one is able to engage practices and discourses, not in the name of 'higher' values but by focusing attention "on realities that have gone unnoticed" and by showing "what is intolerable and what it is in an intolerable situation that makes it truly intolerable."[1] There is no singular speaker, no anchoring linguistic father, in democratic space. Such space restores a nontragic lineage of Babel, of a plurality of voices that does not have an Adam as a first speaker or as an original author. In democratic space there is no singular first principle or set of first principles that controls language and speech. Something in Foucault's language that disperses language in its operation comes to prominence in an organization that gives value to nonreducible plurality. The importance of values is not in question. Rather, the struggle of values is heightened in the absence of an origin that confirms them, universalizes them, or gives them meaning beyond the recognition and experience that presents their interests. Democratic space is a region of disclosure that undermines determinations in their determination and that provides no reason for totalization. In it all commitments may know that possibilities for disbanding are part of the bonding processes. The value of intervention is heightened while the expectation of natural verities dies. What we most fear in our transcendental heritage emerges: unending struggle replaces action in the name of ideals for justice.

Democratic space is defined by the exchanges that take place within it—which is to say that it lacks essential definition. It verifies neither the plays of power that dominate within it for a time nor the insurrections that interrupt the effectiveness of these powers. In a metaphysically contexted language we might say that it *is* empty space, that it lacks essential content. Claude Lefort, in speaking of democratic sovereignty, says that it "signals an absent site or an empty place." It gives dislocation to determinations within it rather than a texture of continuity and a quality of continuing presence that is already there. It does not franchise any overt rule or generative framework. It is revealed instead in processes of relocation, transgression, and interruption regarding definitive powers. A vacancy is then manifest rather than an archaic archetype or truth. To be a political subject in democratic space is to show nonbelonging in the midst of belonging to a community or party. There is always the possibility to take power and to lose it with consequent transformations of truth and value, a possibility that is appropriate to the site of communal belonging. Division and disincorporation within continuities are thus the marks of democratic space.

Another mark of this space is hearing. Foucault, for example, infrequently questioned the guilt or innocence of the prisoners whom he defended. If they were silenced by a judicial order or if they were projected and identified by judgments or categories that were themselves produced by the institution that condemned them, Foucault found cause for intervention. Voices have places in democratic space. One is tempted to say that they have the right to be heard, and Foucault spoke in terms of 'rights' in this context. Rather than a question of rights by nature, however, it is the process of silencing the voices of a space without censor that he found intolerable and that most aroused him. Violation takes place when a system makes claim to space by refusing the legitimacy of other voices. In a fascist space no voices that oppose the dominant authority are to be heard. The space of tyranny is other to democratic space, and it is democratic space that comes to the fore when Foucault demands a hearing of voices in their otherness. Whatever in Foucault had to rebel and refuse cooperation with dominant powers, his political activity found its value in intervention for subjects of subjecting powers when those powers refused to give them hearing. For him this space gives hearings. It yields and maximizes voices by meaning nothing and establishing no definitive texture of authority. It is a space of voicing and hearing and of the struggle that attends radical differences.

One could make a theoretical move as Claude Lefort does and show how democratic space provides by its dislocations and nonpossession a generative framework for institutions. I shall take another turn prior to such a move, since in Foucault's thought theory as such is in question. It is in question because Foucault's work belongs to democratic space. We find an important, probably the most important, political dimension in Foucault's thought as he struggles against theoretical movement and as he attempts to follow the possibility of knowledge without theory—not knowledge without presuppositions but knowledge without theory. His experimentation thus is embroiled in this problematization: what I am calling 'democratic space' is a point of reference in his critique of many relations of power, but democratic space functions effectively in such critique only in its withdrawal from the possibility of being a normative point of reference. We can say initially that Foucault's account of games of truth and his critique of liberation thought make impossible the 'use' of democratic space as a grounding principle, that something akin to Heidegger's use of grounding is operative: grounding that withdraws itself as ground. I shall return to this thought in a moment. For now I wish to give emphasis to the political importance of Foucault's *not* applying the thought of something like democratic space in a project designed to suggest a new arrangement of institutions and practices. The political dimension of Foucault's thought has its most powerful moment when it refuses to provide normative alternatives to current practices. That is the moment that inspires the charge of nihilism from all sides of the political spectrum. Within the context of metaphysical-theoretical values, the absence of a 'constructive' alternative signifies an absence of reconstruction, a bad lack of affirmation, an instance of political irresponsibility. Foucault, however, provides an account of political and moral subjectivity in its formation through processes of domination. That subjectivity constitutes our current ability to conceive of normative options and to project new practices, and along with theory our political and moral subjectivity is most in question in Foucault's thought. His strategy of interrupting our—including his—recognitions and appreciations, interrupting our systems of dominant valences, includes the knowledge that a rush to reconstruction blindly holds in place the subjectivity that has totalization and a lineage of suppression as a part of its destiny. The political dimension of Foucault's work is found in allowing through processes of critical, interrupting thought and investigation the emergence of values that arise in departure from our totalizing heritage. This means that reticence before the passion for reconstruction is a highly important part of Foucault's political discipline.

Foucault's later emphasis on the formative aspect of practices of self, an emphasis which shifts attention from repression to ethnic production, illustrates the point. Although his attunement to domination and repression did not change, he saw that the thoughts of repression and suppression carried with them a virtually unavoidable suggestion that a truly free state of being suffers the repression, that liberation means not only lifting the barriers but also returning to a state of being more original than the repression and one that is definitive of the repressed human being. Such an essential state effectively totalizes the thoughts of liberation and repression and places a tacit demand for a normative account of the being that is repressed. It requires a theory and a substantial state of freedom. But when Foucault approached the formation of subjectivity with the question of how certain practices and discourses and problematizations produced certain kinds of subjects, he managed a context of knowledge that was free of the thought of original subjectivity.

A possible return to a primal origin in the form of definitive arts and practices, however, hovers in Foucault's accounts of our Greek heritage in spite of his intentions to avoid such a return. The art of existence, liberty, self-mastery in the avoidance of slavery, the priority of an aesthetics of existence, even the care of self and the practice of freedom appear to suggest to Foucault a normative field of reference for making judgments about our current social and moral practices. He experienced, I believe, the power of theory in his resistance to such a return, a resistance and a return both of which moved in his genealogical-archeological knowledge. Is it possible to avoid such a countermovement toward theoretical normalization? Is it possible, that is, to avoid the shaping power of theory when *we* think? I believe that such an avoidance is not possible, given who we have to be in our heritage. Addressing, countermanding, falling prey to, and interrupting this inevitability is the political aspect of Foucault's thought that we are now considering.

In the instance of democratic space we face a similar question. Democratic space is the term that I have given to this space of Foucault's thought. Its opposites are all closely associated: the space of tyranny, theological space in the power of one or another organizing, absolute sign (such as God, nature, reason, human being, or subjectivity), the space of anything timeless and essential, or the space governed by any suppressing power. Democratic space, as we have seen, is without an uninterrupted definitive authority or truth. It is not finally housed in any determinate body of knowledge. Hence it produces no lasting and definitive formation. It is not only other to all signifiers, it also arises in the failure of re-presentative thought, in the collapse of the power of the order of representation. Democratic space in its withdrawal leads away from the truths produced by systems of representation as well as from the truths produced by relations of domination. We thus face the problem of thinking the thought of democratic space with the thought's determination based on the withdrawal of interdeterminate space.

Foucault's Politics

Foucault worked politically with many people who were committed to a totalizing system of belief: with Maoists who, had they won the power of state, would doubtlessly have attacked him as an intellectual and disciplined him by closely supervised work and reeducation; with Muslims who, with proper power, might have cut off something vital to punish his free-thinking promiscuity; with Christians who, with authority over him as a believer, would probably have limited his thought and publications. But he engaged actively with them all to call attention to practices that enraged him, and he ignored their monopolizing intentions as they worked together momentarily in common projects of exposure. He cooperated for specific goals without attaching himself to their fields of doctrines.

Lacan once said to a class of radical students at Vincennes, just before he walked out of the class and the new university, "What you long for, as revolutionaries, is a master. You will get one."[2] Foucault took action from a body of desires different from those revolutionaries. He usually avoided membership in movements. He attempted to sidestep ideologies. Eribon reports on his compartmentalization, on his ability to hold apart his many involvements and endeavors. He focused on specific problems and regions of problems rather than globalizing something like human nature. He sought changes in specific instances of perceived mistreatment and did not experience his politics by reference to anything universal. Knowledges and truths are of regions and locales, and different configurations produce different systems of recognition, suffering, justice, and submission. As he avoided a master, did he avoid also the possibility of community and commonweal? Or did he know that in *his* locale common bonding had to mean also common bondage? That the ties that produce in our lineages knowledge of human nature and common good are ties in which the subject who acts, to be *able* to act, is already invested by an historically organic predisposition to a mastering totality? Regardless of its psychological dimensions, Foucault's fragmentation of political causes intervened in any tendency to organize the environment by a body of values that are given the effect of a central authority by the powers of commitment and belief.

This intervention is considerably different from a humanistic relativism. It refuses an overarching, theoretical justification and rests its case on specific, highly focused problems of power within circumstances that call for action and that can change and lose both necessity and urgency. These are problematizations that arise within specific circumstances and invoke values that are given in the circumstances and have valence by virtue of the circumstances. But Foucault's is not a politics of relativism. It is a politics of problems that is known and experienced outside of the theoretical framework that produces absolutism and relativism. In his politics an alternative comes to view that is different from the positions spawned by the defining categories of absolute and contingent. It is an alternative that arises in the demise of 'man' and human nature.

Foucault's politics thus reveals no centralizing commitment but rather a series of limited commitments that arise from the values and knowledge spawned by his archeological-genealogical approach and his revolt against mastering power. His politics recognized individuals who were suppressed and appealed under the circumstances to their rights as individuals to freedom from oppression. But the connective tissue among the many issues of oppression were networks of control that created victims and silenced their voices. He recognized the values that moved him as counterforces to those networks and knew that his danger lay in a theorization of power and rights, a theorization that would invoke the totalization that gives rise to the enforced silence of exceptions. Here we find a manifestation of democratic space. It is not composed of a table of natural rights or fundamental truths. It is not a fabric of essential powers. It is not a determinate being that has come to light by virtue of disciplined reevaluations after an evolution of misadventures. Democratic space, in its lack of determination, puts in question those constructions of influence and learning that would impose on it a feeling of essence or a privilege of access. Democratic space withdraws from the specifications that silence its silence by a language of truth regarding it.

The Political

The knowledge produced by Foucault's intellectual work is far more important politically than his political activity. I do not mean that his knowledge is spared instances of the foolishness that at times colored his politics. I mean rather that the manner by which he shaped words and thoughts, transformed assumptions, and revised the content and the style by which we know has implications for our common lives that are excessive to the importance of his political actions. I shall now look at the political dimension of his work on the history of the knowing and willing subject in order to show part of the impact that his genealogical work has as it puts in question our selves as valuing subjects and opens toward a manner of valuing that is formed in the withdrawing space that I have called democratic. In this direction of reformation Foucault interrupts movements of inevitable suppression in our lineage and begins a process of producing both knowledge and individuals that, in Nietzsche's metaphor, are on the cusp of the lion and the child: they are at once aggressive and interruptive as well as tempted by a kind of life that is innocent of the imprisoning spirit of our lineage and open to a vague 'perhaps' before the possible loss of resentment and denial of life.

We should hold in mind his growing interest in governmentality and the conduct of conduct during the time that he composed *The History of Sexuality* in its three volumes and recognize that these volumes not only begin a genealogy of the modern subject but also address the formation of contemporary systems that shape the conduct of people in the West. The issue that guides my remarks is the movement from personal self-formation to governmental shaping of selves and the way in which Foucault defines this movement within a knowledge of orders that finds exchanges of powers, problematizations, and subtle shifts of emphasis where traditional wisdom has found grounds for natural proposiveness and enduring truths. As we saw previously, the knowledge that Foucault's genealogies produce finds that orders of practice emerge from other orders of practice by virtue of problematizations in the absence of *an* origin or *a* principle of order. The formation of people as subjects of desire, for example, has no sexual nature to fulfill, no liberation to a universal sexual propriety to promise, and no original subject that moves toward self-realization. This knowledge, rather, takes place in democratic space where individuals have subjected themselves to a variety of disciplines and in the process have become agents with a variety of trajectories and momentary inevitabilities. Foucault's is a political knowledge—in other words, one that manifests an indeterminate space and gives it place in the unordered orders that it uncovers. It privileges orders of conduct in traces of unconductable space, space that withdraws from the voices that give it testimony.

First, a note on games of truth and liberation. Games of truth are plays of rules, principles, and practices that produce truths. Truths are formulations that give articulation to the rules, principles, and practices that produce them. Neither the games nor their truths signify anything determinate other than their own practices and orders. The political import is clear in this regard: no basis is found in truths for beliefs and commitments that give determination to something that transcends the particular game. This restraint—*this* game, this discipline—requires that we act with reasons and values that carry with them an understanding of their mutability and instability. In such an understanding, passions fade that are bred by a sense of essential rightness. This is the juncture where people of passionate commitment begin to find reasons to resist Foucault, even when they have found his work helpful. I believe that the persistence of this refusal is often inspired by a sensed threat to the feeling of vitality that is based on a requirement for original meaning. As a sense of rightness and a spirit of seriousness fall into question, our traditional sense of life that is fused with foundational meaning can feel threatened. When truths cannot mean Truth and just causes cannot disclose ultimate human value, the reasons for life and the value of life seem to lose their power to give us or our causes a sense of purpose and vitality. The combination of politics and a sense of rightness, a spirit of seriousness, is put in question by Foucault's knowledge of games of truth, and the political import in this shift of knowledge is visible as we in our persuasions at all points on the spectrum of political activism leave out of the game those axioms and beliefs that move us to activity and give total meaning to our political commitments. The democratic space of Foucault's thought does not give reason for cherishing any principles. It gives space rather for strategies of coping individually and communally with the problems, dissatisfactions, and suffering that arise as we live out the truths, deviations, and perplexities that characterize our orders of knowledge and life. But in it a sense of vitality in serious rightness withdraws. I shall say in a moment that another kind of vitality arises.

Foucault was both distrustful of the theme of liberation and engaged by it. On the one hand, he wanted to make relations of power unstable enough to allow alteration and reversal in order to liberate individuals from dominations that restrict them to identities that serve the purposes of other people. On the other, he knows that liberty is not a natural state of being but is rather a space for formation and transformation. Dominating powers are those restrictive relations that institute largely invariant patterns of recognition and activity. One is dominated by a recognition of being right or good on the basis of highly stabilized values, just as one is also dominated by the recognition of being criminal or deviant. The point of emphasis is that liberty arises in Foucault's game in the absence of values that are known to stand outside of games of truth. Or, to state the issue positively, individuals enjoy liberty in some processes of forming themselves in practices of freedom when the values of practices are held in unstable confederations.

There is thus for Foucault no normative or proper practice of freedom. Or there are many ways for individuals to give themselves expression in their manner of forming themselves. Foucault's emphasis was frequently on people other than the individuals who form the individual, as distinct to the practice of an individual's giving expression to him/herself. In such cases of domination the individual finds a measure of liberty not in achieving a proper obedience, not in knowing the truth, and not in being true in a determinate way. The individual finds a measure of liberty in resisting the dominating relation. That resistance would be a practice of freedom. Liberty, like domination, is found in relations of power, and it is found as an individual enacts itself in something like space that exceeds the determinations of the power relations. The metaphor is one of space without essence—not an opposing space or an antifactor—a space other to the determinations that mark it and that seems to yield liberty in its withdrawal.

The political dimensions that I am pointing to, however, are not found primarily in Foucault's inciting dominated people to revolt and resistance. The political occurs with the emergence of democratic space in Foucault's thought and knowledge, as distinct from the dominance of specific values that function for all practical purposes as absolute in the organization of his thought. Until the ontotheological space of dominating values 'is transformed into democratic space—or into some other nonontotheological space—no fundamental political change would seem to occur. And as long as our politics are formed by values that function as though they were transcendental, that is, as long as our political thought is formed, in Foucault's word, "theoretically" and provides us with 'isms' and commitments that overarch our local problematizations, ontotheological space is alive and well.

Democratic space emerges in our lineage and provides difficulty for our traditions of transcendental commitment. We can see it emerge in the space of representation in the episteme of Man as Foucault shows in *The Order of Things*. In the project of certainty in the modern episteme, the primary object to be known with certainty is split from the subject of knowing, although they are also posited as the same. An unovercomable space is generated by the subject, which must found itself by immediate self-knowledge. This subject splits itself from itself by an act of self-representation, and the space of this division is without the essence, the immediate presence, that would define it.

This space of no possible certainty problematizes the project of self-founding, the project of complete subjective immediacy, that is necessary for the project's success. It is a space that requires noncertainty, splits the proposed unity, and makes necessary either a metaphysically imaged belief in a nonmanifest totality or a recognition of the project's failure. Both the metaphors of totality by which the split is pictured as bridged and the recognition of failure reveal an epistemic space that arises in representation and makes possible one's thinking in this space rather than in the epistemic demand for a founding unity free of spatial interruption. We can thus read *The Order of Things* as an account of the arising of democratic space for Foucault's own game of truth. In this genealogical-archeological reading, the space of Foucault's work appears in the failure of representative knowledge with its competing factions of idealism and realism. The political dimension I am suggesting is found in the reformation of knowledge, a reformation in which the demand for grounding is dissolved as the withdrawing, indeterminate space of failed representation is affirmed. This event, which seems at first to be purely intellectual, is highly political: it unsettles the certainty of the knowing-desiring subject, opens a way to questioning the axioms of our knowledge and desire, allows Foucault, as we know from his later work, to reconsider the pleasures of bodies and to emphasize the individuality of suffering, and provides a hinge or a turning door into the possibility of values whose affirmation does not require transcendent grounding. By allowing the necessity of a grounding subject to lose its intellectual and effective power, Foucault affirmed a turn to the voices of all those that are excluded in the ontotheological episteme of representation and subjectivity. The door is opened to the transformation of the subject of knowledge and desire.

In *The History of Sexuality* the process of critique that arises from the space of Foucault's thought is considerably expanded. In volumes II and III particularly, he begins a project that shows how highly individual and largely private disciplines of self-mastery within the ethos of classical Greece and Rome give impetus through a traceable series of problematizations and mutations in our lineage to varieties of procedures whereby conduct is conducted by well-founded authorities who are invested with mastering power. These volumes comprise the beginning of a study of subjection in which subjects—desiring and knowing agents—are found in their formation to be articulations of describable plays of value and forces in Western society that are designed to produce certain kinds of reasonably predictable individuals. When the desiring subject is known to want what it wants and to will the way it wills because of a series of capacity-forming subjections and when the knower knows that he or she knows and desires *in* the formations that are known—when, that is, the knower knows that he or she is interrupting a pattern of inevitability in his or her own capacity to know and desire—a significant political event takes place: both values and the structure of valuing come into question. This problematization occurs: the disciplines of knowledge and morality that make Foucault's work meaningful demand a certain validation, a clear expression of human worth and constructive need. That worth and need constitute something essential, something not interrupted by withdrawal of essence and validity. But the knowledge provided by Foucault's genealogical account arises in a sensibility of time and individuality that occurs as a space of interruption and withdrawal, space without nature, space that not only loses presence and nature but also, in its withdrawal in Foucault's work, loses the need for presence and nature. Foucault's description of problematizations is accurate. In their context, practices and axioms are moved and transformed. The problematization is itself a site of exchanges of powers that move all parties. We can expect, for example, that the image of transformation from the lion to the child that I noted will be impacted by the demands of traditional morality and politics, that as it gains significance in the function of thought, it may well come to lose the draw that it enjoys in *Thus Spoke Zarathustra*, and that it will leave a metaphoric vacancy where it once contributed to breaking the hold of many traditional values. We can expect as well within the knowledge produced by *The History of Sexuality* that our knowledge of knowledge will change, that our affections will subtly shift, and that the topography of the desiring subject will alter. This study constitutes a problematization in disciplined learning, and in that problematization it finds its political dimension as it occasions a shift in structures of knowledge, conviction, and desire.The political aspect of this study by Foucault is thus found in the transformations of language, knowledge, thought, and desire that take place within it. The question is not whether we will appropriate it, make it a model for our decisions, and thereby make Foucault a bridge for our empty spaces. The political aspect of the study is found as one thinks and reads in its space, in its vacant interruption of unbroken time and its spacing of agency and subjectivity in problematized and disparate practices and institutions.

I began by noting excess to determination. In excessive withdrawal from the determinations of our lives there is both uncanny threat to our circumscribing worlds of meaning and release from the demeaning aspects of these same worlds. Both space and possibility occur as excess—and in that sense, as liberation. Through the metaphor of democratic space I have said that in Foucault's work we undergo an affirmation of excess without metaphors of continuing presence, that is, we undergo indeterminate possibility in the midst of our firmest values, find those values dislodged from the passions that would present them as absolute, and find as well that the role of commitment, racial, sexual, and national self-identification, and our dominant senses of self are put in question. We have seen that in Foucault's work, space and strategies of interruption, strategies that break up dominations of empowered presences, are closely allied. We have seen that the political in Foucault's work puts in question our senses of justice and propriety as well as our common allegiances that give us vision and a context for hope. There is no doubt in Foucault's work that an interruption of this magnitude is dangerous. Perhaps one of its primary dangers would be to still the communal desire to preserve the values that have determined our culture and subcultures. But we also know within Foucault's work that democratic space, in its withdrawal from values, exposes the dangers of our values and our selves as agents of value. These are dangers that produce suffering and silence. They also produce powers that oppress as well as tell our selves how to conduct themselves in the hope that there is Rightness beyond our rights and Truth which we should know and to which we should commit ourselves for the sake of human self-fulfillment. In this work, perhaps, bodies of pleasure and pain have come to recognition without fundamental identities, and perhaps in this recognition a different manner of organizing ourselves is on the horizon—a manner that arises in the failure of epistemes of presence and re-presentation and of powers that are given to dominant individuals in the name of universal justice.

13 | On the Advantages and Disadvantages of Politics for Life

W E ARE ALWAYS having to take care of things. Our lives constantly come to life without fundamental security. Even our securities are insecure. We take care of things within an horizon of something like no care at all. We take care of things because nothing else takes care of them for us. We probably sense unconsciously most of the time something like carelessness or mere possibility shining through our careful practices, like wolves' eyes shining out of the dark. When we see a highly developed society, such as the societies of the Native Americans, fall, or when we hear of a people's obliteration, such as that of the inhabitants of early Hawaii, we intuitively know that our established worlds are fragile, that only systems of care care for themselves. The lives of such systems can pass away without a lasting trace, although at one time they seemed complete in their vital intricacy. The possibility of alteration and eradication, of transvaluation and transformation, disrupts the power of our organizations to stand in full control of their presence. Their presence is always fragmented by possibility and by unorganization, which we name by words indicating death, instability, outer dark—words that indicate something other than the care of our lives.

We achieve our *stability* of presence by caring for things. We arrange ourselves by practices of self-care, such as those of nurturance, protection, education, and health. But we achieve something like 'depth' when we attend to the unorganization of the careless other to our living. Classical Greek society achieved a depth of insight and affirmation in its sense of tragedy that was not available earlier to Homeric singers and that is probably not available to us in contemporary Western society. In the care for things in the United States, we have developed a refined sense of the practical and the technical, of democratic participation and hope for our destiny, a sense that finds expression in metaphors of light, openness, space, and frontier that are probably unique to North American culture. But this ethics of optimism that so defines us is frequently inattentive to the eyes shining from the outer dark. Or we define those eyes as shining opportunities for growth or as transcendent signs of infinite concern. We use metaphorical instruments of stable illumination—like spotlights—to obliterate the horizon of careless darkness, eliminating the shadows by the crafted brightness of beliefs in education and redemption that create at best signs of an unshadowed world in which the thought of fate is figured by social planning and cultural improvement. We have learned, in the metaphor of e. e. cummings, to measure spring as well as the coming of death.

Probably this optimism gives expression to a Western tradition that sought freedom from the constitutive force and uncertainty of finitude, a tradition that fulfills the destiny of predicting the future by those with gifted clarity, a lineage of search for salvation from alterity to human life. We are living, perhaps, in the destiny of a primitive conviction that rightness of behavior could determine a future that is unmarred by horror and silence. North American optimism probably carries the intention of priests, seers, and prophets as it attempts to erase shadows by illumination, as it foresees a world promised to democratic justice and peace. Our ideals of education, employment, and social morality may well reinstate a masked horror before the strange experience of utter lack of care, of simple unorganization that interrupts the living presence of all stable things. Perhaps our cultural shallowness signifies in a withdrawn and silent way the withdrawal of life and meaning within the economics of care that give to us our sense of life.

If I am right in saying that attentiveness to the unorganization that runs through and interrupts our organizations is a vital factor in our attentiveness to things, political absorption in good causes poses a serious danger to our sense of life and to our common lives. Ordinarily I think of indifference to politics as a major threat to the values that organize our lives in common. I think of indifference to German National Socialism in the 1920s and 1930s, of indifference to racial injustice in the United States during the nineteenth and twentieth centuries, of contemporary indifference to overpopulation. Indifference allows bad values to flourish by their own unchecked energy. Only by committed action and involvement can I be responsive to what I find good and prevent what I find bad. But another element in the question of responsibility has arisen, one with attentiveness to what is not subject to the perimeters and possibilities of politics. Can we be responsible to our lives if we care primarily for things that we can value and organize?

By minding this issue of caring for the horizon of uncare as we take care of things—a certain responsiveness to unresponsibility—I would like to think within the possibility that politics is dangerous to our lives *in* the advantages that politics makes for our lives. Pursuit of this possibility is not motivated by an intention to promote a quieting of political interest, but it is motivated by an interest in the advantages and disadvantages of the *polis*—of the political region—and of our being political in our given requirement to care for things if we are to live. Both politics and the political necessity of our being, far from avoidable, are part of our need, our given insistence on being together. From this insistence come friendship, social identity, and loving and hateful engagement, as well as individuality with others, originality, and value. In a word, *regimes* of relation and broad social connection come from our political need, regimes of control and possibility, of practices and traditions. Regimes are organizations, and organizations always require arrangements of greater and lesser forces. Caring for our lives is inseparable from hierarchies and associations of forces, inseparable from management, institution, evaluation, and control. We ignore such inevitabilities at the cost of mistaking the ways in which things are available, usable, identifiable. The measure of stasis that occurs in the flow of our lives is a measure of enforcement, organization, and identity. Without forms of stasis we are chaotic and not long for this world.

This is not primarily a question, however, of how to develop and maintain greater flow in our organizations. It is a question of a strange difference, an organizationally embodied difference of organization and unorganization, presence and unpresence. The descriptive claim is that our organizations of relation, identity, and recognition are traversed by unorganization. The evaluative claim is that we advantage our lives by responding affirmatively to unorganization as we organize things. In developing these two claims I take a final look at Heidegger's account of possibility in *Being and Time* and at Foucault's account of governmentality. How might we advantageously govern ourselves in affirmation of the nonpolitical?

The Possibility of No Possibility at All: Ontologically without Love

One reads much about a regrettable lack of ethical relevance in Heidegger's *Being and Time*, or of the book's suspected vulnerability to fascist values. Such criticism is usually made from an ethical point of view that intends to require that all viable ontologies show that being brings with itself ethical expectation, guidance, or imperative. That the occurrence of being is interruptive of all formations of value—that formations of value might be at odds with their existence in their existence—is considered an unethical or antiethical claim that is dangerous to human well-being. The second suspicion, that *Being and Time* has vulnerability to fascism hidden within it, is based—at its best and when it is not based on simple inaccuracy regarding the text itself—on the belief that ethical neutrality as such is vulnerable to bad values. It is also frequently suggested that in *Being and Time* Heidegger finds authenticity in the figure of an individual who is closed to the world in an internal accomplishment of subjectivity—a reading of *Being and Time* that in my opinion cannot be sustained in the face of the text.

I mention these various readings in order to note two claims here that differentiate us from this contemporary stream of publication. First, the ethical and political relevance of *Being and Time* is found in the absence of an ethics or a politics; and second, this absence, when appropriated in our ethics and politics, is to the advantage of human life.

For our limited purposes, we shall pay attention to Heidegger's phrase "*the possibility of the impossibility of any existence at all*" (GA 2, 348; BT 307). It occurs in his discussion of authentic being to death and elaborates his description of possibility as interruptive of dasein's present actuality. The aspect that I want to emphasize in the phrase is interruption that is not like the interruption of something finite by *something* transcendent. In the instance of this phrase, a human life has nothing in particular that is upcoming and to be actualized; no imperative is given to guide a genuine or authentic realization; there is no partially realized nature to complete. It is possibility "that knows no measure at all" and that is opening to itself—to possibility, to mere opening—and as opening, possibility 'is' at once open to absence—to no possibility at all. In this context the Macquarrie-Robinson translation (of pages 347 and 348 of GA 2; 306 of BT) is misleading. It states in several sentences that dasein is being toward *a* possibility, toward *something* possible, or toward *this* possibility. Not only are the articles and the 'something' missing in the German; Heidegger's descriptive claim is that dasein's ontological possibility to be cannot be conceived as a determinate possibility. Being-to-death is not a movement to a determinate end. ("*The closest closeness which one may have in being to death as possibility, is as far as possible from anything actual,*" GA 2, 348; BT 306-307.) To *be* not yet, Heidegger says, is to *be* dasein's end—it *is* ending: "Death is as dasein's end, *in* the being of this being towards its death" (GA 2, 343; BT 303, emphasis added). Human being *is* ending in the interruption of actual presence by mere possibility. In living, human existence is always coming to end—dying—and hence it is able yet to be. This means that being to or toward death is to be indeterminate in the determinate "now." It does not primarily mean having to die at a later time.

If dasein's being were complete actuality that had to die—a finite perfection, as it were—then its death would be an event foreign to its own occurrence, something that overtakes it as foreign to its being. This is the tacit image in which we Westerners usually live, according to Heidegger. It is as though we grow into our being, which already prefigures as an archetypal presence its own full completion. In that image being does indeed appear to give itself an imperative of how to be in order to be fully itself. Or if we think of being as an immortal part indwelling a mortal body, we might well think of death as the imperfection of human life, as the cost of embodiment, and as something to be judged in relation to the requirements of a deathless soul that seeks its own inherent fullness. Heidegger, to the contrary, is attempting to find a way of thinking that thinks measureless nonpresence which occurs with presencing and which, as unpresence, occurs in the ending of presence in presencing.

We Westerners find ourselves in question in simultaneous presencing and nonpresencing. Given our Greek heritage, Heidegger says, we traditionally experience our being in this living-dying happening. In our lineage, our being and our capacity to be attuned with it occur in the presenting or disclosure of beings, in their *alétheia*, in their disclosive interconnectedness and in their interrupted presence. We and the beings that constitute our world occur coming-to-be-passing-away: the Western human ability to be attuned with its own occurrence is found in the disclosive interconnection that Heidegger terms being-in-the-world and not in a subjective structure or power or in any other kind of presence. To be attuned with our being is to be attuned in the self-presentation of being wherein presence undergoes the erosion of possibility without presence. There is no division to be found between dasein—human *being*—and the presentation of being; and there is no distance to be found in the presentation of beings and their ending as they come to be. Hence the descriptive claims in *Being and Time* that we find the identity and significance of things in the dynamic structures of caring and concern, and that we find the meaning of the necessity that we take care of things in the mortality of temporal occurrence—these claims arise from the strong, aporetic event that is valorized in our tradition, the event of coming to be in unpresence, the possibility of no presence at all.

The aspect of these claims that I want to emphasize now is the illimitable transgression of limited existence by possibility. Maintaining the limits of our determined lives includes a constant struggle to find measure and structure proper to survival and living well. We are not suited for illimitable existence. It is as though we were pitched into immeasurable possibility with a constantly irritating ability to suffer and sorrow, to prize and to love, to possess and temporize. We *are* to establish limits such as ways of governizing ourselves, to cope with determinations which already define us, such as social practices. We *are* to find regions of determination by limiting actions, by the decisions: in a phrase, we are to establish limits by care and concern. We usually find such complexity quite enough—quite enough to preserve procedures that we have found salutary, to keep out enemies of our ways of preserving our values, to experience our lives as worth living, and sometimes it is quite enough just to make it through the day.

Is it not salutary to establish images that help us in these processes of concrete life? Salutary to provide practices that link the decisions of our collective lives to something constant? To add dimensions of transcendental meaning to the meanings that we have made or found? Salutary to give ourselves to presence beyond the little hopes that are frequently disappointed?

Heidegger's response is not one of direct encounter and refutation. Instead, in *Being and Time* he attempts to establish a rigor of description before the phenomena that constitute our existence, i.e., the phenomena of finite disclosiveness and the self-presentation of things in their significations. In this account he shows that the phenomena—the disclosures—of beings are not completely subject to our accumulative and sophisticated processes of careful determination, that, as we have seen, indetermination crosses the determinations of beings, that illimitable possibility irritates the clarity and identity of our limits.

The meanings of our love and cultivations, our rage and fear, are not transcendentally answered. Rather, our limits are unlimited in their establishment, and we must yet care, continue to care, in their (and our) ending in openpossible unexistence.

Thus, he shows, limit, grasp, and determination lose a lot while they gain purchase of beings, whether that purchase be by value, practice, or thought. The 'a lot' that they lose is unlimiting, ungrasping, nondetermination in being able (now) not to be at all. Grasp by care and concern give life. Without such preservation and identity we would not be. But there is also 'something' deathly in our structures of care which we ignore only at our own peril. The paradox of our existence is that in deathliness we open to renewed life, that is, we open to the disclosiveness of beings that is not subject to the limits of the way in which the beings function with us. *Limit* has the overtone of making available, signifiable, and practical (in a broad sense of the word *practical*). By virtue of limits we identify, contain, make namable and referable. But illimitable openpossibility in the limited manifestness of things, in the ending of presence as presence comes to be, is 'beyond' the disposition of names, significance, and placement. In transgressing limit and determination, the possibility of no possibility at all requires something other than a grasp in our attunement with 'it.' It 'is' no thing at all, not *really* an 'is', not 'real-ly'.

In this absence of reality and political significance I find the importance of the possibility of no possibility for our communal lives, for our politics, if you will. Heidegger speaks of an appropriate alertness to our being by using the word *Entschlossenheit*, which suggests, in addition to determination and decision, unlocking, opening, releasing, and delimiting. The translation of *Entschlossenheit* by the word *resoluteness* also suggests loosening determination, dissolution, and breaking apart at the same time that it suggests determination and conclusion. In resolution, in the context of *Being and Time*, a human being allows itself to come to the end of its presence as it determines itself in specific ways. The human acts determinately *and* releases itself to its loss of determination. "When resoluteness is transparent to itself," Heidegger says, "it understands that the *indefiniteness* of one's ability to be is made definite only in a resolution as regards the current situation" (GA 2, 408; BT 356). In a release of the hold of a determination *in* the determination, one resolves the release of being in the presencing of beings. That means not only that one does not experience determinations as absolute but also that one attends to the disadvantages for life of determination and limitation as such. A sense of dispossession accompanies possession. A sense of mortal excess to the life of an identity accompanies identification. A sense of openpossibility accompanies experiences of reality. A sense develops that more is to be preserved than what we can preserve by the value of the valued.

Governmentality: Political Determination

Before I say more about the political advantages of such a sense of release from determination in determinate situations, I shall turn to Foucault's description of governmentality.

We should continue to keep ourselves focused by an emphasis on disclosure or appearance as we turn to Foucault. This emphasis in his writing often takes the form of accounting structures of recognition, which let things appear in their cultural identities. These structures of recognition are not subjective or ideal structures but are those of historicosocial formation. They are structures of discourses which give identity and significance to things and individuals. A system of recognition for Foucault is always one of power relations, so we can say initially that disclosures—the way things come to presence—are infused from the start with forces that place and move things in axes of importance and relative degrees of control. Individuals come to presence within systems of rules and practices that allow them their ways of being and that appear as subject to change: whatever is necessary in the concreteness of a given situation can cease to be as it is and is, in that sense, optional. Openpossibility pervades determinations.

Governmentality in Foucault's account means the science and politics of the state's care of the people, things, and their multiple relations in the state.[1] The purposes of governmentality are the care and control of people—"population" is the word Foucault uses. This is in contrast to a state that is oriented by the discipline of the sovereign, a discipline which teaches him or her how to govern with wisdom, patience, and other paternalistic values of intelligent control, and in contrast to the state that is oriented to the benefit of the sovereign. The governmental state management is directed toward a population. Such a purpose is, of course, a highly complex undertaking, and Foucault charts the rise of the state of governmentality and the decline of the sovereign state primarily by reference to the growth of population that a state had to manage and to the growth of strength of population in its numbers and economic force. Population grew through conquest, colonialization, and economic expansion, and it became a "field of intervention and . . . an objective of governmental techniques" that supplanted the feudal structures in which the state and act of sovereign government were separate from the laws governing people and things and in which the maintenance of the sovereign was carried out with little attention to the interests and style of life of its people.

The governmentalization of the state is constituted by a combination of pastoral-like concern for people's welfare, by a sovereign-like authority to define what constitutes welfare and well-being according to the needs of the state, and a military-like strategy of applying laws and rules through regulations that are administered by police and bureaus with the power of education and punishment. The kind of knowledge emblematic of the governmental state is statistics, which is able to handle large numbers of things and discern trends, densities, and relations at both macro and micro levels. The power of the governmental state is administered primarily in cultural techniques and institutions that produce subjects who want to do what the state wants them to do. It 'subjects' as it forms subjectivity. I call this process "governmental determination."

The word *state* in its many uses carries the sense of 'mode of existence', the determined or specific standing of things. It has a connotation of stasis and definition. A governmental state looks to the body of people that constitutes it as both its source and object of power. It seeks to maintain a certain kind of stasis through control of health, efficiency, productivity, wealth, and value. And since its primary strategy is the cultivation of self-discipline regarding desirable practices, its goals are directed to a highly regulated care of its subjects' desires, pleasures, ideals, satisfactions, ambitions, and interests: its goal is determination of individuals by stately values through regulated institutions, rewards, and necessary enforcement and punishment, all of which form a self-regulating individual. More than nurturing creatures who are able to promise, the governmental state nurtures by direction and control the very structure, process, and content of promising. Such a state thus becomes the most important agency in its citizens' lives. Hence Foucault says that "the problems of governmentality and the techniques of government have become the only political issue, the only real space for political struggle and contestation." We and the state are who and what we are because of governmentality.

Promising, caring, and coming to an end, in Heidegger's sense, are temporal occurrences that arise in the indeterminacy of possibility. We have seen that the possibility of no possibility at all means a temporalizing interruption of presence and of the determination that provides identity and status. We see immediately that the governmental subject will be confused before the question of time's indeterminacy and illimitability, that the crossing of determination by indetermination and openpossibility are at best perplexing and probably seem to be a threat to the state of one's subjectivity, identity, and ethical behavior. A governmental subject is not given to be attracted by the openpossibility that appears to be suggested by promising and caring, and such a subject is certainly not given to attending to what is without utility and measurability in our ethical and political disposition, management, and organization of individuals and things for the sake of most people's benefit. In this state of mind, dying, ending, and death appear strangely like a sovereign that stands outside of the regulations of life and interrupts such ordered life usually to no one's benefit within the order.

I am not suggesting, however, an alternative to the governmental state. I do not know of a viable alternative to a state that regulates itself and its subjects by rights and privileges, that is committed to the people's general welfare, that organizes itself by information, analysis, regulation, education, and enforcement. I think of a nongovernmental state as one in which individual freedom and self-determination come to realization, as one in which individuals are subject to the chaos of rampant disease, arbitrary services for the sake of someone who is served, external and competing forces that are articulated in the monotonous savagery of continuous war. I think of the losses sustained when public welfare is not the concern of government, when government serves itself outside of people's rights, and when governmental structures are not committed to the shared needs and interests of individuals.

I am saying, rather, that the state's self-absorption and self-establishment by the processes of its concern for the people are, when those processes are uninterrupted and allowed to interpret themselves, to the state's own disastrous disadvantage. Governmentality and its subjects are predisposed—instated, if you will—to manage their own management, to count their own countability, to regulate their own regulations, to institutionalize their own institutions, and to become absorbed in the demands of the present situation. It is, after all, a *state* of affairs and a *state* of mind, a 'now' that fixes attention on one of a series of absorbing situations. The governmental state is slow to allow for the interruption of unstately difference to itself. Such interruption feels treasonous and unethical to it and to its subjects. It is like an attempt to infuse a spirit of poetic inefficiency into a hardnosed, well-running bureaucracy. The possibility of no possibility at all is not governable, not subject to statistical knowledge, immune to the discourses of rights, moral behavior, and pastoral power. Indeterminacy will not be political and is without reaction, consciousness, benevolence, identity, or reality. It is without. It is uninstatable.

The advantage of such nonpolitical interruption is found *critically* in a sense of the state's and the subject's limits. Foucault speaks of the enormity of the exaggeration of the state's importance.[2] He says that the procedures of the state, its governmentality, its invidious control of individuals, present us with the proper area for contestation. He has in mind the disinheritance by governmental states of groups of individuals, such as those who violate proper, enstated subjectivity, e.g., prisoners, nonconformists, homosexuals, and free spirits. We rank people's importance according to the standards of governmentality. He also has in mind those who regulate their personal lives according to the art of pleasure and not according to the interests of the population. The less we serve the state's interest, the more expendable we are. Foucault gives priority in his critical assessment of the limits of governmentality to the individuality of people, not so much to their liberation as to their difference from the current, collective, and measurable models and types. He develops a knowledge of individuals by marginalizing in his disclosure the power of the state to control their subjectivity.

Individuality, however, does not constitute a value adequate to the formation of the temporal subject. An individual's temporality, which Heidegger describes as temporal *ekstasis*—the excessive unindividualizing of the individual in the individual's determination—this temporality limits individuality as well as governmentality. Individuality ends in its beginning, must care for its continuation, and does not occur like a continuing presence that gives universal meaning to existence. Individuality, like governmentality, is always in question. The ways of caring for individuality solely by means of the values of individual rights or the values of pleasure do not hear temporal *ekstasis*. They are unattuned to reticence before ungovernable unindividual openpossibility and lack a certain lightness of existence before their own unsolvable question. This dispossession of the certainty of value in value's certainty puts in question the power of possession and control in governmentality *and* in the value of the individual. It puts in question both the ideals of state determination and self-determination in this sense: we find ourselves able to be thanks to nondetermination as well as to determination. No determination is enough for individuals to be.

Unsettling the value of determinations allows people to know that a way of life in its currency—a hero, a static, transcending presence, a group of values—can fully determine our existence only with the severe disadvantage of disinheriting us from the incalculable occurrence of ending. In that disinheritance we expect to find our proper ways of being through proper determination. In that state of mind, people govern themselves with an inherent sense of right of possession which seems to carry with it a mandate to dispossess the unfitting and to eliminate unpresentable excess. This priority of possession and its attendant value of dispossessing turn both the individual and the governing ethos into holding patterns—models of present determining force—which count well their losses and gains but which do not know how to end as they begin or to hear the release of a situation's hold.

To say that attunement to openpossibility in ending is advantageous to politics means that neither secular politics nor politics supported by a sense of transcendent mandate are advantageous in their constant self-enstatement. It means that as temporal phenomenon, secular politics and politics by transcendent mandate are also inconstant, disinstated, and dispossessed. If they ignore such loss, that loss will be determined through the overdetermination of stated presence, and something like suffocation by values, ideals, and other means of establishment will give a politics the disadvantages that result from regulating itself by reference to its uninterrupted presence to itself.

Notes

Introduction

1. Not only by the differences of *something* other and not by an other's being to itself or in itself beyond our relation to it.

1. Nonbelonging/Authenticity

1. I take the term *twisting free* from David Krell's translation of *Herausdrehung* and from John Sallis's use of the term in "Twisting Free: Being to an Extent Sensible," *Research in Phenomenology*, 17 (1987): 1–21.

2. In Foucault's account of surveillance, the power to observe and judge is also a power to incarcerate. One developing claim in *Discipline and Punish* and toward the end of *The History of Sexuality* trilogy is that the state's manner of enforcing its interests in the welfare of its citizens changes as government changes from regency to forms of democracy. Authority is internalized. Instead of an external state's surveillance, an interior surveillance forms whereby we become incarcerated by a body of values to which we are taught to give voice: the power of conscience in this sense of the word is the power of a hierarchy of values. Genealogy is the approach Foucault uses to break this power in his writing. Instead of a different authority that counteracts the authority of modern conscience—and hence the authority of modern self—genealogy counteracts conscience by means of disclosing the power-interests that invest self and conscience in the context of those values. So, for example, our predisposition to distaste and disgust regarding dissemblance recoils against the dissemblance that constitutes the values of sincerity and non-dissembling honesty, the very values that generate our predisposition to disgust regarding dissemblance. In this way the modern conscience and self are in question in his writing. Although Heidegger, in contrast to Foucault, uses *conscience* constructively in his analysis, we may also appropriately ask who is looking and judging in the context of his description of conscience. His direct answer is *das Man,* the anonymous one of our inherited structures of value. In the function of conscience, however, in its distance from its contingent religious and moral contents, and in the ontological function that Heidegger ascribes to call, language, and guilt, he finds neither a normative self nor the priority of meaning and value. He finds the articulation of dasein's difference vis-à-vis its daily and traditional observations. *Conscience* names a movement of dasein that has no surveillance and no judgment, and by conceiving it that way one is in a movement of twisting free from the everyday that puts the priority of value-judgment in question. How are we to think outside this priority? Nietzsche's account of the ascetic ideal claims that philosophical reflection as such originated in an ascetic, priestly contemplation that removed people by its activity from alertness to earthly, fragmented existence. Nietzsche's thought recoils in the strain that it puts on itself as thought and always diminishes itself in the

metaphor of will to power and eternal return. Heidegger's thought, in the context of conscience, diminishes no less its own conscience regarding dasein's forgetful and banal life. The contents of everyday conscience, its clarity regarding right and wrong, its fearful guilt, its concern over metaphysical security and peace of mind, its predisposition not to question its axioms for conduct—its forgetful banal life—are in question by the recoiling movement whereby it puts itself in question by the values that it holds. This wrenching motion is an aspect of the conscience of *Being and Time*. It is in question in *Being and Time* no less than Nietzsche's philosophical reflection is in question in his reflective account of the ascetic ideal. If the wrenching, recoiling movement is emphasized, rather than the specific and static claim that Heidegger makes regarding the ontological status of conscience, we find the process in which both the subject of the description and the subjectivity of describing are in question.

3. In pathological grief, for example, a person is often traumatized by the interruption of death, and the grief is less over the loss than over the mortality that infuses the other and one's relation with the other.

2. Language in a Passing Sense of Transcendence

1. Since these remarks are focused by the question of sacrality, I shall limit what I say about the sense of transcendence largely to a sense of transcendent presence to human being and in human being. I wish to show that in Heidegger's thought regarding language, this sense considerably weakens and that in this weakening the usually unrecognized force of the sense of transcendence comes to bear in many people's distaste for his 'later' thought. We shall see that the transcendence-continuity diad also passes out of focus in his thought. When he speaks of language he is able to set a direction of thought that is not guided by the traditional problematic of continuity and continuing presence in finite existence. The loss of presence through signification, for example, is not an issue for his thought. Language, as Heidegger speaks of it in *Der Weg zur Sprache*, is founded by neither continuing presence nor the loss of presence in the work of signification. In this essay, re-presentation is not the orienting occurrence of his thinking, and the occurrence of 'the other' is reconceived in an initial way in the thought of disclosure that is free of the constraints of subjectivity and the dominance of agency. At this point, the connection between the sense of transcendence and contemporary ideas about subjectivity becomes unavoidable, although I cannot address that connection here. My broad and undeveloped suggestion is that deterioration of the sense of transcendence accompanies Heidegger's turn out of the problematic of subjectivity and that this turning affords us otherwise unthinkable options for thinking presence and loss of presence. These options are not formed in an anxiety over continuity and presence. Hence the contemporary, felt need for transcendence in the service of human survival and what we call justice is in question. Difference and transcendence need not be thought together in order for us to recognize connection and relation. But when we conceive of difference within the power of a sense of transcendence—i.e., to conceive of difference as transcending otherness—we usually also think of a corollary conception of continuing presence as the 'tissue' that connects difference and provides the condition for the possibility of relation and order. Without such presence, we and the world could not be. Hence the religious meaning that in our traditions usually attaches to the sense of transcendence, a kind of meaning that shines through the thought of Aristotle and Husserl as well as that of Hegel and Bataille.

2. GA 12, 227–257; BW 393–426.

3. When such changes in thought and speech emerge, our habitual experiences and conceptions of sacrality are stressed and distressed. Could sacrality itself also become no more or less than a trope? And thereby signify a loss of sacrality?

4. GA 12, 237; BW 404.

5. This paragraph is a gloss primarily on the essay's second paragraph. GA 12, 229; BW 397. The last clause in the paragraph of GA reads "und unser Verhältnis zu ihr sich als *das* Ver-hältnis bekundet." Heidegger's marginal comment is recorded on the same page as: "Ver-hältnis: Ortschaft des Zu-einander-Gehörens von Brauch und Ereignis." The clause and its note are not in the 1959 edition of *Unterwegs zur Sprache* or in the translation by Krell. My language usage in this context is awkward in part because of reflexive structures that could suggest a transcendental relation. That both the reflexive structures and the suggestion of transcendence are in question will become clearer in the course of this chapter, particularly when the middle voice is highlighted.

6. GA 12, 239; BW 406. "Es gilt, dem Eigentümlichen der Sprache näherzugehen." He also notes as he moves away from von Humboldt's theory and into his own subject that "we can no longer root about [*umsehen*] for general notions like energy, activity, labor, force of spirit, view upon the world, or expression, under which we might subsume language as a particular instance of this or that universal. Instead of explaining language as this or that, and thus fleeing from it, the way to language wants to let language be experienced as language. True, in the essence of language, language is grasped conceptually, but it is caught in the grip of something other than itself. If on the contrary we pay heed only to language as language, it demands of us that we begin by bringing to the fore all those things that pertain to language as language." Ibid.

7. GA 12, 239; BW 406.

8. GA 12, 243; BW 410–411.

9. GA 12, 243; BW 411. I have changed the translation of *Sichsagenlassen* from "lets itself be told" to "lets itself come to saying." *Told* suggests an objectivity and narration that I believe is not found in Heidegger's German.

10. This turn of thought is especially disconcerting to those readers of Heidegger who want to preserve a presumed priority of Aristotle in his thought and thus to reserve him for reintegration into one of the Aristotelian traditions. I suspect that disappointment in Heidegger by those who have wanted him to serve their religious or theological beliefs has been as important an element in the lineage of interpretation of Heidegger as the intent to utilize part of his thought for broadly onto-theological purposes. Both directions—the one of religious immanence and the Aristotelian one—and the disappointments that mark them lose touch with the turning edge of his thought in which the very thoughts and ways of thinking that characterize what he is saying are themselves in varying processes of transmutation or passing away. Heidegger's thought is an extremely dangerous preserve for its own tradition. 'What' it proposes to preserve usually lets die our seemingly lasting values, procedures, and ways of knowing. We find his thinking in its turning out of what has essentially defined it—*that* turning, *that* coming to pass— eventuates as the *Wesen* of Heidegger's thought.

11. GA 12, 246; BW 413–414. The last clause, whose translation I have altered, reads "dahin jegliches An- und Abwesen sich hereinzeigen, sich einsagen muss." The English reads "to which every presencing and absenting must expose itself and commit itself."

12. Enownment," *Boundary*, 4, no. 2, (Winter 1976), pp. 357–377.

13. GA 12, 257; BW 436.

14. Although I use phrases that suggest a genealogical approach to language like that of Nietzsche, Foucault, and, perhaps, Derrida in his early work, such phrases as 'our

lineages' knowledge of language' and 'force of language', this turn on Heidegger's part is not so clearly in Nietzsche's lineage. While his studies of the history of being have an important genealogical aspect, Heidegger's temporal and historical thought does not fit into the limits of genealogical structures. I will use such phrases to emphasize both lineage and constitutive force in language, but the turn we are now taking is distinct to Heidegger. The phrase "to bring language as language to language" occurs as in GA 12, 250; BW 419.

    15. GA 12, 249; BW 417.

    16. GA 12, 257; BW 426 (my emphasis).

3. Ethics in a Passing Sense of Transcendence

    1. I shall only gesture to indications of this preoccupation by reference to the indelibility of the problem of one and many throughout Western thought in what Heidegger calls onto-theological philosophy, to what we might call the anxious sense that existence requires transcendental unity for its well-being if not for its survival, and hence the sense that thought will lose its own grounding if it is not ordered by transcendental unity of some kind. Knowledge, law, and order are experienced within an axis of unity even if that unity is not perfect and is subject to process. Foucault's study of the fragmentation of similitude in modern knowledges, for example, in *The Order of Things*, also shows the persistence of a sense in established disciplines that transcendental unity is required for knowledge of whatever is. Our ability to recognize things embodies this transcendental unity.

    2. Studies implicating the struggle of the sense of transcendence for dominance over a sense of singular orders without transcending order include Nietzsche's *Beyond Good and Evil* and *Genealogy of Morals*, Heidegger's *Early Greek Thinking*, Derrida's *Of Grammatology*, and Foucault's *Madness and Civilization* and *The Order of Things*. A common factor in these otherwise different works is the authors' recognition that our heritage has been formed in part by a pervasive and largely unconscious struggle to establish, in our knowledge and discourses, the presence of a being that encompasses the fragmentation and limitation of the orders of life. A sense of presence, a presence that gives continuation of being in and among otherwise mortal and finitely connected beings, pervades the sense of transcendence. Levinas has a considerably different take on both transcendence and presence, as we shall see in the third section ("The Return and Withdrawal of Transcendence") of this chapter.

    3. Nietzsche's thought of will to power requires its own nonfoundational status, its own overturning, and hence cannot be thought as a concept of continuing presence. I give a full discussion of this claim in *The Question of Ethics* (Bloomington: Indiana University Press, 1990), chap. 2.

    4. How these words struggle! How language that was molded by a sense of transcendence and that loses a sense of transcendence writhes as if it were mimicking the senseless patterns of a dying snake!

    5. The new language and thought that Heidegger hoped would arrive out of this withdrawal—the coming of a sight and vigor that were lost in their Greek beginnings but that were retained as lost and that are now traced in their loss in the withdrawal of Gods and of presence—the hoped-for language and thought would not, I believe, on his terms replace withdrawal with new presence. A new *Sage* situated, let us say, in Germany or the United States, could not return to a presence without reinstating the medium of metaphysics whereby the finest gift of Greece was lost in its formation. It is the formation

of another *Sage*, another culture-giving language (I would hesitate to call it a myth) that is tentatively foreseen. Although Heidegger had predictive things to say about the new *Sage*, he was not inclined to believe literally his predictive sayings. To speak, for example, of his hope for a new religion or a new philosophy is to miss both the radicality of poetry as he experienced it—poetry overturns the dominant Western experience of reality and literal presence—and the metaphysical weave of religion and philosophy as it has developed in our tradition.

6. I shall use *presence* and *transcendent presence* to mean *immediate presence*. Levinas's word, *proximity*, thus does not suggest either *presence* or *transcendent presence*.

7. This is not what Levinas directly says but is my reading of him. For Levinas such philosophical knowledge comes from the face-to-face and substitution, from pre-philosophical 'occurrences' which embody ethical imperatives. The issue I am developing at this point addresses the possibility of the other. I find the other in Levinas's thought, and in contrast to his claims, to be a manifestation or disclosure of a specific ethos and to be structured in its importance by a certain lineage of faith.

8. This claim on my part could be taken to reinstate the very kind of transcendence that I (and Levinas) want to avoid, namely, the kind of transcendence in which 'something' transcends the limits of consciousness while being immanent to consciousness. I note for now, first, that the genealogical thought that I am developing about language, values, beliefs, and knowledges is not a claim about consciousness but is a way of thinking that is an alternative to philosophies of consciousness and, second, that disclosures are not of something that stays hidden behind other disclosures. There is no 'behind' to disclosures.

9. I am drawing primarily from *Otherwise than Being*, particularly from chap. 4.

10. OTB 100.

11. Even to speak of *truth* is difficult in this context because that word also carries the Greek domination.

12. There is a fundamental religious dimension to the other's transcendence of the self: for example, "There is an anarchic trace of God in passivity" (OTB 196, n. 21). Levinas also speaks of "the religious situation of transcendence" in the context of transcendence's loss when the religious situation is thematized theologically (OTB 197, n. 25). This religious situation and the trace of God reflect the Hebraic tradition as Levinas has experienced it and not another religious tradition such as Buddhism or classical Christianity in its Greek dimension.

13. See, for example, OTB 100 ff.

14. Or one could say that Levinas's discourse is organized by an axis of withdrawal and return with regard to the other. Although the other is never immediately present, Levinas's continuous return to the other's proximity gives the other a sense of presence in the discourse, in spite of the overturning of presence that his text performs. There is in his work a double performance of withdrawing the other from a sense and discourse of presence and of returning to a sense of withdrawn presence, now transformed by the experience of call and substitution.

4. A (Non-) Passing Sense of Tragedy

1. GA 5, 321–373; EGT 13–58. Further references will be given in the text. For key to the abbreviations, see "Selected Works Cited."

2. I translate *phthoran* at different times as ruin, disappearance, not arising, passing away, destruction, and catastrophe. I translate *genesis* as arising, advent, origin, com-

ing to be, and coming to appear. I translate their combination as rising ruin, appearing-disappearing, coming to be passing away, arising–not arising, and coming to pass. *Gines-thai*, in this context, says the two words in their combination in the coming of beings.

3. A note on the translation. In EGT 40 the words are, "what is present coheres in unifying presencing, as everything becomes present to everything else within its directions; it becomes present and lingers with the others." The German reads, "Das Anwesende gehört im Einen des Anwesens zusammen, indem jedes zu jedem in seiner Weile, weilig mit dem anderen, anwest" (GA 5, 353). A preferable translation would be, "whatever comes to presence passing away belongs together in the One of coming together passing away, in that each being comes to be passing away with the other in its lingering as it lingers with the other." The translations "coheres in unifying presencing" and "what is present" accentuate presence at the expense of the aporetic simultaneity of coming to appear disappearing (viz., coming to be passing away) in Heidegger's words *Einen, Anwesende, Anwesens,* and *Anwest.* Throughout his reading Heidegger does not mean *a* unity or harmonious unity when he uses *Eine* and *Einende.* Gathering occurs in coming to appear disappearing. Further, without the emphasis falling on this aporetic simultaneity, *Wesen* seems to name essential presence in spite of statements to the contrary. When, however, *Wesen* is read in this context as the sending of *genesis/phthoran,* a sending that comes *in genesis/phthoran,* we are not speaking of finitude (living dying) in relation to something that mysteriously continues outside of and transcendent to appearing disappearing. In EGT 30 Heidegger emphasizes that he is speaking of appearing-disappearing rather than finite beings when he speaks of *genesis/phthoran.* This important difference governs his thought throughout the discussion. Hence the rendering of the various forms of *Anwesen* in terms of presence without withdrawal of presence loses the question that defines the dialogue of his language and thought.

4. This is not a question of order, as the translation suggests, so much as it is a question of distribution in the turning of appearing disappearing. Beings are meted out, measured, as it were, in the turning, the hinge. They belong fittingly to dispensation. I have thus chosen *dispensation* in association with *turning* rather than *order* to translate *Fug* in this context.

5. Thinking Noninterpretively

1. BW 307–341; VA 9–40. Further references will be given in the text.

2. I have translated *Wesen* by such words as coming to be passing away, coming to presence, and waying. By this word Heidegger speaks of the disclosiveness of technology as distinct from the manner in which things come to appear within technological ordering.

6. The Ascetic Ideal

1. "Brief über den Humanismus," GA 9, 313–364; "Letter on Humanism," BW 213–265. Further references will generally be given in the text.

2. Heidegger phrases this occurrence in this way: "Das Denken . . . lässt sich vom Sein in der Anspruch nehmen, um die Wahrheit des Seins zu sagen. Das Denken vollbringt dieses Lassen. Denken ist l'engagement par l'Etre pour l'Etre . . . penser, c'est l'engagement de l'Etre." GA 9, 313–314. "Thinking . . . lets itself be claimed by being so as to say the truth of being. Thinking unfolds this allowance in the fullness of its coming

to pass. Thinking is the engagement by being for being . . . thinking is the engagement of being."

3. Medard Boss has put this claim to work in psychoanalysis by showing that every aspect of the human body is pervaded by one's appropriation of being. In this way he rethinks psychosomatic medicine and the psychological meaning of physical impairment. See *Grundriss der Medizin* (Bern: Hans Huber, 1971), part IB.

4. GA 9, 355–357. Cf. Nietzsche, T 37: "Origin in something else counts as an objection, as casting a doubt on value." This "degenerate" idea, according to Nietzsche, is companion to the ideas of 'highest concept', unity, and the unconditioned. Heidegger eliminates the idea of *causa sui* without question, but do these other "last fumes of evaporating reality" pass away in Heidegger's thought?

5. See T, " 'Reason' in Philosophy," section 5.

6. We may say that being 'vacates' by its withdrawal, by its continuous abandonment of human being in its difference from beings. In that sense humans are bereft of being in the granting closeness of being. But *that* abandonment protects and preserves being in its difference as well as in its granting nearness, its purity vis-à-vis beings. Being continues to enjoy an unquestioned privilege.

7. Transition

1. *Derrida and Différance*, ed. David Wood and Robert Bernasconi. Evanston: Northwestern University Press, 1988.

12. Democratic Space

1. Didier Eribon, *Michel Foucault*, trans. Betsy Wing (Cambridge: Harvard University Press, 1991), 234.

2. Eribon, *Michel Foucault*, 211.

13. On the Advantages and Disadvantages of Politics for Life

1. Although my remarks draw from many of Foucault's works, they are focused by his essay "Governmentality," which may be found in its English version in *The Foucault Effect: Studies in Governmentality*, ed. G. Burchell, C. Gordon, and P. Miller (University of Chicago Press, 1991), 87–104.

2. Ibid., 103.

Index

Charles E. Scott holds the Edwin Erle Sparks Chair in Philosophy at Pennsylvania State University. His publications include *The Question of Ethics, The Language of Difference,* and *Boundaries in Mind: A Study of Immediate Awareness Based in Psychotherapy.*